EDITION

USE OF
MEDIA

ndbook

nsultant,
e London
d on the
ked with
advertis-

g Depart-
atchi and
d Promo-
various
rse Direc-
Interact

FOURTH EDITION

THE EFFECTIVE USE OF ADVERTISING MEDIA

a practical handbook

by Martyn P. Davis,

BSc (Econ), FCAM, FIPR, FCIM, DipFEd

Marketing Communications Consultant

CENTURY
BUSINESS

This Fourth Edition was first published in Great Britain in 1992 by
Century Business
An imprint of Random House UK Limited
20 Vauxhall Bridge Road, London SW1V 2SA

Random House Australia (Pty) Limited,
20 Alfred Street, Milsons Point, Sydney
New South Wales 2061, Australia

Random House New Zealand Limited
18 Poland Road, Glenfield
Auckland 10, New Zealand

Random House South Africa (Pty) Limited
PO Box 337, Bergvlei, South Africa

First Edition 1981
Second Edition 1985
Third Edition 1988
Reprinted 1989, 1990

Set in Century Schoolbook by SX Composing Ltd, Rayleigh, Essex

Printed and bound in Great Britain by
Mackays of Chatham PLC, Chatham, Kent

British Library Cataloguing in Publication Data
A catalogue record for this book is available from the British Library

ISBN 0-7126-5497-6

Companies, institutions and other organisations wishing to make bulk purchases of this title or any other Century Business publication should contact:

Direct Sales Manager
Century Business
Random House
20 Vauxhall Bridge Road
London SW1V 2SA

Fax: 071-828 6681

Contents

v

Broadcasters' Audience Research Board – British Rate
& Data – BUSADS – Cinema Advertising Association –
Cinema And Video Industry Audience Research –
Conferences and Exhibitions Diary – Direct Mail
Information Service – Exhibition Industry Federation –
Exhibition Bulletin – Exhibition and Conferences Fact
Finder – Independent Television Commission – ITV
Association – Joint Industry Committee for Poster
Audience Research – Joint Industry Committee for
Regional Press Research – Media Expenditure Analysis
Ltd – Media Audits – Media Register – MediaTel –
Media Monitoring Services – National Readership
Surveys – Outdoor Advertising Association – Pan
European Television Audience Research – Periodical
Publishers Association – PressAd – Radio Advertising
Bureau – Radio Joint Audience Research – Royal Mail
– Target Group Index – Tube Research Audience
Classification – Verified Free Distribution – Other
Information Sources

Part 2   THE ORGANISATION OF MEDIA

Preface to the Fourth Edition

The media world and advertising practice have both become increasingly sophisticated in recent years, but people in all branches of advertising – advertisers, agencies and media-owners - often seem hindered rather than helped by the wealth of media data and techniques at their disposal. Immense energy is devoted to gathering information and great skill applied to devising new techniques, but unfortunately all this effort is often undermined by failure to build on a sound base. There appear to be more than a few 'blind spots': some matters are so fundamental they are taken for granted, and therefore receive insufficient attention. The chart overleaf shows the six fundamentals – the media themselves, the criteria by which they can be compared, the principles of media planning, and the three groups of organisations involved: advertisers, agencies and media-owners. Not only must all six operate efficiently in their own right, they must also interact effectively before optimum use can be made of advertising media.

My view is that any book on the use of media must necessarily at the same time be a book on advertising administration. This will no doubt present problems to librarians and booksellers – having ordered it, where should it go on the shelves? Should it go under *Media, Media Planning* or under *Advertising Administration?* Under *Advertisers, Agency Practice* or *Media-owners?* I leave this decision to the booksellers and librarians. If they opt for the safest course and buy more copies than they would otherwise have done, I would prefer, in the interests of modesty and good taste, that the suggestion should not have come from me!

The book is really three books in one:

The first part, 'The World of Media', outlines the range of media

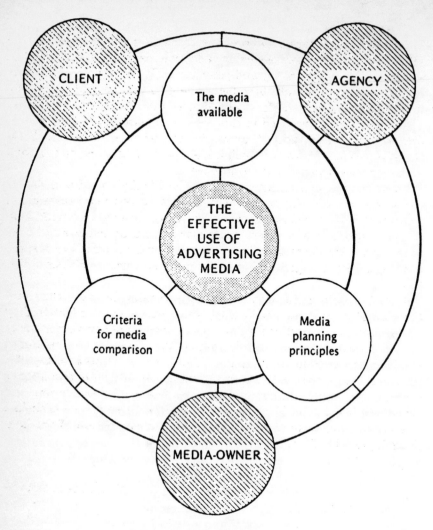

THE SIX FUNDAMENTALS

available to communicate your advertising message, reviews the data known about them, and discusses the criteria by which you can compare one with another.

The second part on 'The Organisation of Media' covers the firms and the individuals concerned with these media: the media-owners, the advertisers, their agencies and the media independents.

The third part, optimistically titled 'The *Effective* use of Advertising Media' devotes itself to how the individuals and organisations discussed in the second part can best ensure that the media described in the first part are used to maximum effect.

To attempt to produce a comprehensive media manual incorporating all the facts and figures needed for effective media planning would be an impossible, unnecessary and pointless task. Impossible in that any volume incorporating all these facts would be vast beyond proportion; unnecessary in that the facts and figures are readily available elsewhere in the sources listed in this book, and pointless in that, should any statistics be included, they would soon be out-of-date. This book, therefore, concentrates on principles, and you will find media costs and statistics conspicuous by their absence.

I welcome this opportunity to update the *The Effective Use of Advertising Media* since this makes it possible to give proper coverage of important new developments: some received only a passing mention in the last edition, while others are major structural changes not even under consideration at that time. Anyone wanting proof of how fast the world of media changes need only compare the various editions of this book.

A Fourth Edition also provides an opportunity for me to reconfirm the market for which I am writing, which was alas misunderstood by one reviewer of an earlier Edition. For the benefit of new readers, may I make clear the purpose of this volume. It is intended as a reference work for new entrants to advertising, and as a practical handbook for those working for professional qualifications or attending practitioner courses (hence its recommendation by the CAM foundation and Chartered Institute of Marketing).The book will also serve established executives wishing to make a fresh and detached review of the fast-changing world of media.

MARTYN P. DAVIS

Acknowledgements

Special thanks to Kevin O'Sullivan of D W S Advertising for his constructive comments, criticisms and suggestions; to Vanadis Ward for so carefully checking both manuscript and proofs; and to the following organisations for providing valuable information: The Advertising Association, Advertising Standards Authority, Association of Household Distributors, Association of Independent Radio Companies, Association of Media Independents, Atlantic 252, Audit Bureau of Circulations, British Broadcasting Corporation, British Rate & Data, Broadcasters' Audience Research Board, BSkyB, CAC, CACI, Capital Radio Sales, CCN Systems, Cinema Advertising Association, Cinema and Video Industry Audience Research, Conferences & Exhibitions Diary, Conference & Exhibition Fact Finder, Demographic Profiles, Direct Mail Information Service, Exhibitions Bulletin, Exhibition Industry Federation, Exhibition Marketing Group, Incorporated Society of British Advertisers, Independent Radio Sales, Independent Television Commission, Independent Television Association, Institute of Practitioners in Advertising, IPC Magazines, Joint Industry Committee for Poster Audience Research, Joint Industry Committee for Regional Press Research, London Transport Advertising, Media & Airtime Sales, Media Audits, Media Expenditure Analysis Ltd, Media Register, Media Sales & Marketing, MediaTel, National Readership Surveys, New Media Sales, Newspaper Publishers Association, Newspaper Society, Nielsen Marketing Research, Outdoor Advertising Association, Pan European Television Audience Research, Periodical Publishers Association, Pinpoint, PressAd, Radio Joint Audience Research, Radio Authority, Radio Sales Company, Royal Mail, Scottish & Irish Radio Sales, Saatchi & Saatchi Advertising, Sky Television, SuperChannel, Target Group Index, J Walter Thompson, Total Media, and Verified Free Distribution.

The author readily acknowledges his debt to those whose brains he has picked, with or without their knowledge.

Terminology

Throughout this book general terms such as 'advertiser', 'product' and 'purchaser' are used for reasons of simplicity: 'advertiser' may mean a manufacturer, retailer, service organisation or a non-profit government department; 'product' covers services as well as goods; and 'purchaser' must be taken to mean not only the man or woman in the street – in many cases, the buyer may be a large industrial group or some official department.

Other general terms are used when referring to media, again for simplicity. Any mention of advertisement 'size' should be taken to include all variations of the concept and thus covers the length of a television or radio or cinema commercial just as much as press or poster media. Similarly, 'insertions' should be taken to include transmission of commercials, or any other form of appearance of an advertisement. References to advertising copy cover the spoken just as much as the printed word, and design includes moving as well as conventional illustrations. Unless specifically stated, media terms should be interpreted as broadly as possible.

Generally, the reader is addressed as 'You' to avoid reference to any specific job title in any particular type of organisation. Whether your concern is selling advertising space or time, or buying it on behalf of a manufacturer's advertising department or advertising agency, the underlying fundamentals remain the same: you simply approach them from a different standpoint. Where specific posts are mentioned, jobs are sometimes described in terms of their being held by men: this is, again, for simplicity and to avoid cumbersome 'spokesperson-speak' rather than any male chauvinism or discrimination.

Foreword

by *JOHN W. HOBSON, CBE, FIPA, FRSA*
Former President of the Institute of Practitioners in Advertising
Chairman of the Advertising Association
President of the European Association of Advertising Agencies
Author of 'The Selection of Advertising Media'

It is a puzzling fact that, while so much attention and so many books are devoted to the creative and marketing sides of advertising, the media side is so thinly documented. The explanation lies, no doubt, in the glamour element in creative work, and in the commercial interest in effective marketing. Yet the choice of media, the correct analysis of each medium's value, the use of each for its proper purpose, the combination of various media into a powerful orchestration, are not only the governing factors in the wise spending of millions of pounds, but are in themselves a fascinating study and science.

It is, therefore, with particular pleasure that I welcome a new, up-to-date and comprehensive book on this important subject; and I would think that no one is better qualified to write it than Mr Martyn Davis.

I believe I am right in saying that the first analytical study of the subject was my own book *The Selection of Advertising Media* and to many students of advertising it was their first introduction to this side of the business. But the changes in media are so fast-moving that it was out-of-date in detail (though not in its principles) almost from the time of publication. In particular, it was written when television was only a gleam in someone's eye. It was consecutively updated by myself and others, but this could be no more than a process of tinkering.

Martyn Davis' earlier book[*] was written particularly from the viewpoint of educating the advertisement departments in the techniques of selling media, and it is now high time to have a new coverage of the subject as a whole – seeing it from the advertiser, the agency and the media angles.

[*] Handbook for Media Representatives.

It is a sobering thought, but one that needs to be constantly impressed, that with a budget of say £1 million, unsound media selection can waste £100,000 or £200,000 – sums that an advertiser would never think of wasting in some other context. The causes are many, and complex. They start with the failure to study the up-to-date figures of readership or viewing, and their value relationship to the target audience for the product. They go on with disregard of the basic 'Concentration – Domination – Repetition' pattern of good media selection. They derive from a slap-happy repetition of some traditional schedule or even from some concession to what the client Chairman's wife likes to see his advertising in. The truth is that scientific media selection can now be based on such a wealth of information about readership, attention values, size and frequency values and so on (not to mention the subjective elements of atmosphere and the company you keep) that it is a very challenging and complex operation to get the answer right.

Equally, in selling space in media, it is not easy to get away from the wishful thinking that expects one's own medium to be acceptable in all cases, and to limit one's own selling operation to those contexts where the statistics show it is an appropriate choice.

For the selfish financial values alone, the knowledge of media selection that this book promotes is essential. But also for the general reputation of advertising, and to avoid the impression of reckless spending in inappropriate contexts, the subject is of importance.

I hope that the book will be well received and well studied, and I wish it all success.

JOHN W. HOBSON

Part 1
THE WORLD
OF MEDIA

Chapter 1

Advertising, and the Media Available

The Advertising Standards Authority once defined advertising as *'The use of paid-for media space or time as a means of persuading people to take a particular course of action, or to reach a point of view.'*

The ASA's *British Code of Advertising Practice* is now broader in its coverage, but this is still the best *functional* definition. The key words, as far as this book is concerned, are 'paid-for media', as an essential element in the effective use of advertising media is a contractual agreement with a media-owner, who undertakes to transmit your advertising message in return for a given sum of money. The media-owner has a legal obligation to transmit your message, and you have a legal obligation to pay him for so doing. What that message should be is discussed later. Which media to use (and how best to use them) are the subject of this book.

ADVERTISING AS A MEANS OF COMMUNICATION

This book is aimed primarily at advertising people – whether with advertisers, agencies or media-owners – and there is thus no need to 'defend' advertising against some of the more foolish criticisms. Never-theless, it is worth reminding ourselves of the benefits it offers in comparison with other means of communication.

Any businessman might justifiably comment that his best advertise-ments were satisfied customers and ask why he should spend good money on advertising when word-of-mouth recommendation is spread-ing news of his products to potential purchasers. Most certainly any manufacturer will benefit from new purchasers learning from old about the benefits of his product and should do all he can to encourage this: much public relations activity has this very aim. Nevertheless,

3

the use of advertising to communicate messages brings certain specific benefits which make more than worthwhile the expenditure involved:

Speed Advertising communicates rapidly: many manufacturers launching new products need a return on their investment as swiftly as possible and rely on advertising to help them achieve this, rather than the gradual build-up in sales which word-of-mouth may bring.

Timing Personal recommendations, valuable though they are, may be spread over time in a haphazard way. Equally, it is uncertain when (and indeed if) the media will carry your News Releases in the editorial columns. Advertising, on the other hand, can be used as a precision instrument, stimulating your market when necessary. This may be a matter of seasons, promoting winter goods in the winter and summer goods in the summer, or alternatively may be a matter of days, giving customers a timely boost on a given day of the week.

Frequency Editorial references in the media may appear only when a company has news to release – how is the market to be stimulated in the meantime? Many manufacturers, particularly those whose goods are purchased on a repeat basis, cannot rely on News Releases or word-of-mouth. Their products are bought on a weekly or monthly basis and they need to stimulate the market at appropriate intervals: advertising can do just this, simply by booking appropriate appearances as part of your campaign plan.

Selectivity Personal recommendations spread indiscriminately, and you cannot rely on them to achieve full coverage of your particular target market: word often spreads to people with no interest in your product. Advertising, however, can be selective, and aimed at just the people most likely to buy your product. This may be a matter of media selection, choosing those media with good coverage of your target market, and here a fine degree of selectivity is possible, bearing in mind the wide range of media available to you. Alternatively, audience selection may be achieved by advertisement positioning just as much as media choice: an advertisement on the gardening page of a newspaper will select gardeners out of the total readership, and the same is true of other positions which prove equally effective in selecting suitable readers for other manufacturers. Naturally, many advertisers use both methods of audience selection, booking specific positions in selected media.

Definite delivery News Releases, as part of a co-ordinated promotional campaign, can help secure valuable editorial coverage. While 'third party endorsement' can play a major role in securing customer acceptance and keeping possible purchasers up-to-date with news about your product, such editorial references are necessarily uncertain. Should events of greater importance occur, your News Release – however well written and targetted – will be consigned to the bin. With paid-for advertising, you are certain your message will be delivered.

Completeness On many occasions you will find that, although the media have carried your story, an editor has 'subbed' the News Release rather than printed it in full. Word-of-mouth recommendation is similarly unreliable: those who made a purchase may, in spreading word to their friends, perhaps forget some key points about your product. The same can be said of your sales staff: at the end of a long day on the road, it is perhaps too much to expect tired representatives to deliver *every* sales point. With advertising, you know your chosen message will be delivered in full, simply because you have paid the media-owner to undertake this very task.

Accuracy Word-of-mouth recommendation and News Releases share a common weakness, in that your mesage is frequently distorted. With press advertising, you decide precisely which words you wish to use and control how they are to be conveyed. Furthermore, you receive proofs which you correct for accuracy. With other media you have equal control of advertisement content, and there is no possibility of your message being distorted.

Economy Advertising media costs spread over a very wide range but, whatever the figure, cost per contact is low in comparison with personal selling. Your company's salesforce plays a vital role and it could be argued that the best way to spread news about your products would be to employ more sales staff. Clearly, however, this would be most uneconomic: salesmen's time can be measured in tens of pounds per call, whereas advertising contacts are usually measured in pennies per thousand. Not only is advertising a more economic way of spreading messages than using your sales force, it can also be most effective in making your sales executives more productive – paving the way before they make their calls, or even providing them with direct leads to follow up.

COMMUNICATIONS MEDIA

Compared with other communications media, such as editorial coverage, word-of-mouth recommendation and even your own sales staff,

TOTAL ADVERTISING EXPENDITURE BY MEDIA

£ million	1981	1982	1983	1984	1985	1986	1987	1988	1989	1990
National Newspapers	467	515	584	678	747	844	959	1,099	1,222	1,187
Regional Newspapers	684	737	817	921	1,003	1,101	1,280	1,544	1,707	1,715
Consumer Magazines	230	239	254	280	307	350	378	440	482	480
Business & Professional	258	302	355	414	458	506	602	702	838	788
Directories	97	124	154	182	209	267	310	365	439	492
Press production costs	146	154	181	216	245	277	305	357	389	412
TOTAL PRESS	1,881	2,071	2,345	2,691	2,969	3,345	3,834	4,507	5,077	5,074
Television	809	928	1,109	1,249	1,376	1,675	1,872	2,127	2,286	2,325
Direct Mail	299	341	299	324	444	474	483	530	758	979
Poster & Transport	115	124	137	150	164	193	216	244	271	282
Radio	60	70	81	86	82	91	111	139	159	163
Cinema	18	18	16	16	18	19	22	27	35	39
TOTAL	3,182	3,552	3,987	4,516	5,053	5,796	6,538	7,574	8,585	8,863

paid-for advertising has the advantages of speed, timing, selectivity, definite delivery, completeness, accuracy and economy and – to some extent – *all* media offer these advantages.

To use these media effectively and efficiently, it is essential that you know precisely what you are using. The first three chapters in 'The World of Media' review the range of media available to transmit your message, the next two examine what we know about them, while the sixth chapter discusses the criteria by which you can compare one advertising medium with another.

There are many ways in which your advertising messages can be communicated to potential purchasers. Individual statistics would soon be out-of-date, so this review of media is necessarily limited to broad generalisations about the different categories. These media categories are by no means watertight compartments: some media can be considered under more than one heading, or even shift from one category to another. Some publications, for example, are really magazines in newspaper format, while others originated as newspapers and became magazines, and colour supplements can be considered under the twin headings of newspapers and magazines. The national press now often provide regional advertising facilities, while regional newspapers have co-operative facilities for national advertisers. The media market place is a very dynamic one, with existing media continuously adapting and new ones appearing.

The media available to you will be considered in the order listed in the table above, which shows their importance in terms of overall advertising expenditure. A review of other media will then be made.

TOTAL ADVERTISING EXPENDITURE BY MEDIA

Percentage of total	1981	1982	1983	1984	1985	1986	1987	1988	1989	1990
National Newspapers	14.7	14.5	14.6	15.0	14.8	14.6	14.7	14.5	14.2	13.4
Regional Newspapers	21.5	20.7	20.5	20.4	19.8	19.0	19.6	20.4	19.9	19.4
Consumer Magazines	7.2	6.7	6.4	6.2	6.1	6.0	5.8	5.8	5.6	5.4
Business & Professional	8.1	8.5	8.9	9.2	9.1	8.7	9.2	9.3	9.8	8.9
Directories	3.0	3.5	3.9	4.0	4.1	4.6	4.7	4.8	5.1	5.6
Press production costs	4.6	4.3	4.5	4.8	4.8	4.8	4.7	4.7	4.5	4.6
TOTAL PRESS	59.1	58.3	58.8	59.6	58.8	57.7	58.6	59.5	59.1	57.3
Television	25.4	26.1	27.8	27.7	27.2	28.9	28.6	28.1	26.6	26.2
Direct Mail	9.4	9.6	7.5	7.2	8.8	8.2	7.4	7.0	8.8	11.1
Poster & Transport	3.6	3.5	3.4	3.3	3.2	3.3	3.3	3.2	3.2	3.2
Radio	1.9	2.0	2.0	1.9	1.6	1.6	1.7	1.8	1.9	1.8
Cinema	0.6	0.5	0.4	0.4	0.4	0.3	0.3	0.4	0.4	0.4
TOTAL	100.0	100.0	100.0	100.0	100.0	100.0	100.0	100.0	100.0	100.0

Source: The Advertising Association

PRESS

This overall category covers several distinct types of printed advertising media.

Newspapers

As a group, newspapers permit you to deliver a detailed message on a given day, and at short notice, to a media audience whose size and composition are usually known, as circulation and readership figures are generally available. Space is usually sold by the single-column centimetre (S.C.C.), and in multiples thereof. A wide variety of special positions is usually available, as is classified or semi-display advertising.

Different newspapers appeal to different types of readership, but they fall into two broad categories, according to their physical format – 'broadsheets' and the smaller 'tabloids'. The former are usually read more by the A, B and C1 socio-economic grades discussed later, defined as 'Managerial, administrative and professional' at higher, intermediate, and junior or supervisory levels. Accordingly, broadsheets are often referred to as the 'quality' press. The majority of tabloid or 'popular' press readers are in the C2, D and E socio-economic grades, comprising skilled, semi or unskilled manual workers, and pensioners and casual or lowest-grade workers.

Another way of classifying newspapers is as national or regional. The dividing line between these two categories is, however, becoming increasingly blurred.

National newspapers In addition to the advantages just mentioned, the benefits of national newspapers can be summarised by considering the two parts of the name – 'national' and 'news' papers. There is a sense of urgency and immediacy about the advertising message which is distributed on a national basis (allowing, of course, for area variations in penetration). There are different papers to cover different types of readership, and British Rate & Data (see Chapter 4) lists six 'popular' national mornings; five 'quality' national mornings; six 'popular' national Sundays; and four 'quality' national Sundays. Also listed are two 'sport' national mornings.

Although 'national', it is nevertheless often possible to advertise on a regional-edition basis. An in-depth knowledge of each newspaper is essential as some, for example, divide into separate 'themed' sections. Colour is increasingly available, either as separate supplements or in the normal run of printing.

Sunday newspapers An in-depth knowledge of each paper and its format is again essential but, overall, Sunday newspapers have the additional advantage of being read in a more leisurely atmosphere, and present you with an opportunity to appeal to husband and wife or the entire family together. The fact that Sunday is perhaps a non-shopping day is rarely a hindrance, for consumer durables are seldom purchased on impulse and Sunday's leisure environment is ideal for writing for further information. Furthermore, an increasing number of retail outlets are starting to trade on Sundays. In addition, some Sunday newspapers have a longer life, being kept and re-read later in the week, or even retained for reference, which is rarely the case with daily newspapers. The various colour supplements often have a 'life-style' emphasis, and so can be considered under the twin headings of newspapers and magazines, as discussed below.

This general area of the national press has been subject to ups and downs in the circulation/readership patterns of individual publications, but has recently been shaken up by circulation wars between competing publishers, by the introduction of new titles/supplements, and by increasing segmentation of the marketplace. Nevertheless, the basic points made at the beginning of this section still apply.

In recent years, the press medium has changed in line with developments in printing technology. This has been particularly evident in the field of national newspapers. Fleet Street journalists formerly wrote editorial which was typeset and proof-read by others; copies printed in bulk in London were then physically transported by rail (or other special arrangements). The move from Fleet Street to London's Docklands revolutionised all these practices. 'Direct inputting', by which journalists typeset and check their own material direct resulted in considerable savings. Further cost reductions were achieved by vacating high-cost old-technology premises in Fleet Street and siting new-technology facilities in the low-cost Docklands area. Further economies resulted from sending heavy bulk supplies of newspapers by road rather than rail – or even achieving a double saving in both print and transport costs by printing at provincial centres where there was spare capacity, having sent the 'London set' material there electronically.

London In a category of its own, not truly national but too large to be considered local, is London's evening paper. In that readership figures are included in the National Readership Surveys, it is best considered under that heading – or at least as semi-national. The 'monopoly' was challenged a few years ago (unsuccessfully) by a new concept which illustrates yet again that media categories are not watertight compartments. This was a 24-hour London newspaper which cut across the old *morning* vs *evening* concept. If successful, it could have gone on to challenge the *national* vs *regional* concept by building up a network of 'metropolitan' newspapers to provide national coverage (rather than national press offering regional editions, or regional press co-operating to offer national advertising facilities). The London *Evening Standard* now features a monthly colour supplement.

Regional and local newspapers These sub-divide into two main categories: paid-for and free. They are frequently the mainstay of local retailers' advertising, and are also used by national advertisers for test marketing or boosting particular sales areas, to support local stockists, and to compensate for any weakness in the area coverage of other media such as national newspapers and television. Regional and local newspapers tend to be most effective for advertising close to point of sale, directing customers to local outlets, and providing maps showing the location of such outlets.

As with national newspapers, your advertising message can be quickly spread on a selected day and detailed product and price information included. In common with other press media, most regional and local newspapers have much-improved printing techniques as well as colour facilities.

Verified circulation figures for paid-for newspapers and distribution figures for free newspapers are available for most titles. Readership information is now provided by the JICREG database, and the Target Group Index shows that nine out of ten people read a regional newspaper. Area fluctuation is small, ranging from 87 per cent in Greater London to 93 in the South-West. Chapter 4 gives details of these data sources.

At time of writing, the breakdown of regional titles was:

Morning and evening dailies	89
Regional Sundays	6
Paid-for weeklies	434
Free weeklies	802
Total	1,331

These figures relate to advertising editions rather than editorial editions, of which there are rather more.

Regional mornings These papers usually have a more serious-minded approach and consequent lower circulations, but with coverage spreading some way outside the publishing centre. Editorially, they feature the business and political affairs of fairly wide areas in more detail than other newspapers, and many titles increased their circulations during the 1980s.

Regional evenings These generally have more of a mass appeal, and consequently larger circulations than the morning papers. This larger circulation is usually concentrated on those who live and work near the publishing centre. Editorially, copies carry substantial amounts of local news and sports coverage, together with much classified advertising.

Regional Sundays Though few in number, these combine the benefits of local interest with the advantages of Sunday publication described earlier. Like the local mornings, regional Sundays also perform an area service with in-depth coverage of issues not duplicated by the national Sundays.

Local paid-for weeklies These 434 titles form a significant category. They tend to relate to smaller communities than those covered by evening newspapers, but are widely followed for details of local news and events, and for their local retail and classified advertising, including births, marriages and deaths. Local weeklies are likely to have a longer life, being kept a full week for reference.

Free newspapers Some newspapers (and magazines or directories) are issued free of charge, either distributed door-to-door or given away at important central points (such as hotels, or stations where they are handed to people on their way to work). This type of free circulation must be distinguished from the controlled-circulation publications described below, which are distributed through the post.

It is worth noting a similarity between both types of free publication (household/central distribution and postal delivery). Most conventional publishers have two sources of revenue: sale of copies and sale of advertising space. Free and controlled-circulation publications have both forgone cover-price revenue in the belief that they can make greater profit through increased advertisement revenue, by the promise of 100 per cent coverage of the advertiser's target market.

Free newspapers have been published in England for more than 100 years, but the modern upsurge started in the United States and then spread to the UK in the late 1960s. The growth was stimulated by a boom in classified advertising, later extended to most display advertising categories, and the inability of the conventional press to handle it.

During the 1980s, the biggest growth sector in all UK advertising media was free newspapers. They have grown in number dramatically, and a high proportion of companies which publish conventional regional newspapers are also involved in the publication of free ones – a major change since the early days when free publications were seen as a threat and some conventional publishers banned from their columns anyone who advertised in free newspapers! There are now more than 800 titles. Most free newspapers carry a degree of editorial, although the advertising/editorial ratio tends to be higher (eg 9:1) than with paid-for titles. In some areas, free publications have entirely supplanted the paid-for newspapers.

The majority of free newspapers are received by household delivery on a weekly basis, and VFD (Verified Free Distribution, described in Chapter 4) has procedures to confirm that distribution is carried out systematically, consistently and professionally. This official verification is important: a major problem in the development of free newspapers was providing proof of their most important advantage: ability to deliver total coverage of a given area. In the early days it was sometimes said that free newspaper distribution was a dumping operation, and there are apocryphal stories of delivery boys throwing them away by the bundle! Hence the importance of official verification, since a good free newspaper is often just what the advertiser wants: it ensures full coverage of the community. The established paid-for newspaper might be more thoroughly read by people with their roots in the area, but if it offers low household penetration, advertisers may seek more comprehensive coverage.

There are now very few areas of the country which do not have a free newspaper delivered, and in many cases advertisers use both free and paid-for newspapers to provide comprehensive press coverage within geographically-defined target areas. Some free newspapers can also be used to distribute leaflets as loose inserts (see Association of Household Distributors, described in Chapter 4).

Series and groups, and media organisations

A factor that sometimes deters media-planners from using local media is the sheer physical labour of sending individual orders and advertising material and subsequently correcting individual proofs and paying individual invoices, which becomes increasingly burdensome the more local papers are used. A number of developments are, however, overcoming these administrative problems.

Many of the 1,331 regional newspapers share common ownership, and combine into series or groups which make planning and buying much easier. The fact that most regional newspapers have London offices, or are represented by national sales houses, further facilitates planning and buying 'packages' of titles. There are indeed standard regional packages covering ITV areas (some sold together with local television) or providing national coverage, and even facilities for placing orders on a one order/one piece of copy basis. The Newspaper Society's *PressAd* services, described in Chapter 4, include a central production facility. On receipt of master copies of each advertisement, PressAd sends material to each newspaper on the schedule. Some 95 per cent of regional and local titles subscribe to this service.

Co-operative advertising

Setting aside the order/production chores just mentioned, another factor which sometimes deters advertisers from using local media is that joint manufacturer/dealer promotions involve companies in the considerable task of contacting an extensive distribution network to determine individual stockists' participation in co-operative advertising. *PressAd* services are also important in this respect.

These various developments make it far easier from the administrative point of view to use local media, thus enabling regional newspapers to make their particular contribution to effective advertising schedules.

Magazines

Magazines, as newspapers, afford you an opportunity to deliver a detailed message. The exact manner of delivery can vary widely for there is great variety in magazine format, size, number of pages, printing quality, colour availability, and advertising facilities. Space is usually sold by the page and in fractions thereof and a variety of special positions, e.g. inside front cover or facing matter may be available.

One of the main reasons which leads advertisers to select magazines is mood – the reader's state of mind when your advertising message is delivered. This aspect of magazine media is frequently linked with another point in their favour, in that a finer degree of audience selection is often possible, since readership is usually in more clearly defined groups than the broad coverage of newspapers. These two points together give you considerable advertising advantages, since you reach a clearly defined group of prospects when they are likely to be receptive to your message.

A point which may count against magazines on the other hand is that of timing, since magazines are not precision instruments capable of delivering your message on a selected day, as can newspapers. The physical life of magazines is far longer, and your advertising message may be delivered at any time during this period. Indeed, cases are known where advertisers have received replies to magazine advertisements years after the cover date. Another aspect of timing is long copy dates, which may count against use of magazines by advertisers seeking to make swift announcements, or whose advertising content is subject to sudden and unexpected changes. Marketing considerations will determine which of the two contrasting points is more important to you: lack of precise timing, or the far longer life of magazine advertisements discussed later. Technological changes are having their effect here, however, as copy dates are shortening.

This preamble has, of course, contained generalisations and it would be unrealistic to group all magazines together and view them as one homogenous media group. They can be sub-divided into many further categories – general consumer magazines; specialist publications appealing to groups having in common a certain occupation, hobby, sport or other special interest; the trade press; and controlled-circulation journals.

General consumer magazines These appeal to the broad mass of men or women or both, but there is increasing segmentation by life-style. There is usually scope for a finer degree of audience selection, as readers tend to have more clearly defined characteristics than for newspapers. Advertisers know there audience characteristics, because most general magazines are included in the National Readership Surveys described in a later chapter. Accordingly, total readership can be sub-divided into the various categories of age, sex and socio-economic group, or by specific characteristics such as ownership of appliances, and this makes precise audience selection much easier. This fine degree of selectivity is coupled with the other media factor of a receptive audience. With some general interest magazines, split-run, regional and test-town facilities are available as well as national advertising.

Specialist magazines These, as the name implies, appeal to groups having a special interest in common, but can be sub-divided into different categories according to the nature of that interest, which may be an occupation (industrial, commercial or professional) or a hobby, sport or other specialist activity. When considering publications where the special interest is a technical/occupational/professional one, you should bear in mind the difference between 'vertical' and 'horizontal' media. The former cover a single trade or occupation at all management levels from top to bottom, whereas the circulation of horizontal media implies coverage of readers occupying similar positions but spread across a wide range of industries, for example accountants. (See also 'Points in Common' below.) The full range of business-to-business media is discussed in depth in my other book, *Business-to-Business Marketing and Promotion* (Century Business 1989).

Trade journals These are, in fact, also special interest publications, but are singled out for separate attention since advertisers use them in a particular way. In using general or specialist magazines, you try to persuade readers to buy in their own right, as consumers of your merchandise. Only a few advertisers, selling such things as shop fittings, use the trade press to promote their merchandise direct. Most advertisers use the trade press to contact retailers in their vital role as intermediaries between the manufacturer and the public. Accordingly, trade press advertising messages usually urge 'Be ready for the demand that public advertising will stimulate – stock up, display and make a profit!' rather than 'Buy for your own use'. Trade press advertisements, therefore, tend to feature incentives such as details of coming consumer advertising, display material available, and profit to be gained.

Specialist and trade press: points in common Despite the major differences in the way in which the two media groups are used, special interest and trade publications have certain characteristics in common, relating to the number and type of readers. With general magazines, you usually have circulation and readership figures to evaluate, but with special interest journals and the trade press it is sometimes impossible for you to form a considered opinion in the same way. Circulation figures are usually available, but not always. Furthermore, where circulation is known, this frequently reveals that the publication does not fully cover the group in question. A counter argument to incomplete market coverage is that the proportion reached are the enthusiasts and 'trend setters', and that those who do not read the publication cannot have the same degree of interest as those who do. This, however, only highlights another point sometimes made against these magazines: that sometimes all you know about coverage is what is implied by the magazine's title. When considering a trade or special interest magazine, you need to know where the readers are located within the country, whether they are large or small buyers, traditional or modern in outlook, and so on. In some cases an 'ABC Profile' (see Chapter 4) may be issued, but in others, however, no readership information is provided and you are left to deduce what you can by common sense, from the title and contents of the magazine and, if available, publishers' own surveys.

In short, the specialist and trade press may reach only a proportion of your total market, and you know little or nothing about the characteristics of the proportion you do reach. This is perhaps a harsh statement, but it accurately summarises the problem you may face when attempting to evaluate some of these media. Instead of hard data, you often have little choice but to rely on old-fashioned criteria like editorial 'feel' and your own personal knowledge of what is read and respected in the industries of your customers. The fact that there may be several publications competing for the same market makes this in-depth study of the actual magazines all the more important.

Controlled-circulation distribution The incomplete market coverage and lack of readership information just mentioned have led to an interesting development, namely controlled-circulation publications sent to individuals in certain defined categories. The magazine is not sold but distributed free of charge, through the post, in the same way as subscription copies. Conventional publishers have argued that readers are unlikely to value anything they do not pay for, but the counter-argument is that the cost of many special interest publications is borne by employers: the actual readers are unaware of the source of the copy that arrives on their desks, and value it according to the subject matter.

The benefits of a controlled-circulation publication depend on its distribution, which overcomes the two main drawbacks to conventional publications: incomplete coverage and lack of readership information. Controlled-circulation journals fully cover the market chosen by the publisher as his target market, and readership information is automatically available simply through analysis of the mailing list to which the journal is sent. Thus, in theory, the medium is near perfect. Any medium has it drawbacks, however, and those of controlled circulation arise from the credibility of the journal's mailing list.

Controlled circulation gives you full coverage of the market only if your market matches precisely the publication's market. Should the controlled-circulation journal's definition be wider or narrower than yours, this must mean either waste circulation or incomplete coverage. Further, there is the vital question of how the mailing list was compiled. Giving a definition is one thing, but obtaining a list of all those coming within this definition is another. This problem is further complicated by the normal difficulty of keeping any mailing list up-to-date. The Audit Bureau of Circulations described in a later chapter provides data on controlled-circulation journals, but some media planners undertake additional 'spot checks' on reader attitudes and mailing-list accuracy by telephoning individuals who should be on the mailing list to ask if they receive copies, and their opinion of them.

Free magazines Another interesting variation in distribution method is for magazines to be given away free. This could be by door-to-door distribution in selected areas, or by handing copies to people on their way to work, or by making copies available through hotels or on aircraft etc. Such free magazines cover a wide spectrum and range from those that contain nothing but advertising to those with 30 per cent or more editorial as well as glossy magazines boasting carefully selected distribution and the up-market title of 'Courtesy publications'. VFD (Verified Free Distribution) desribed in Chapter 4 is highly relevant in this respect.

The press medium overall

Before turning to other media, it is important to see the press media in context. What was formerly a relatively static marketplace is now a fast-moving and dynamic one, quite apart from changes in printing technology. Publishers compete for the same markets, adapt existing publications and launch new titles.

TELEVISION

In terms of overall advertising expenditure, television should be the next medium to cover. The many recent changes, those now taking place and other changes in the pipeline mean the situation is so complex that it calls for separate attention in the next chapter. This chapter, therefore, now turns to the next largest medium in terms of share of overall advertising expenditure – direct mail.

DIRECT MAIL

Among the advantages of using postal services to deliver advertising messages is selectivity, since your mailing can be directed to a selected list of individuals. Further advantages are complete coverage of your market and the absence of wastage, since the mailing covers and is restricted to those within the defined market. All depends, of course, on the accuracy of your mailing list. This can be obtained in a number of ways, and in some cases you can build up a mailing list from your own records. Where internal records are not suitable, external sources can be consulted. Published reference books can provide much information, but this source suffers from two drawbacks. One is that frequently there is more than one reference book and the task of cross-checking one against the others is unavoidable, for clearly there is no point in mailing the same individual more than once. Removal of duplicate names, sometimes called 'merge and purge', is straightforward in comparison with the problem raised when two sources show different names for the holder of a given job. Only one can be correct, and the discrepancy no doubt stems from the fact that one reference source went to press later than the other and staff changes took place in the meantime.

Such changes highlight the second drawback of using published sources – the problem of keeping any list up-to-date. This involves carefully checking relevant publications regularly for news of staff changes, and this is no small task. For these reasons many firms turn to direct mail houses or list brokers, relying on them to provide mailing lists that are both comprehensive and up-to-date. External lists fall into two main groups – general consumer, and business-to-business or special interest. There are usually many lists available in the latter categories (industrial / occupational / professional / trade / technical, or alternatively, specialist activities/hobbies/sports or other interests) and your task is not so much obtaining lists but choosing between them. General consumer lists, on the other hand, once presented a major problem.

If you could not build your own list from customer enquiries and responses to earlier advertising, where could you go to get one? The population census was insufficiently selective and often very dated, and the same criticism applied to telephone directories which, additionally, gave incomplete coverage. The situation changed dramatically, however, with the introduction of *geo-demographic* classifications. One such system is ACORN (A Classification of Residential Neighbourhoods) which, as its title implies, analyses where you live in terms of type of neighbourhood or residence. To give a simple example of its application, there is little point in your sending direct mail about lawn-mowers or garden furniture to someone who lives in a house without a garden! There are a number of geo-demographic classifications, described on page 202, which can help you target your direct mail accurately.

Use of direct mail as a medium brings other advantages, such as personalisation. Direct mail letters can be run off in bulk, but with the name and address of each recipient 'matched in' at the head of each letter to give the appearance of individual typing, and your signature realistically reproduced to give the effect of a personal letter. Indeed, many direct mail letters are individually typed on automatic machines and personally signed for greater authenticity.

Further benefits stem from direct mail's flexibility, which permits sending different messages to different target groups and, for overseas markets, addressing them in their own language. Another benefit is that distance is no object, whereas a representative's visit would be most costly.

Flexibility is a major benefit even within the UK, and becomes even more important as direct mail becomes computer-based. Mailing lists are increasingly segmented, and sophisticated retrieval systems can send relevant letters to buyers of different products, or adopt other variations – different letters to those who have bought within the last month or stated multiples thereof, for instance. The computer can even signal those who have not responded within, for example, the last year, thereby making it possible for you to clean your list by removing 'dead' names and addresses. (The use of databases for direct mail purposes is discussed in more detail later.)

You can, if you wish, test different promotional messages, creative formats, mailing lists or other campaign aspects, before your main campaign. Pre-testing – a difficult task with other media – is relatively simple with direct mail.

Direct mail's flexibility also permits you to 'turn the tap' on and off with ease. This could be important if, for example, production restraints or salesforce capacity call for a limited number of enquiries, or for controlled flow over time.

Timing is another advantage of direct mail, since you can select the most suitable dates and frequency for delivery of your advertising message and need not be restricted by any media-owner's publication dates.

Yet another advantage of direct mail is that inclusion of reply-paid postcards or envelopes can stimulate replies. Certainly you can include reply-paid folders or freepost coupons in press advertisements, but this takes up costly space and is often unattractive. With such press advertisements you cannot be so selective and your prospective customer must still write in his name and address, while with direct mail you can enter the recipient's particulars on the card beforehand, so that all he need do is post it. Such direct response makes evaluation of results and control of your campaign that much easier.

Direct mail shots can also include leaflets, booklets, or even samples. In short, there is no limit to the information you can include. Some direct mail shots in fact amount to reference books and are kept by recipients as useful sources of information.

The attention factor of direct mail is somewhat controversial. Many claim that some people receive so much direct mail that they pay no attention to mailings, but throw them straight into the waste-paper basket. No doubt some people do receive a large number of mailings, but this is perhaps a creative rather than a media problem. If a direct mail letter is thrown away, this is proof that the mailing *did* receive attention – if only to detect that it was a direct mail shot. Attention *was* given and the problem is thus a creative one, of devising a mailing shot to retain that attention. I do not accept the generalisation that 90 per cent of direct mail is wasted: 100 per cent of *bad* direct mail is thrown away, and most *good* direct mail carefully studied – the recipient may not even consider it a direct mail shot.

Direct mail houses can help here, and their services can be considered under three broad headings: provision of mailing lists, physical handling of the mailing, and creative advice on the type of direct mail campaign to be mounted. Also highly relevant in this context are the Direct Mail Information Service and the Royal Mail's Direct Marketing Department, described in Chapter 4.

The main drawback to direct mail is its cost. Though often low in total outlay, direct mail can be very expensive when considered on a cost per contact basis, though a well-planned campaign often gives a low ratio of cost per enquiry, or even cost per sale. The advantages, however, are many, and as always your task is to assess the benefits against cost. In this respect, this formerly static medium has in recent years undergone major changes in the light of new technology: computerisation of mailing lists, and new printing methods. These developments are of great importance, bearing in mind the rapid increase in direct marketing (discussed in Chapter 8) in which direct mail plays so vital a role: expenditure on direct mail increased from £444 million in 1985 to £979 million in 1990.

POSTER AND TRANSPORT

Facilities exist for poster displays in most urban areas in Great Britain. Perhaps the most traditional form of advertising, the poster medium has undergone a major overhaul during the 1980s. Historically the poster industry is divided into 'roadside' and 'transport' sections, with Advertising Association statistics showing an expenditure ratio of just under 2:1.

Poster sizes

Poster size terminology is historical, and 'sheets' referred to the number of sheets of paper that had to be pasted (or *posted*) up on the hoarding. The standard poster sizes are:

4 sheet	1.524 × 1.016 metres
6 sheet	1.676 × 1.219 metres
16 sheet	3.048 × 2.032 metres
32 sheet	3.048 × 4.064 metres
48 sheet	3.048 × 6.096 metres

In addition to these standard sizes, there are larger 96-sheet *Supersite* panels and special displays. These are normally on main roads and can be hand-painted, with three-dimensional illuminated displays if required. Although historically there is a wide range of sizes – including Double Crown (508mm × 762mm) and Quad Crown (1016mm × 762mm) the overhaul of the industry resulted in a dramatic growth in the panel sizes most demanded by advertisers. Of the total UK universe of 130,000 roadside panels, there are now some 70,000 4-sheet and 6-sheet panels (in many of the new towns and redevelopment areas, including the vast majority of shopping precincts) and 30,000+ large 48-sheet sites, and more than 2,000 larger supersite panels and special displays.

Within the transport section of the industry, there is a wide variety of sizes and sites (too many to list here – think how many different types you pass on your way to work!) on buses, trains and stations.

Poster research

The great majority of roadside sites (some 95 per cent of the total) are owned by poster contractors in membership of the Outdoor Advertising Association, and an independent measurement of audience delivery is available through OSCAR, the outdoor site classification and audience research described on page 81. Within the transport section, audience statistics are not so widely available, although BUSADS and TRAC (the Tube Research Audience Classification, described in Chapter 4) provide much useful information about sites on London's transport system.

The advantages of poster advertising

Posters, whether on roadside hoardings or transport sites, offer you the full benefit of colour. This can be of particular advantage since printing the posters rests within your own control, and high quality can thus be assured. With other media you must accept the colour quality uniformly available to all, but with posters you can if you wish achieve a quality often unobtainable in press media, simply by printing in more than the standard four colours. Some sites have also featured electronic displays. Supersite advertisers have sometimes achieved spectacular effects with three-dimensional constructions (one adhesive manufacturer even stuck a car to his hoarding!). The majority of poster advertisers, however, achieve highly effective communications without this additional expense, through standard printing.

The poster medium offers many additional advantages. You control the area of coverage and can localise your campaign to a street, a town, an area, a region, or alternatively mount a nationwide campaign. You can in fact book sites in exactly those areas where you most need advertising support.

A further advantage is that you achieve almost complete coverage of the active population within the selected area, together with a high repetition factor (depending on the number of sites booked) for nearly everybody goes out and does so frequently, and therefore has the opportunity to see outdoor advertising. The greater the number of sites booked, the faster will maximum coverage of the population of the target area be achieved, and the greater will be the repetition factor.

For these reasons, posters are regarded by many as the ideal reminder medium. This view is re-informed by the fact that posters are usually read at a glance, and thus well suited to a brief message. When the factors of high coverage and repetition, colour and reminder close to the point of sale in selected areas are considered together, it becomes clear why a large number of manufacturers place great faith in poster advertising.

Poster advertising need not always be restricted to a brief message: on a number of occasions, particularly where the audience is captive as in railways and buses, there is an excellent opportunity for you to convey a more detailed message.

The drawbacks of the outdoor medium

The many advantages of the poster medium are almost self-evident but there are, of course, drawbacks. One of these is defacement – by weather or vandals. Some former disadvantages of the medium – shortage of good sites due to the T/C (till cancelled) bookings described below, and lack of research data – have now largely been overcome by the overhauling of the industry, and by the new OSCAR scores.

Buying poster advertising

Advertising rates vary according to site, but are subject to discounts for six-month or twelve-month orders. Sites can be bought individually (a method of purchase known as site-by-site or *line-by-line*), by preselected campaigns, or by selected packages. At one time, poster availability was a problem in that many good sites were tied up in 'till cancelled' contracts, but the proportion on T/C bookings is now less than 15 per cent.

Restructuring of the poster medium has made campaign planning and buying much easier, and the 1980s saw the emergence of national poster contractors for the sizes most in demand – for 4-sheet 'Adshel' bus shelters, for 4-sheets in shopping precincts, and for 48-sheet panels. Additionally, there are specialist poster agencies which can put together complete poster campaigns bought site-by-site, using the OSCAR system.

Other forms of outdoor advertising

A final point is that the term 'outdoor advertising' is sometimes extended to embrace other media not yet mentioned. British Rate & Data, the standard reference work described later, has sections dealing with aerial banners, airports, freight transport, hansom cabs, mobile adtrailers, parking meters, sea transport, sports venues, supermarket sites and taxis.

RADIO

Radio as an advertising medium is available on a local basis through an extensive network of Independent Local Radio (ILR) stations, which also carry some national campaigns. 'National' radio advertising is partly available through *Atlantic 252*, which transmits from Dublin to a large part of the UK (although this is not part of the official network, as it holds an Irish Republic rather than a Radio Authority licence). National radio advertising as such will soon be available through three Independent National Radio (INR) stations.

Before discussing radio advertising, it is important to recognise that the medium is in the throes of change. Independent Radio, formerly supervised by the Independent Broadcasting Authority (IBA), is now under the official control of the Radio Authority (RA), which has three main tasks:

- to assign frequencies

- to appoint licensees with a view to widening listener choice

- to regulate programming and advertising.

The RA began its regulatory and licensing role in January 1991, when the 1990 Broadcasting Act came into force, and now supervises all independent radio services. These comprise national, local, cable, satellite and restricted services. The latter category includes all short-term services (for example, 'special events' radio) and highly-localised permanent services (for example, student radio).

22

ILR licences are awarded to applicants whose proposals would, in the opinion of the Authority, best cater for the needs and interests of listeners in the area. Applicants must also have adequate financial resources to implement their programming proposals. Unlike television, no competitive bidding is involved for local licences. INR licences, however, are awarded to the highest cash bidder.

As well as satisfying the RA's programme codes, licence-holders must also ensure that they meet the requirements of its advertising and sponsorship codes. Under the IBA, there was a maximum of nine minutes advertising per hour. This requirement has been removed, and the amount carried is now left to the discretion of individual radio stations. All programmes, with the exception of the news, can now be sponsored.

The Authority can apply sanctions to any licensee who breaks either programming or advertising rules. These require that advertising must be clearly separated from programmes and obvious for what it is. As with other media, advertising created for radio should be compatible with the medium that carries it, and there is evidence of growing awareness of the special needs of radio: the Authority's controls have not inhibited advertisers from creating entertaining, informative and interesting commercials which make a special contribution to the sound of Independent Local Radio.

Independent local radio

Advertising on ILR is sold in standard metric units of 10, 20, 30, 40, 50 and 60 second commercials. As well as 'spot' advertisements, a number of sponsored programmes are available, subject to individual negotiation. Advertisers wishing to sponsor programmes normally undertake a sponsorship of not less than 13 weeks.

Radio, a relatively recent advertising medium in the UK, is frequently a 'companion' to its listeners, so your advertising message is received in an intimate and personal atmosphere. Successful advertising requires an appreciation of radio's one-to-one relationship between listener and broadcaster. The medium is a transient one, and your message is received through one sense only: that of hearing. Messages should be brief and make maximum effective use of words. Their delivery and the supporting sound effects or music are equally important.

People listen to radio in the car, on the beach, in parks, in the kitchen at home and in the factory at work. It thus reaches people at different times and in different moods from other media.

As ILR is a local medium, many broadcasters speak with an intimate knowledge of their local community, so establishing a link with their audience. It can serve the advertising needs of local firms and equally give 'area boosts' where necessary for national advertisers.

The composition of the radio audience varies between different periods of the day, and selective timing can deliver your advertising message to various important groups, eg business executives (at 'drive time'), housewives, teenagers and young adults. The pattern of listening to the ILR network naturally differs, according to each station's programme pattern.

One great advantage of radio as an advertising medium is its ability to communicate your advertising message at very short notice. A commercial can be scripted, recorded and transmitted in a matter of hours. As discussed later, however, certain categories of advertising, such as for medical items, need to be 'cleared' to ensure that they comply with the RA's Codes and with the many UK laws which impinge on advertising.

This operational flexibility means that radio executives can accept and transmit your advertising message at short notice and thereby meet urgent needs for swift transmissions when marketing conditions call for this. Frequent market stimulation is also possible, simply through repeat transmissions.

A further advantage is that radio can be relatively inexpensive to use, and commercials are normally cheap to make. Although there are many radio production companies, all ILR stations can make your commercials as well as transmitting them. Thus, for advertisers seeking a low-cost medium, radio advertising is often extremely attractive.

The ILR network

As well as being flexible by time and day, radio is also flexible by area, as airtime can be booked with individual ILR stations. The Radio Authority's most recent 'Pocket Book' lists 140 Independent Local Radio services and this number will increase.

Two major changes have occurred since the last edition of this book – 'split broadcasting' on AM and FM frequencies, and the issue of what were once termed 'incremental' licences. Both changes have considerably increased the choice of radio services to listeners, increasing equally the choice of radio media open to you as an advertiser. The future changes described below will increase this choice even further.

Split broadcasting

At one time radio programme contractors transmitted the same service over both AM and FM frequencies. What was once termed 'simulcasting' has in most cases been replaced by split broadcasting, whereby two services are now provided instead of one. As an example, London's single Capital Radio service has been replaced by Capital FM and Capital Gold (AM). Most ILR stations now provide two programme services, except where audiences or areas are insufficient to support this. In other cases, contractors retain their individual FM services, but combine to provide a joint AM service, eg Trent FM and Leicester Sound FM now share GEM-AM. Split broadcasting added perhaps 30 new radio services to those originally provided. Others were provided by the granting of additional licences.

Additional licences

Further radio services arose through what were once called 'incremental' franchises, granted by the IBA to provide a *new* radio service within an existing ILR area. Three main groups of additional programming, not previously available within the area, were covered by such franchises:

1. Specialist music (for example, Jazz FM and Kiss FM in London – the first self-explanatory, the latter providing dance music)

2. Ethnic groups (eg Sunrise FM in Bradford, which broadcasts for the Asian, Afro-Caribbean and other ethnic communities)

3. Specific communities (eg RTM, which provides a specialist music, community, ethnic and news service specifically for Thamesmead).

More than 20 new services were provided through the IBA granting such franchises. When the Radio Authority took over from IBA, all existing franchises, including the former 'incrementals', were replaced with licences.

Booking ILR airtime

Airtime can be booked direct for local advertisers or, where appropriate, through national sales offices responsible for maintaining contact with national advertisers and advertising agencies. It can also be booked on a regional basis, through regional rate cards covering stations within a coherent region. National packages can also be negotiated. The national sales houses are as follows:

Capital Radio Sales (CRS), 356 Euston Road, London NW1 3BW

Independent Radio Sales (IRS), Crown House, 72 Hammersmith Road, London W14 8YE

Media Sales & Marketing (MS&M), 365 Euston Road, London NW1 3AR

Radio Sales Company (RSC), Television House, 32 Bedford Row, London WC1R 4HE

Scottish & Irish Radio Sales (SIRS), 55 Bondway, London SW8 1SJ

The radio industry also recently announced a new marketing initiative, the formation of the Radio Advertising Bureau, to promote radio generically and complete airtime sales deals.

From time to time you may hear of 'pirate' radio stations (so called because they originally transmitted without licence, from ships moored outside British territorial waters). Tighter anti-piracy provisions in British law and in international regulations usually succeed in driving these illegal radio advertisers off the air. These preventative measures are re-inforced by the fact that it is now illegal to advertise on such stations.

Independent Local Radio – the future

At one time the plan was for local radio services to be provided on a 'one station per area' basis. Under the new Broadcasting Act, however, the way is now open for as many additional radio channels as any area can support, provided the new services do not duplicate existing provision.

The Radio Authority intends to advertise up to 20 new ILR licences each year for the forseeable future. Nineteen were advertised during 1991, focused initially upon 'gaps in the map' (areas currently not served by any ILR station), but other licences will be granted to provide additional services in existing ILR areas. The Authority has invited expressions of interest, on which to base its decisions about where and how to advertise new ILR licences.

National Independent Radio

Expansion of radio services will not be restricted to local stations as, for the first time, Independent National Radio licences are on offer.

There will be three INR stations, one of which will be an FM service. The other two, one of which must be speech-based, will broadcast on AM (using frequencies currently being relinquished by BBC Radios 1 and 3).

The future Independent National Radio services are currently referred to as INRs 1, 2 and 3 (even though they may not be known as such when they commence broadcasting). Unlike local radio, the three national licences are awarded on a 'highest bid' basis. Although there is no quality threshold as with television, once the licence has been awarded and the licensee is broadcasting, a 'promise of performance' will have to be met to avoid facing the RA's sanctions.

The licence for INR 1 was awarded to Classic FM, which intends to launch its classical music service in the Autumn of 1992, installing a network of 22 transmitters reaching 86 per cent of the population.

INR 2 (AM) was advertised in 1991 as open to 'all comers', and awarded to Independent Music Radio (IMR), an Adult Rock service jointly owned by Virgin and TV-am. As this is not speech-based, INR 3 will clearly have to meet that requirement. It is likely that this third licence will be advertised towards the end of 1992.

Radio – the future

As regards both national and local independent radio, this book will clearly be overtaken by events. Nevertheless the future structure of the medium is clear in outline, even if there will be many changes in detail. Overall, commercial radio is obviously an expanding medium. Its share of total listening was nearly 38 per cent in 1991 and the commercial radio industry predicts that by 1995 its share of total listening – allowing for the three INRs and more ILRs – will increase to 50 per cent.

CINEMA

There are more than 1,650 cinemas in the UK available for screen advertising, which represents about 95 per cent of all cinemas. They may be bought line-by-line, individually or in any combination. By the end of 1991 the number of screens operating in the UK was the highest figure since the late 1960s.

Since then the UK cinema industry has undergone a major modernisation programme. The less attractive and less profitable cinemas have closed and many single-auditorium cinemas converted into modernised multi-screen complexes with greater appeal to the cinema-goer. Provision of modern facilities has not been restricted to existing locations, however, and there have been completely new cinema developments. In many cities throughout the country these take the form of 'multiplex' cinemas within new entertainment complexes which include discotheque, restaurant, bar and other facilities.

Cinema advertising offers you the advantages of colour, sound and movement, giving creative scope to demonstrate your product in full colour and with high technical quality on the large screen, to show people enjoying its use, and with music and the human voice heightening the effect. Other creative approaches such as animation and computer graphics are also possible. In addition, your message is screened to what is descriptively termed a 'captive' audience, sitting facing the screen in a darkened auditorium – contrast this with television viewing. The cinema audience is a distinct one, composed largely of young adults with freely disposable purchasing power, at a point in their lives when they make many important decisions, thus providing a market of considerable attraction to many advertisers.

Since the mid-1980s, cinema has enjoyed a sustained revival in popularity, with 1991 figures forecast to be the highest total for ten years. Coverage build-up is slow, however, and full penetration of your target groups by no means complete. There are three main ways to buy cinema campaigns:

1. Line-by-line In some cases, additional advantages stem from the fact that cinema advertising can be localised: you control the area of coverage and can localise your campaign to a town, an area, a region, or alternatively mount a nationwide campaign. The benefit of this to the local trader is obvious – he can appeal to his local audience and attract enquiries by featuring his name and address on the cinema screen. Other advertisers with broader distribution can follow the same principle by building a schedule based on cinemas that match their particular geographical requirements and, after demonstrating their product in the opening part of the film, conclude with the name and address of the local dealer, perhaps on a shared-cost basis. On-screen local advertising can also be extended to include point of sale, through foyer promotions.

2. Packages For advertisers whose needs are more general, the major cinema contractors offer a number of special packages, which ease administration and often include bonuses or discounts. Operation varies slightly between different contractors, but the principles on which these packages are based remains the same.

Similar facilities exist for children's packages while other facilities offer opportunities to buy packages of advertising built around individual film titles, or 'Art Screen' cinemas. These facilities are popular with advertisers who wish to capitalise on the large audiences of outstanding films, to ensure that their films are shown in an environment that is helpful for the product, or to take advantage of the audience patterns created by films with different film certificates.

3. Audience discount plans One important development in the selling of cinema advertising space was the Audience Discount Plan (ADP). Many major advertisers have taken advantage of this innovation which offers seasonally weighted admission targets at a fixed maximum cost per thousand admissions.

Cinema advertising commercials are shown within one reel which is screened at all performances (except children's matinees) with the house lights down, prior to the main feature film. You can buy screen time in this reel on the basis of standard timelengths of 15, 30, 45 and 60 seconds or, alternatively, book in metric lengths of 10, 20, 30, 40 or 60 seconds. Longer timelengths can usually be accommodated, subject to negotiation.

The basic booking unit is one week's advertising on one screen, and each cinema screen has its own rate, geared to its level of admissions. Most campaigns, however, cover a number of cinemas over a period of several weeks or months.

A final point to be made is that cinema advertising can also be used to reach specialist groups such as airline passengers, the services, holiday camps or the ethnic communities.

OTHER ADVERTISING MEDIA

Exhibitions

Exhibitions, one of the oldest advertising media, originated with the mediaeval trade fairs. Exhibitions range from those of general consumer interest to those appealing to special interest groups or trades, with many intermediate categories. Some exhibitions may be considered in more than one category, as when entrance is restricted to the trade for the first few days, after which the exhibition opens to the public. In the course of time, exhibitions may perhaps shift their position in the scale, as when a special interest exhibition arouses such general interest that public attendance gradually outnumbers special interest visitors. Cutting across the scale of special interest and general exhibitions are geographical variations, since exhibitions may be local, national or even international in their coverage.

According to the Exhibition Industry Federation (EIF) described in Chapter 4. there are more than 45 exhibition venues of over 2,000 square metres in the UK, at which some 800 events are held annually, and the EIF is establishing an industry categorisation of events to help you more easily identify suitable exhibitions for your own product or service.

With some special interest exhibitions you have the benefit of a selected audience, implied by the exhibition's subject matter. A drawback that the medium shares with the special interest or trade press is that sometimes all you know about the exhibition's coverage is what you can deduce by common sense from its title. Often there is little or no information about where visitors come from, the type of firm they represent, their position in the organisation, and so on. The Audit Bureau of Circulations, described later, has an Exhibitions Data Division and the Association of Exhibition Organisers now makes it a condition of membership that its members audit their exhibitions. The position is thus improving, but in many cases there is still a serious lack of information.

The advantages this medium offers really speak for themselves. Exhibitions afford you the double benefit of demonstration combined with personal contact. You can demonstrate your product (a tremendous advantage when it is too bulky to take around) and can do so under ideal conditions, in settings specially designed for the purpose. Prospective buyers can see and handle your product, try it for themselves and ask questions. As an exhibitor you can for your part answer their queries, distribute samples or literature, obtain names and addresses to follow up for subsequent action, or take orders on the spot.

An additional benefit with many special interest exhibitions is that they represent the one opportunity in the year when you can contact virtually all your prospective customers, since the opportunity to view all the current models ensures a consistently high attendance. Exhibitions can also provide opportunity to express appreciation of support given during the year, with your company's sales director and other senior staff using the stand as a basis for dispensing hospitality and greeting those they cannot call on regularly themselves. Admittedly, this is sometimes abused, with exhibits being reduced to the role of free bars and buyers making the rounds of the stands. Accordingly, the main advantages of exhibitions – demonstration and personal contact – should always be kept to the fore.

A further benefit of exhibitions arises from the descriptive entry you contribute to the catalogue, which visitors frequently keep for reference. In addition, there is always the possibility, for a fortunate few, of valuable editorial publicity: most exhibitions merit considerable comment in the press and other media, and those with revolutionary products or striking stands may be the subject of many editorial features.

Other than the lack of audience statistics already mentioned, the main drawback to exhibitions is their high cost. They are often very much more expensive than would appear at first sight, for the cost of designing and constructing your stand can far outweigh the site costs, particularly where advertisers compete for visitors' attention by the lavishness of their exhibits. In addition, there are many running costs: electricity, telephone, literature and samples, direct mail shots inviting people to your stand, advertisements in the catalogue, hospitality, insurance and staff. On top of the expense of hired demonstrators are the hidden costs of your own staff, who must be present to deal with those questions temporary staff cannot answer: there may also be hotel and other expenses. The longer the exhibition's duration, the higher the costs of stand construction and running costs.

There can also be practical problems, and the small print on the contract should be checked carefully: regulations may restrict what exhibitors are allowed to do on their stands. The practicalities of exhibiting should also be considered – if the product is a bulky or heavy one, it may be too big to get through the exhibition hall's doors, and are there any load-bearing restrictions?

Furthermore, most exhibitions permit only once-a-year stimulus. Where repetition/continuity is achieved by participation in a series of exhibitions, expenses rise proportionately. Frequently, too, exhibitions occupy far more top management time, before and during the exhibition, than is customary with other media. The attention paid by management shows, however, that although exhibitions may be costly, the benefits clearly outweigh the drawbacks, where personal contact and demonstration are of major importance.

Other forms of demonstration Formal exhibitions are not the only medium to offer you facilities for demonstration and personal contact. Some advertisers mount private exhibitions, either on their own premises or by using a portable display which they erect in premises hired for the occasion. This type of exhibition can often be combined with an invited audience film show. Some advertisers, in preference to portable exhibition stands, construct mobile exhibitions in special trailers, buses or railway carriages which they then send round the country.

The very extreme of personal contact and demonstration is, of course, salesmanship. Rather than use conventional advertising media, your company's representatives may demonstrate the product. Even here, however, the range of media includes activities which can assist you in your marketing operation. Demonstrators can be hired to promote your product in retail outlets and distribute samples; demonstration can also be achieved by distributing samples from door to door. Sales aids such as display cases and back-projection film cr video units that assist representatives in their selling task, are further examples which show that personal selling by representatives and indirect selling through advertising are not separate activities but overlap considerably.

Point-of-sale material

Display material can serve as a vital reminder at the very point of purchase, delivering your advertising message at the time and place most likely to result in sales. The range of display material is too wide to cover fully here, and extends from showcards of various shapes and sizes, through window stickers and crowners, in-store television units, and other display pieces to dispenser units which both sell and display your product.

Adequate display at the place of purchase can make or mar the success of your marketing campaign, and point-of-sale material is therefore of great importance. As a medium, however, it differs markedly from others. It has been said, with some justification, that 90 per cent of all display material is wasted. Usually, the reason is failure to realise why point-of-sale is a unique medium. With other media, you pay the media-owner and have the assurance that he will deliver your advertising message: with display material, however, this depends entirely on the retailer who selects, from the vast amount of material available to him, the few display units he will use.

The high wastage of display material arises usually from one or both of two basic faults – production of poor material, and failure to merchandise this material. And in this context poor material means not only that which is inferior in quality but also high-quality material that does not suit the retailer's needs. Much display material is alas based on what the advertiser would like, and ignores the hard fact that only the material that the retailer wants is put on display. And even when you have produced exactly the right display material, you must still devise a complete selling programme to ensure its effective use at point of sale. Sending out a showcard with your merchandise, to be unpacked in the warehouse and thrown away, its existence unknown to the display manager, illustrates lack of attention to this point. There are many ways of ensuring the dealer's co-operation in display (see Part 3); all have the common aim of making the dealer confident your product will sell, and eager to use your display material to promote it to best advantage.

Miscellaneous advertising media

The range of advertising media is considerable, and within this chapter it has been possible to review only the major ones. Overseas media have deliberately been omitted, since it would call for a separate book to give them proper coverage. The chapter could be extended to include a whole range of miscellaneous publications, juke box commercials, book matches and many others. If you are concerned with evaluating these media, the basic questions are the same and apply equally to those media not specifically discussed here. The fundamental questions you should ask in selecting the media best suited to your marketing objective will be discussed in Chapter 6.

Before proceeding further, however, it is necessary to examine a major medium deliberately left until the next chapter because of its complexity – television.

Chapter 2

Television Media

Television merits a separate chapter because of its complexity, rather than because of the amount spent on TV advertising – Advertising Association statistics show that in 1990 press media accounted for 57.3 per cent of all advertising expenditure, compared with television's 26.2 per cent.

The public body responsible for licensing our commercial television channels is the Independent Television Commission. The ITC regulates all non-BBC transmissions, including Channel 3 (the ITV regional network and our national breakfast channel), Channel 4 and the proposed Channel 5 – which can all be grouped together under the heading of terrestrial broadcasting. It also regulates satellite and cable transmissions, and 'additional services' such as teletext, carried on the spare capacity of the television signal.

This chapter therefore reviews television media under similar main headings of terrestrial broadcasting, satellite transmissions, cable TV, and additional services, together with one further category: non-broadcast sources. Before discussing these various types of television, it is important to recognise that the medium is in the throes of change.

For many years, most viewers were restricted to three television channels. This choice was then widened by the introduction of Channel 4 and later by breakfast TV, and now we have satellite and cable channels. The ITV network delivered mass regional audiences at predictable times but, as this chapter makes clear, numerous developments are changing that pattern: the mass regional audiences of past years may be whittled away by viewers switching to other channels, which may in turn cover smaller or larger areas. Furthermore, TV audiences are no longer viewing at predictable times, since many viewers now use video-recorders.

The ITC replaced the Independent Broadcasting Authority (IBA) and the Cable Authority in 1991, and is concerned with television services only. (Independent radio services, formerly also regulated by the IBA, are now the responsibility of the new Radio Authority described earlier).

New technology opened the way for a greatly increased number of television channels and related services at local, national and international levels, and the 1990 Broadcasting Act provided the framework for a new style of regulation. The ITC has the duty to ensure that:

- '... [a] wide range of television services is available throughout the UK and that, taken as a whole, they are of high quality and appeal to a variety of tastes and interests'

- '[there is] fair and effective competition in the provision of such services.'

The ITC ensures that each ITV contractor (or, after 1992, Channel 3 licensee) provides a suitable balance of programmes, of proper quality. While advertisers are not *directly* interested in programmes as such, the size and composition of the audiences they attract are of immediate concern. BBC1 and BBC2 programmes are of equal importance – the BBC does not carry advertising but, if audiences watch their channels, they cannot watch independent television at the same time. Both BBC and ITC channels must also ensure their programmes satisfy the newly-appointed government watchdog, the Broadcasting Standards Council.

Unlike the IBA, the ITC does not build, own, or operate transmitters. The IBA's former Engineering Division became National Transcommunications Ltd (NTL) which, after a temporary period in the ownership of the Secretary of State, will be privatised. The company will transmit both ITV and Channel 4 (and S4C in Wales) to UK viewers, and develop new business in the fields of telecommunications and broadcasting.

Any commentary on television media runs the risk of becoming quickly outdated – new developments are being announced day by day.

TERRESTRIAL BROADCASTING

Channel 3

The independent television network is a regional system of broadcasting in which 15 ITC-appointed licensees provide programme

CHANNEL 3 – THE ITV REGIONAL NETWORK

Area	Contractor	% share of net ITV homes[1]
London weekdays	Carlton Television[2]	19.48
weekends	London Weekend Television (LWT)	
East, West and South Midlands	Central Independent Television	15.40
North-West England	Granada Television	11.64
Yorkshire	Yorkshire Television	10.12
South and South-East England	Meridian Broadcasting[3]	9.19
Channel Islands	Channel Television[4]	
Wales and West of England	Harlech Television (HTV)	7.70
East of England	Anglia Television	6.60
Central Scotland	Scottish Television (STV)	6.42
North-East England	Tyne-Tees Television	5.04
South-West England	Westcountry Television[5]	2.96
Northern Ireland	Ulster Television	2.26
North Scotland	Grampian Television	2.09
Borders and The Isle of Man	Border Television	1.11
		100.00
National breakfast-time licence	GMTV[6]	

Notes:
1 *Source*: BARB/RSMB Establishment Survey August 1990-March 1991
2 Previously held by Thames Television
3 Previously held by Television South (TVS)
4 Currently sold by the present S & S-E England contractor
5 Previously held by Television South West (TSW)
6 The licence was awarded to Sunrise Television, which has since changed its name to GMTV (Good Morning Television). The service was previously provided by TV-am.
7 These regional companies currently also sell airtime on Channel 4.

services in 14 separate areas of the country (London is served by two contractors on a split-week basis), together with one national break-fast-time service broadcast over the same network.

Licensees have responsibility for ensuring that their programme services comply with the Broadcasting Act and the ITC codes and guidelines. The ITC has a range of sanctions and financial penalties for licensees who fail to comply with their licence conditions. It monitors compliance through its headquarters and regional staff, with the assistance of regional Viewer Consultative Councils.

The ITV network

New ten-year franchises come into force in January 1993 for the companies listed opposite. Licences were awarded (amid some controversy) 'by competitive tender', subject to the licence applicant passing a 'quality threshold' and satisfying the ITC that it was able to sustain a quality service over the full licence term.

Until January 1993 when the new licences start, the ITC is discharging the IBA's regulatory functions with regard to current ITV contracts, as well as Channel 4 and the continuing DBS (Direct Broadcasting by Satellite) contracts discussed below.

From the very first day of their new licences, the programme companies must face Channel 4 selling its own airtime in direct competition, as described below, and ITV's monopoly will thus finally be broken.

Four of the previous programme companies were not awarded licences, and some sought legal redress against the ITC's decision, as did one new bidder who did not receive a franchise. Of those which were unsuccessful, at least two are likely to continue as independent production companies, offering their programme output to the full available market: to Channels 4 and 5, to the satellite and cable channels described below, as well as to the successful Channel 3 licensees – or even the BBC. Thames Television has in fact agreed to work with the BBC in providing a new satellite service, described below.

Advertising on ITV

The great impact of television comes from its ability to demonstrate your product's benefits to a family audience, at home in a relaxed atmosphere, and with the additional benefits of sound and colour. (Although we have had colour transmission for many years, a number of black and white sets – currently six per cent of the total – are still in use.) Other creative approaches, such as animation and computer graphics, are also possible.

ITV areas seem to present convenient regional advertising facilities but transmitters do not recognise lines on a map and, although television coverage is almost at saturation level, there are still a minimal number of households within areas which cannot receive signals, and other households which are in overlap areas.

Programme contractors' areas are larger than those served by essentially local media. For this reason many advertisers regard television as a regional medium rather than a local one. This has led a number of advertisers, who place great reliance on television, to revise their marketing areas to match ITV transmission areas, thus reversing the original practice of seeking a medium whose coverage co-incided with an advertiser's sales area.

Television, though regional in structure, gives you the benefit of an impact on the audience equivalent to that of a national medium. Viewers think of TV as a medium of national importance, and many advertisers value it for that reason.

Television as a medium is flexible by time and day as well as area. It is possible, by making appropriate bookings, to stimulate the market on a date and at a time of your choice. Control of timing is, however, increasingly affected by the pre-empt system and by video-recorders, both discussed below.

Advertising time is sold in standard metric units of 10, 20, 30, 40, 50 and 60 seconds duration, booked into different time segments with advertising rates appropriate to the size and composition of the audience you are likely to reach. Subject to availability, longer spots may also be booked.

The frequency, amount and nature of the advertisements must be in accordance with the Broadcasting Act and the extensive rules and principles laid down under it by the ITC. There must be total distinction between programmes and advertisements, and advertising is limited to seven minutes an hour averaged over the day's programmes. A maximum of seven and a half minutes per hour is permitted during peak viewing hours (ie, 0700–0900 and 1800–2300) so long as the preceding averaging rule is adhered to. The Broadcasting Act provides for the insertion of advertisements not only at the beginning or end of a programme but also 'in the natural breaks therein'. There are also opportunities for sponsorship, discussed below.

Channel 3 television differs from other advertising media in that it is almost a commodity market: rate cards are structured to extract whatever advertising revenue the market will bear. The supply of airtime is fixed so price is determined by demand – contrast this with press media where a media-owner selling many pages of advertising can simply print thicker issues.

Supply and demand of television airtime are balanced by omitting less profitable advertising. Spots booked at a relatively inexpensive 'broad spot advertisement rate' may be pre-empted (or displaced) by spots sold to other advertisers at a higher cost, such as bookings made at a first-level 'pre-emptible fixed spot' rate. These fixed spots, may, however, be pre-empted by spots sold at various higher level pre-empt rates. These higher-rate pre-empt spots may in their turn be pre-empted by spots sold to other advertisers at the very highest rate – that for non-pre-emptible fixed spots, which are the only ones certain to appear. This is a straightforward matter of supply and demand for the media-owners, but for the advertiser and agency it makes the already difficult problem of planning and buying a television campaign more complex.

Television rate cards thus call for detailed study, and television schedules – under such circumstances – demand constant attention, review and adjustment. The volatile nature of television can be contrasted with other media where advertising is usually a 'one-off' operation in which you plan and book your schedule and then wait for your advertisements to appear. With television advertising, schedule adjustment is more important than the original basic plan, and most spots are repeatedly shifted as information about programmes is released, and new audience data becomes available. The advent of many new channels, discussed below, will make television schedules even more volatile.

Television programme contractors' rate cards are frequently more complex than those for other media and, in addition to the different categories of spot rates already mentioned, may include a wide range of other facilities – support spots you can book on a 'run-of-day', 'run-of-week', 'run-of-campaign' or 'seasonal' basis – all of which may have separate rates for peak and off-peak screening. Rate cards may also include a wide variety of different discount rates as well as other advertising packages (such as the Guaranteed Home Impressions, described in a later chapter) by which television programme contractors attempt to balance supply and demand for television airtime.

Rate cards (or separate brochures) may feature further facilities. As well as transmitting your advertising message, most television contractors also offer a number of additional services to advertisers, including production of commercials and a wide range of other facilities. (These are described in Chapter 7.)

Sponsorship

In addition to spot advertising, television now also offers sponsorship opportunities. A programme is deemed to be sponsored if *'any part of its costs of production or transmission is met by an organisation or person other than a broadcaster or television producer, with a view to promoting its own or another's name, trademark, image, activities, products, or other direct or indirect commercial interests.'*

The ITC's new *Code of Programme Sponsorship* effectively allows any programme – except pure news and current affairs – to be sponsored. A sponsor, who must be clearly identified, cannot influence programme content or scheduling, but is offered front/end credits and 'bumper' credits around the advertising breaks within the sponsored programme. These credits may indicate the connection between a sponsor and a brand (eg, 'Sponsored by Company X, makers of Brand Y'), but must not show the sponsor's product or service, and must not include other descriptions, nor slogans of any kind. Programme trailers can also include credits of up to five seconds. These are, however, likely to be alloted randomly by the contractor's traffic department, which may not always be in the company's best interests. For most advertisers, sponsorship is likely to end up as either a fairly expensive way of delivering short commercial messages, or an interesting way of matching a programme's strength and character to that of their brand, thereby enhancing total corporate communications.

The Television Audience Reached

The regular flow of research information about the size and composition of television audiences (described in Chapter 4) enables you to gauge the audience you are likely to reach. To some, particularly the less experienced in television advertising, this wealth of information causes some embarrassment, especially when taking into account additional research information provided by programme contractors. In passing, this view highlights the two ends of the complaints scale about media research: with some advertising media, practitioners complain about lack of information, while with others they complain there is too much!

Breakfast Television

The programme contractor holding the breakfast-time licence (originally TV-am, but subsequently GMTV) differs from the other 15 in having a national franchise, which permits the company to broadcast from 6.00 to 9.25 am seven days a week throughout the year, to all areas of the United Kingdom. The service is available to the public on Channel 3 and thus offers advertisers the same coverage potential. Contrast this with Channel 4 (described below) which, although it also has a national franchise, faced two major tasks when first launched: building new transmitters and persuading potential viewers to adjust their sets and aerials. The new Channel 5 will face two similar tasks.

The programme company sells its own airtime, and makes this available as both packages and spots which precede or follow the programme units. Advertisers can book national advertising from a single source, rather than having to negotiate separately with several ITV companies. Moreover, the service provides the opportunity to advertise simultaneously throughout the United Kingdom. However, as GMTV will transmit on the ITV network it could, if it so wished, sell advertising time on a regional (or perhaps macro-region) basis.

One advantage of breakfast-time programming is that it reaches a high proportion of housewives (and housewives with children), and advertisers and agencies are therefore able to target this important audience before they go shopping. A large proportion of breakfast-time advertisement revenue is contributed by manufacturers of food products whose principal markets comprise these important target groups. Other products which account for a significant proportion of advertisement revenue are toys, confectionery, and cosmetics/toiletries.

The company holding the early morning franchise does not have a monopoly of breakfast-time advertising, however, as Channel 4 is also on air at that time. It also competes for audiences with BBC1 and BBC2.

Channel 4

The Channel 4 Television Company Ltd is currently a wholly-owned subsidiary of the ITC: it provides a national programme service except for Wales, which is covered by S4C (Sianel 4 Cymru), a separate broadcasting authority with its own network.

When Channel 4 first began broadcasting it was intended that *the new service will cater for special interests and concerns for which television has until now lacked adequate time, and also foster new and experimental programme ideas*.

The programme schedule is complementary to ITV, with reasonable choice between the two channels, co-ordinated in viewers' best interests. This complementary planning should be contrasted with the results of competitive planning of like against like – viewers would get the worst of all possible worlds (choice between two similar programmes) and advertisers would reach similar audiences split between the two.

Channel 4 seeks to provide a distinctive service to fill gaps it identified in the programming of the other three channels: for example, programmes appealing to 'light viewers', including the AB socio-economic groups, and the younger age bands. Channel 4 aims to be a channel 'for all of the people – some of the time', rather than restrict itself to minority audiences and interests.

Advertising on Channel 4

Although Channel 4 can be a mass as well as a selective medium, it does not deliver conventional mass audiences. Cumulative cover builds up by a mix of audience sizes, ranging from the specialist to the large, allowing advertisers to buy whatever audiences they want. It provides the following advertising opportunities:

- *Strong up-market coverage* – particularly of the AB socio-economic groups, who traditionally are 'light viewers'

- *Special-interest groups* – selected by considering programme content rather than standard demographic research data

- *Coverage build-up* – the 4th channel, over time, delivers conventional audiences in large cumulative numbers, regardless of whether or not more specialist groups are also reached

- *Better balanced schedules against any target audience* – providing additional opportunities-to-see for any group inadequately covered by the ITV schedule.

Regular TV advertisers use Channel 4 in parallel with ITV to increase their total coverage, and to give better balance to their schedules. Advertisers new to television use the channel to reach specialist target audiences, either nationally or regionally. Channel 4 is also used by advertisers seeking more general audiences, whose advertising budgets are insufficient to provide an acceptable weight of advertising on ITV.

At present, the ITV companies fund the Channel by annual subscription and in return sell its advertising time in their areas. From January 1993, however, Channel 4 will become a public corporation, licensed and regulated by the ITC and selling its own airtime, although it is guaranteed a 'safety net' under the Broadcasting Act. If its share of terrestrial national advertising revenue (NAR) falls below 14 per cent, then Channel 3 companies must top it up by a maximum of two per cent. If Channel 4 sells more than 14 per cent of NAR, 50 per cent of any revenue above that level must be given back to ITV. Channel 4's remit will remain to serve interests not catered for by other programmes.

Although there may still be regional flexibility in the way in which airtime will be sold, there is no guarantee that Channel 4 will continue to provide the current regional advertising options. Whatever the outcome, advertisers and agencies will in future negotiate with a single sales point in place of separate regional ones.

Channel 5

The ITC (after various delays) advertised a single licence for Channel 5 in 1992. The Broadcasting Act requires the channel to carry news and current affairs, children's and religious programmes, and to appeal to a wide variety of tastes. The licence period will be for ten years, awarded on the same competitive tender basis as Channel 3. The proposed time-table would allow the appointed company to commence transmission in 1994.

The ITC proposes that Channel 5's licence should be for a service utilising 33 transmitters, giving an overall coverage estimated at about three-quarters of the UK population. It will be for applicants to decide, on editorial and financial grounds, to what extent (if any) they wish to provide local or regional programmes from any or all of these transmitters.

The cost of establishing the new service, including installation of the transmission system, must be met by the licensee on top of the costs of providing the programme service. One big drawback for any would-be Channel 5 licensee is the responsibility for retuning video recorders or other equipment which may experience interference from C5 transmissions. Another drawback is that many viewers will need to install a new aerial to receive the new channel.

Some media commentators have cast doubts on the new channel's financial viability. They doubt the commercial prospects for a service with multiple local opt-out options, claiming that only a 'cheap and cheerful' national broadcaster could afford to bid the winning price in the next television auction. The question then is whether viewers (who, for a little more money could already get multiple satellite/cable channels, with even more to come) would support such a format. Without audiences, the new licensee would have great difficulty in obtaining sufficient advertising revenue to make the channel profitable.

SATELLITE TRANSMISSIONS

Terrestrial broadcasting has been supplemented in two ways. One is geo-stationary communication satellites which 'bounce' TV (and radio) signals back to earth, either to individual homes – *direct* broadcasting by domestic satellite (DBS) – or to community reception stations, from where the final link to the home is through the second supplement to traditional broadcasting: cable TV.

Satellite transmissions differ from terrestrial broadcasting in that coverage is national (or rather international). The reception areas are known as 'footprints' or 'groundprints' and, to give an idea of their size,

UK transmissions overlap Northern France, while France's ground-print reaches into the UK not far short of Scotland. The net effect is a web of overlapping transmission areas, which become even larger if the signals are then spread further by cable.

Although discussed separately for ease of analysis, the two supplements to traditional broadcasting are clearly inter-related. Both are the ITC's responsibility.

Direct Broadcasting by Domestic Satellites

The IBA's DBS (Direct Broadcasting by Satellite) contractor, British Satellite Broadcasting (BSB), began transmissions in April 1990 using the Marcopolo satellite and those DBS frequencies allocated to the UK. The quality of its five-channel service was impressive: television critics, and those viewers who purchased the necessary D-MAC receiving equipment, were complementary about many aspects of the new channels.

Sky Television, which had for some years provided a pan-European service to cable opperators, commenced DBS transmissions shortly before BSB went on air. While many potential viewers liked the idea of wider choice, confusion over whether to opt for Sky Television or BSB (and install a dish or a 'squarial'), together with mixed messages coming from the broadcasters themselves, blurred the concept of satellite television, and most viewers were content to stick with the familiar, uncomplicated terrestrial channels.

In consequence, the sales of squarial dishes through the summer months were slow, and BSB was unable to achieve sufficient penetration to be financially secure.

In November 1990, BSB and Sky Television announced their merger (without consulting the IBA). Their intention was to broadcast a single programme service from Sky's Astra satellites, as opposed to using BSB's Marcopolo satellite and specialist D-MAC technology. Both organisations, having invested many millions of pounds in their high-risk projects, decided this was the only way to secure a continued satellite service to the United Kingdom.

BSkyB then launched its five-channel package – a combination of Sky and BSB programmes – and the end result was a virtual monopoly of DBS television within the UK. Like other TV contractors, BSkyB is financed by a combination of advertising and sponsorship revenue. It differs from ITV contractors, however, in having a further source of income – subscriptions paid to receive 'scrambled' programmes, for which viewers need a decoding device.

BSB's action in merging with Sky Television, without prior IBA approval, constituted a breach of the company's programme contract, which the IBA consequently had the right to terminate. The IBA recognised, however, the need to minimise the difficulties which any abrupt withdrawal of DBS programme services would cause viewers, and also wished to give maximum opportunity for use and development of D-MAC technology.

Following detailed discussions with BSkyB, the IBA announced in December 1990 that the programme contract would continue until the end of 1992, during which time BSkyB was required to continue broadcasting on the DBS (Marcopolo satellite) channels as well as from Astra.

The IBA could also withdraw from BSkyB (with due notice) part or the whole of up to three DBS channels, for use by new duly-appointed satellite service licensees. In such circumstances, BSkyB would charge only a token rental for capacity on its Marcopolo satellite to any new licensee offering a service aimed at minority and special interest groups that did not compete with BSkyB's own services, and did not have an appreciable income. BSkyB would also support further research into D-MAC technology.

Viewers with BSB squarials would be offered free Astra dishes with free installation, before such time as BSkyB ceased broadcasting from the Marcopolo satellite.

Discussions on the terms of a formal supplemental agreement to the programme contract, for implementing these new terms, continued into 1991.

BSB's inability to maintain an independent DBS programme service was a major disappointment to the IBA. It also had serious consequences for cable franchise holders and their viewers, as well as for manufacturers, retailers and programme providers who had contracts with the company.

There is little doubt, however, that satellite television's image – as well as its potential profitability – was much improved by the Sky Television/BSB merger. Furthermore, many potential viewers would probably invest in the necessary receiving equipment if their favourite TV programmes moved to satellite (as is increasingly likely, with Thames Television and TVS setting up as independent producers). Whether by moving wholesale on to satellite, or by selling their established programmes to the satellite broadcasters, franchise losers are likely to push up sales of dish aerials even further. Price reductions, arising from improved technology and increased production, will no doubt accelerate this process. At the time of writing, independent research showed that monthly dish sales had hit a record figure of 116,000, pushing the total above the two-million mark, representing a penetration of almost one in ten UK households. Some financial analysts extrapolate from this that BSkyB might break even financially, on an operating profit level, earlier than anticipated. (This forecast has since been confirmed by BSkyB.)

Satellite Audience Research

Regular information about satellite viewing is provided by the data sources detailed in Chapter 4.

Satellite to Cable Transmissions

The second supplement to terrestrial transmissions, in addition to direct broadcasting to individual homes, is satellite transmission for community reception, from which the link with homes is Cable TV.

Sky Channel and *SuperChannel* both transmit programmes on non-domestic satellites (Astra and Eutelsat respectively) to cable systems throughout Europe including, of course, the UK. These services are financed by subscription, advertising and sponsorship.

Both pan-European channels offer viewers wider choice, with different programmes for different audiences at different times of day, designed to complement rather than compete with existing national channels. The total amount of advertising in any one day must not exceed an average of nine minutes per hour of broadcasting.

Rate cards allow advertisers to buy specific days and times with programmes targeted at specific audiences. There are also opportunities for sponsorship, and the usual range of 'packages' and discounts.

Many other satellite channels (listed below) offer additional programme services and advertising or sponsorship facilities.

CABLE TELEVISION

A cable system is primarily just another means of delivering television to the home. The television channels carried by cable systems include those from a number of satellites, as well as from other sources. Because cable connection avoids the need for individual viewers to have satellite dishes, receivers and decoders, it provides an easy and cost-effective way of delivering the new television choices now developing.

The last edition of this book named all 22 cable franchises then awarded. The final Annual Report of The Cable Authority (now superseded by the ITC) lists 137 franchise-holders – far too many to include here, especially as the ITC intends to advertise additional franchises. Cable areas vary in size from 10,000 homes to nearly 500,000 and, taken together, these franchises cover some two-thirds of the UK population.

The task of The Cable Authority was not, however, to divide the country into TV areas, nor to ensure that all areas (even uneconomic ones) were covered. Its role was to facilitate rapid and orderly expansion – a remit which will be continued by the ITC.

There are different kinds of cable systems, including narrowband, broadband, SMATV, and local delivery.

Narrowband Cable Just over 50 old narrowband cable systems in various parts of the country presently provide new television programmes. Most systems have only four channels, though some of them cover relatively large areas.

Broadband Cable These are the multi-channel and interactive systems currently being constructed or planned in most areas of the country, which already account for more than 50 per cent of all cable connections. The systems can carry between 30 and 45 television channels, although some can carry more. They also have a facility to control which channels are delivered to specific premises, allowing viewers to subscribe to some channels but not others. Broadband cable systems are permitted to provide a full range of television, telecommunication and interactive services. The total number of operating broadband franchises, at end April 1992, was 50.

SMATV A growing number of new 'Satellite Master Antenna Television' systems are being installed. These are smaller systems, often serving blocks of flats, which deliver a range of satellite television channels to the homes connected to them. No ITC licence is needed for any SMATV system covering fewer than 1,000 homes. Several SMATV systems operating on a joint basis could, however, require a Local Delivery licence.

Local Delivery Any system providing television services in an area of more than 1,000 homes will require a Local Delivery licence. This differs technologically from a purely cable franchise, in that the service may be delivered not only by broadband cable but could also utilise one or more SMATV systems, or even microwave video distribution systems (MVDS). The latter technique has not yet been used in the UK, but is nevertheless undergoing development.

Programme channels

Programme licences, as distinct from cable franchises, are issued on demand for any programme service which conforms to the 'consumer protection' requirements of the ITC's Codes on Programmes, Advertising and Sponsorship. A license lasts for ten years. Separate arrangements apply to the DBS broadcasting channels allocated for UK use, which are awarded by competitive tender.

The merger between Sky Television and British Satellite Broadcasting caused mixed feelings in the cable industry. Understandably, cable operators would prefer the continuing availability of nine separate channels provided by two rival groups coming from two different satellites using incompatible technology. This was, however, regarded as unrealistic, and in reality the merger put programme provision on a more secure footing. The current position is that, in addition to BSkyB, SuperChannel and the terrestrial services, further British-based television channels are available to UK cable systems, some transmitted and others distributed by videotape. These programmes services include:

Bravo	Classic movies
Cable Jukebox	Music videos, interactively on demand
Children's Channel	Children's programmes
CNN International	24-hour news
Discovery	Nature, history, travel and science
Eurosport	Sports programmes
Home Video Channel	Adult feature films
Indra Dhnush	Indian programmes
Landscape Channel	The natural world, with music
Lifestyle	Women's magazine
Movie Channel	Feature films
MTV Europe	Pop music
Parliamentary Channel	House of Commons coverage
Screensport	Sports programmes
Sky Movies plus	Feature films
Sky News	24-hour news
Sky One	General entertainment
Sky Sports	Sports programmes
SuperChannel	General entertainment

Some services are free, while others are provided on a subscriptionbasis (to both viewers and/or cable operators), and some also sell advertising time. In addition, various educational and training programmes are available on some cable channels, together with a considerable number of foreign programmes. Among those countries making their services available are America, Austria, Belgium, Canada, France, Germany, Italy, Japan, Mexico, The Netherlands, Norway, the Russian republics, Spain, Switzerland and United Arab Emirates.

Many broadband systems also carry their own local channels of text information or news, features and community access, or minority programming such as Westminster Cable's Arabic Channel. Finally, all broadband systems (and some older narrowband ones) carry a range of radio stations and, additionally, some hospital broadcasting services are also available via local cable systems.

Some MSOs (multiple systems operators) also provide telephone and communications services. Interactive services such as home shopping, home banking, healthcare and security and alarms services, electronic mail, market research, remote meter reading and video-conferencing are also possible.

Advertising Support

Cable operators face a stiff challenge if they simply attempt to divide the existing advertising 'cake' into even smaller slices, rather than look for new sources of revenue – the very same problem that Channel 4 faced (and successfully tackled) with ITV. As with local press (and radio) much advertising revenue is from local traders, but it is important to recognise that cable presents a variety of important new opportunities for national advertisers, including small-scale test marketing by franchise area, direct response advertising, and advertising within specialist programmes.

Many advertising executives (particularly those in agencies) are understandably concerned that these new facilities should be sold on as practicable a basis as possible. They want cable to be highly flexible (with time purchased by the individual system, by regional groups of systems, or across the entire cable network) and as simple as possible to plan and buy. The future may thus see the introduction of regional rate cards, the formation of national sales houses to sell local cable TV on radio advertising lines, or perhaps a co-operative facility established to provide a 'single order' service covering multiple transmissions over a number of cable networks.

The rate of development

To date, the spread of cable has been comparatively slow. New franchises have, however, already been built past a million and a quarter homes, with actual penetration of more than 20 per cent of them. The pace of development is accelerating: it is anticipated that the rate of cable system construction will reach one million homes a year in 1992, with the five millionth home passed before the end of 1994. More than half the population should have broadband cable available by 1996.

Unlike the ITV and DBS channels provided nationwide to all who want them, however, it is likely that cable will operate only in major population centres, with little or no rural coverage.

Cable Audience Research

JICCAR (the former Joint Industry Committee for Cable Audience Research) ceased operation due to lack of funding. However, the ITC now publishes quarterly bulletins about cable audiences, the contents of which are described in Chapter 4. These bulletins also give the number of operating franchises.

Other current research on a wider front suggests that, in homes receiving satellite or cable, the new channels account for 35-40 per cent of total viewing. Some media commentators estimate that by 1993 satellite and cable penetration will reach 23 per cent of UK homes, taking an appropriate share of total television advertising revenue.

ADDITIONAL SERVICES

The ITC is also responsible for telecommunications services provided on the 'spare' capacity of a television signal, ie those lines not used for transmitting the picture itself. These include the 'Oracle' teletext services provided on Channels 3 and 4 which, like the BBC's 'Ceefax', provide news and information (and also programme sub-titling) whenever the services are on air. *Oracle* also sells advertising space and so must be considered from two standpoints – as an advertising medium in its own right, and as a supplement (or alternative?) to conventional viewing. The teletext franchise is due for renewal during 1993 and five consortia bid for the new ten-year licence, which the ITC awarded to Teletext UK.

Teletext, transmitted over the television broadcasting network, should be distinguished from *Viewdata* services transmitted over phone lines. Teletext and Viewdata are collectively called *Videotext*, the generic term for data and graphics presented on a television screen.

Penetration of teletext sets is currently only 33 per cent, and the main brake on sales is the slow rate at which people replace their sets – they do not get a new TV set before the old one breaks down. Penetration of teletext sets is increasing, however, and could be accelerated by the rental market.

NON-BROADCAST SOURCES

Britain now has one of the highest penetration levels of video-cassette recorders in the world (already 64 per cent of households have one) and price reductions will increase this percentage. The more VCRs there are in homes and the greater the use made of them, so the greater the possible reduction in the use of TV sets for conventional viewing. The 'owners' (many VCRs are rented) use them to declare their independence of terrestrial, cable and satellite channel schedules.

The advantages a VCR presents include the facility to make recordings while the viewer is away (without switching on the TV set), to 'time-shift' programmes or make permanent copies of them, to view the wide range of pre-recorded videograms available (which represent an advertising medium in their own right), or even to 'film' the viewer's own programmes by means of portable video-cameras. Additional VCR facilities have further implications: viewers may edit out commercials by use of the 'pause' button if present when the recording is made. Alternatively, if the recording is made during the viewer's absence, commercials may be 'zipped' – avoided by use of the fast-forward button – during subsequent screenings. Finally, a new generation of VCRs have built-in technology that can eliminate commercials from the recordings, by editing out the high quality stereo signals commonly used to carry advertising.

Another source of non-broadcast material is video compact discs and reproducers. Unlike video-tapes, these discs cannot be used to make recordings: as with audio records, they are a replay medium only. Much depends, therefore, on the range of material available on disc, and here we could see a similar pattern to that of video tapes.

The drawback of this system, and the reason why some are doubtful about the future of the market, can be summed up in the question 'Who wants to invest in another piece of expensive equipment that offers nothing extra but has the disadvantage of no recording facility?' The advantage of video discs – that, unlike video-tapes, the records do not wear out, and give better sound quality – seem of minor importance when contrasted with the high price/no recording drawbacks.

New technology will have its effect here also. A new generation of video discs may offer a recording facility, while interactive compact discs will enable viewers to manipulate material (animation, graphics, text, video and audio) using a remote control device.

CONSEQUENCES OF INCREASED PROGRAMME PROVISION

New developments within television necessitate a rethink of the marketing concept and the way in which television advertising is used. Penetration of TV sets is at saturation level, and so it follows logically that the TV audience cannot increase in proportion to the ever-increasing programme output which will arise from additional channels transmitting, supplemented by the trend towards 24-hour broadcasting.

There might, however, be a marginal increase arising from new programmes which attract those who otherwise would not wish to view. A further increase could result from the growing incidence of two (and three or more) set households, which permits individual members of the family to view separate programmes rather than losing the argument about which to watch! 56 per cent of households already have two TV sets, while 13 per cent have three.

New developments will affect the television audience in various ways.

New technology The television signal itself is changing, offering high definition pictures and digital stereo sound or even wide-screen TV.

The end of an era ITV will no longer deliver mass regional audiences at predictable times.

Fragmentation and selectivity Increased programme provision but a total audience of only marginally increased size necessarily means that this audience will be fragmented. The greater the fragmentation, the greater, in theory, the possibility of audience selectivity. There will be alternative inroads into mass regional audiences.

Segmented audiences One alternative to mass regional audiences is minority viewing groups, as new programme sources will segment the total audience into smaller and more selective viewing groups. Wider choice will lead to diversity rather than uniformity, allowing advertisers to pinpoint markets with greater accuracy. This could be by cable TV's community-size areas or alternatively by programme interests and audience types. There will be great opportunity for advertisers who think in terms of 'narrowcasting' rather than broadcasting.

Cable TV could take narrowcasting even further as, in theory, broadband cable systems have the capacity to transmit different commercials to different market segments: imagine delivering AB commercials to AB homes, C1 commercials to C1 homes, and so on, or a range of commercials specifically tailored to the various geo-demographic groupings – or perhaps even individual personalised messages. The technology is there!

Transcast audiences The other alternative to mass regional viewing is 'transcasting' to even larger audiences: direct broadcasting by satellite means a single channel covers all 14 ITV regions, while Channel 5 will cover most of the UK, and some satellite/cable channels overlap international boundaries to give pan-European coverage.

Time-shift audiences TV will no longer deliver mass audiences at pre-dictable times: increasing VCR usage will spread message delivery over time.

Volatile audiences The more programme choice is increased, the greater the likelihood of viewers switching from one programme to another. This is for three reasons:

1. Natural curiosity to find out what is available on other channels. This curiosity could be encouraged by the new multi-screen sets, or by the 'scanning' facility by which cable viewers can call up on their screens a multitude of miniature pictures to facilitate programme selection.

2. Greater physical facility for switching programmes, through re-mote control units. 60 per cent of households already have remote control and, as this facility spreads, so fewer people will have to physi-cally get out of their chairs to change channels, thus increasing the likelihood of 'channel flicking' (or 'zapping').

3. Greater choice through pre-recorded videograms, which viewers might prefer to the broadcast provision, and which represent an adver-tising medium in their own right. Viewers might, alternatively, choose to view a programme recorded earlier. Price reductions in both blank and pre-recorded tapes mean that many viewers are building extensive video-tape libraries, aided by the new bar-coding and VideoPlus code numbering of programmes, and new devices for pre-setting VCR timings, which make recording that much easier. Furthermore, a new generation of VCRs have a two-tape capacity, which permits viewers to watch one tape while recording another, thereby increasing the VCR's facility to make (and store) permanent copies, leading to even further inroads into conventional mass audiences.

Interactive audiences New opportunities will arise through videotext services, far broader than telesales commercials, which give phone numbers for viewers to place orders by means of credit cards. Inter-active services such as cable television make direct purchases easier, and direct marketing could thus extend to the television medium. These interactive audiences could themselves be increased by means of interactive quiz and game shows which offer prizes to those viewing at home, as well as to the studio audience. (The offer of a small cash prize on conventional television recently generated a record response of one and a quarter million phone calls in five minutes!)

Inroads into conventional mass audiences will present opportunities as well as problems to the TV contractors, who could sell to the new media – to cable and satellite TV (in overseas markets just as much as in the UK) and to the world-wide pre-recorded videogram market. The appetite for material in countries without domestic TV, or with limited production facilities, could be voracious. Furthermore, production of minority (and thus usually commercially unviable) programmes could be most profitable when sold to multiple minority markets on a world-wide basis.

TELEVISION – THE FUTURE

This chapter started by stressing that television is in the throes of change, and the many new developments just discussed show this to be more than a slight understatement! Nevertheless, the future structure of the medium is clear in outline, even if there will be numerous changes in detail. Should you find these many new developments insufficient in scope, there are further possiblities to consider.

The BBC's Royal Charter comes up for renewal in 1996 but, in the meantime, two important new developments were announced shortly before this book went to press:

1. A new satellite service BBC Enterprises and Thames Television are jointly planning a new satellite programmes service to be delivered direct-to-home and to cable services. The ITC has granted Thames a non-domestic satellite service licence, and the new channel will select its schedules from existing programming, drawing heavily in peak viewing time from the extensive libraries of the BBC and Thames.

For the BBC, this means additional revenue from subscriptions and advertising, and the Director General commented that 'Revenues will be used to strengthen our existing services for licence payers, with the added possibility of wide screen Television'.

2. A new nightime-for-day-viewing service The BBC is launching a new channel called BBC SELECT. Broadcast overnight on BBC1 and BBC2 (when these are normally off air) it will provide a specialist subscription service covering a wide variety of professional, training, educational and general interests. These will be made by independent companies, who buy transmission time from the BBC. All are intended for recording on video, to be watched whenever and wherever viewers choose. Most will be scrambled, for which viewers will need to pay a small subscription, and to have a VCR and a special decoder. The BBC SELECTOR not only unscrambles programmes but also takes the difficulty out of recording them, by automatically switching on the VCR to record the right channel at the right time. Not all services will be scrambled, however, and no decoder is needed for those which are free. BBC SELECT services may carry advertising and sponsorship, to generate production revenue for the service providers.

So a suitable adage on which to finish this chapter might well be:

DO NOT ADJUST YOUR MIND – THE FAULT IS IN REALITY!

The next largest medium after television, in terms of percentage of total advertising expenditure, is in fact Direct Mail: this and the other advertising media were, however, all covered in the preceding chapter.

Having discussed the full range of *advertising* media, it is important to see them in context and recognise that there are alternative means of contacting your target markets, reviewed in the next chapter.

Chapter 3

Other Media

This book concentrates on the effective use of *advertising* media, defined earlier as 'the use of paid-for media space or time'. However, if your advertising is to achieve maximum results, it should be supplemented by, and synergistic with, other forms of promotion. These other forms demand far more attention than can be given in a book about advertising. The purpose of this chapter is simply to alert you to their importance.

1. THE EDITORIAL ROUTE

As Chapter 7 makes clear, advertising is not the reason for existence of most media, but only a means of helping them exist. Newspapers and magazines are read for their editorial content, and television watched for news and entertainment. Never forget that your *new* product is 'news' and could feature in the editorial just as much as the advertising columns, hence the importance of effective media relations.

2. CREATED MEDIA

Although there are numerous media which enable you to contact your target markets, through both advertising and editorial columns, you may find that even this wide range does not fully meet your company's communications needs, and you must therefore create new media.

There is literally no limit to the range of created media, which could include advisory bureaux, annual reports, audio-visual devices, awards & prizes, competitions, conferences, demonstrations, facility visits, films, incentives, gifts, house journals, newsletters, open days, printed material, provision of equipment or samples, seminars, speakers panels, videos, and many more.

Created media present a paradox becasue many executives forget that, as well as creating a medium, they must also create an audience for it. This, however, raises matters in illogical order, since nobody should ever create a medium without first having a specific target audience in mind. Equally, you should decide in advance how to deliver the created medium to this created target market. Booklets, films, leaflets, or videos – however well created – cannot deliver their message from inside a cupboard! Contrast this with the use of advertising and editorial columns, when you know from readership data precisely who you will reach, and also how your message will reach them.

A further point is that those who create media become media-owners in their own right. Many house journals are subsidised by the sale of advertising space. Other companies' created media may present you with both advertising and editorial opportunities, and your own may present such opportunities to others. When considering other organisations' created media as promotional vehicles, they should be evaluated in exactly the same way as other media, described in Chapter 6.

3. OTHER MESSAGE SOURCES

Marketing communications should also be considered in terms of message sources, and how existing and potential customers receive information about your organisation and its products. Those involved in marketing planning often categorise their activities under the headings of The Four Ps – Product, Price, Place and Promotion.

This review has so far considered only Promotion, but the other three Ps have equally important marketing communications implications.

Your product (or service) itself delivers a marketing communications message through its name, design, presentation and packaging.

Price also has marketing communications implications – lower price does not necessarily result in increased sales. Prospective purchasers often equate price with quality, and may suspect that low prices mean cheap and unreliable merchandise rather than price-advantageous products.

Place is important too – consider products widely available through any outlet which wishes to sell them irrespective of facilities and expertise, and – by way of contrast – merchandise available only direct from the manufacturer or appointed dealers, carefully selected for their ability to provide expert advice and effective after-sales service.

PROMOTIONAL PLANNING

When planning your company's overall promotional campaigns, as discussed in later chapters, you should therefore consider communicating through the full range of promotional media – editorial as well as advertising columns and, if necessary, creating additional media – against the background of the other three Ps and indeed all your target market's message sources.

It is equally important for these campaign components to re-inforce each other to maximum effect: there is little point in planning an effective media schedule if the advertising message it delivers conflicts with, or is undermined by, messages delivered by other media. On the contrary, all parts of the plan should reinforce each other, thereby multiplying their individual effects.

Chapter 4

Media Research and Services

Having reviewed in general terms the media you can use to communicate your advertising message, the next step is to examine what we know about them: the quantitative or qualitative data available which permit you to evaluate properly the various media and make comparisons. To quote current facts would be of very limited value as such information goes out-of-date all too quickly: for example, any statistics about circulation, costs, readership or viewing habits would be invalid by the time this book was published. In any event, some figures are already 6–12 months old before new data is published. This chapter therefore reviews the data sources available, rather than giving actual figures. Mention is also made of various services that may facilitate your effective use of advertising media.

Since various sources cover more than one medium, they will be reviewed by title rather than by media. The following brief cross-reference will, however, facilitate your locating those data sources relevant to the media that interest you:

All Media	BRAD, MediaTel
Cinema	CAA, CAVIAR, MEAL, Media Register, NRS, TGI
Direct Mail	DMIS, Royal Mail
Exhibitions	ABC, Conferences and Exhibitions Diary, Conference and Exhibition Fact Finder, EIF, Exhibitions Bulletin
Outdoor and Transport	BUSADS, JICPAR, Media Audits, Media Register, OAA, OSCAR, TGI, TRAC
Press	ABC, AHD, CAVIAR, JICREG, MEAL, Media Audits, Media Register, MMS, NRS, PPA, PressAd, TGI, VFD
Radio	AIRC, Atlantic 252, CAVIAR, MEAL, NRS, RAB, RAJAR, TGI
Television	BARB, CAVIAR, ITC, ITV Association, MEAL, Media Audits, Media Register, MMS, NRS, PETAR, PPA, TGI
Video	BARB, CAVIAR

These various sources are discussed in more detail below, in alphabetical order. This chapter necessarily has a 'list' format, and it is suggested that initially you read through it rapidly to acquaint yourself with the range of information available, and then return to the chapter for more detailed study later, *together with actual copies of the data sources mentioned.*

ABC (Audit Bureau of Circulations)
(Black Prince Yard, 207–209 High Street, Berkhampsted, Herts HP4 1AD)

ABC is a non-profit company, limited by guarantee, controlled by a tripartite council of advertisers, agencies and media-owners, the latter representing the Bureau's four categories of publishing members – national newspapers, regional newspapers, consumer magazines, and business magazines. This tripartite structure is reflected throughout the working parties that regularly review the different categories' audit rules and procedures, to ensure that they meet the needs of both publishers and advertisers.

ABC's primary function is the protection of advertisers against false claims. It provides certification of circulation figures and attendance at exhibitions, by independent professional auditors using standard audit rules and procedures for each ABC membership category.

The independent auditors are usually the members' financial auditors, and the Audit Bureau welcomes this as all ABC audits involve financial records and are more efficiently handled by one firm of accountants. The ABC maintains regular liaison with a working committee representing the financial institutes and accounting professions, to ensure a consistent standard of audit procedures.

The Audit Bureau employs staff inspectors to conduct random inspections of the methods and procedures of auditors, publishers and exhibition organisers. Should such inspection reveal errors, then the certificate will be re-issued and the auditor's professional body informed if there is evidence of malpractice.

CIRCULATION AUDITS

ABC's four categories of membership have differing requirements. Before reviewing these, some general points must be considered, as certain copies cannot be included in audited circulation figures. These are:

1. Returned, unsold or undelivered copies
2. Copies sold in bulk and then distributed free
3. Copies sent to advertising agencies, contributors and employees
4. Copies not carrying all advertising
5. Copies given away at exhibitions, conferences etc.

There is also provision for certain issues to be excluded at the request of the publisher, when an industrial dispute, mechanical failure, etc beyond the publisher's control results in loss of distribution of a publication.

All audit periods must be continuous, and a publisher may not choose to omit an audit return. Publishers failing to make a return without good cause are expelled from ABC membership.

Unless otherwise stated below, net sales are the only audit category: these are copies bought by individuals either from the retail point or by direct subscription, and represent the audited primary paid readership of a newspaper or magazine. With some publications, however, specified types of free circulation are also audited.

National Newspapers

These have monthly audit periods, and the Bureau also publishes six-month rolling averages.

Regional Newspapers

These have six-month audit periods.

Consumer Magazines

These divide into two separate categories:

General: these may have three-month, six-month or 12-month audit periods.

Specialist: these magazines share the same audit periods but may include, in addition to paid circulation, an element of free circulation as discussed below.

Business and Professional Journals

These have six-month or 12-month audit periods, and are primarily free distribution as discussed below.

All audit periods must be within a calendar year.

FREE DISTRIBUTION

The rule for free distribution is that each copy must be auditable down to the individual recipient. In the main, therefore, only postal distribution can be included. The ABC recognises three main types of free circulation, as follows.

Controlled circulation

This category comprises single copies sent free to individuals who fit the 'Terms of Control'. This control must define the individual commercial of professional classification, together with job specification, a reader must have to qualify for receipt of the journal. Terms of control must not be published within the publication. Controlled circulation is further sub-divided into the following six categories:

1. Individually requested in writing
2. Individually requested by telephone
3. Company requested in writing
4. Company requested by telephone.

Circulation within these four categories must be supported by an auditable source document – a signed and dated application form or a telephone request form agreed with ABC, valid for the current audit period ie not more than three years old. The two further categories are:

5. Non-requested by name
6. Non-requested by job title or function

Circulation within these two categories covers non-requested copies which nevertheless meet the terms of control, and may include copies previously recorded as controlled circulation, after their expiration.

'ABC Profiles' audits have recently been introduced for controlled circulation periodicals, to allow publishers to audit reader demographics. This replaces the previous Media Data Form (MDF) and can only be audited by an ABC Staff Auditor. Mandatory features of the system are:

- Breakdown of circulation type for one specific issue, including details of any deviation from the average
- Full breakdown of geographical circulation

- Breakdown of circulation either by primary job function or by title of recipient.

Optional data can include:

- Analysis of circulation additions and deletions (which becomes mandatory in 1993)
- Age of paid subscriptions
- Renewal rate of controlled circulation
- Breakdown of circulation by company size/purchasing authority
- Any other data requested, provided this can be audited.

Society/Association free circulation

The second main type of free circulation recognised by the ABC relates to societies or associations, and divides into three categories:

1. Unpaid single copies requested in writing
2. Unpaid single copies requested by telephone
3. Non-optional single copies.

Society/Association journals sent to non-members must not appear in this section of the ABC return, but can be included within the controlled section provided they are supported by a valid source document: otherwise they must appear in the non-controlled section.

Non-controlled circulation

This type of free circulation normally comprises copies sent to advertisers and agencies, as well as exchange copies, which do not satisfy the rules for controlled circulation.

With effect from the January 1993 audit period, the basic certificate for controlled circulation publications will be audited by ABC staff auditors, replacing the publisher's own financial auditors.

EXHIBITION AUDITS

Exhibitions are administered through ABC's Exhibitions Data Division. A working party (representing the Exhibition Joint Industry Committee, the Incorporated Society of British Advertisers, the Association of Exhibition Organisers, The Exhibition Industry Federation and the ABC) developed rules and procedures for the following audit reports.

Exhibition Audience Profile (EAP)

This gives the total number of visitors admitted during the run of the exhibition, reported under the following categories:

- *Registered Attendance (Free)* Attendance may be claimed if the organisers can provide auditable proof of the attendee's name and address through an exhibition registration form
- *Registered Attendance (Paid)* An attendee can be claimed if the organiser can provide auditable proof as with free attendance, plus proof of payment
- *Other Paid Attendance* This gives the number of other visitors who gained entry by paying an admission fee.

Exhibition Data Form (EDF)

In addition to attendance numbers, the EDF provides organisers with the option to report visitor demographics, job titles/functions, commercial or industrial classifications, and the geographic location of the visitor's company.

The EDF also covers the number of stands available and the number actually let, categorised by net sold at prospectus rates, and at less than prospectus rates.

Organisers may also make optional statements, such as any conference or symposium held in conjunction with the exhibition.

Note: The information given here on ABC procedures is a summary and should not be used as a 'rule book' for ABC procedures. Furthermore, ABC's working parties continually review its rules and procedures, to ensure all aspects of an audit are considered. For further details, contact the Audit Bureau.

AFMP (ASSOCIATION OF FREE MAGAZINES AND PERIODICALS) *(See JICREG and PressAd below.)*

AFN (ASSOCIATION OF FREE NEWSPAPERS) *(See JICREG and PressAd below.)*

AHD (ASSOCIATION OF HOUSEHOLD DISTRIBUTORS)
(3 Brunswick Square, Gloucester GL1 1UG)

This new trade body was formed to promote the medium of unaddressed direct marketing. AHD members offer three distribution systems: solus, shareplan and – more relevant to our discussions – material distributed with free newspapers.

All free newspapers detailed in the Association's directory, *The Letterbox Marketing Handbook*, have their distribution systems certified by VFD (Verified Free Distribution, discussed below) and this certification is a condition of AHD membership.

A new initiative is verification of leaflet distribution systems, called 'VFD for Leaflets', and many AHD publisher members now offer advertisers this added security.

AIRC (ASSOCIATION OF INDEPENDENT RADIO COMPANIES)
(Radio House, 46 Westbourne Grove, London W2 5SH)

AIRC is the trade association for companies holding Independent Radio licences awarded by the Radio Authority. It represents these radio companies in their dealings with Government, the Radio Authority, copyright societies and other organisations concerned with radio. AIRC provides a forum for industry discussion, is a source of advice to members on all aspects of radio, and has taken over the functions of the RMB (Radio Marketing Bureau). It also acts as a clearing house for radio information, and is the central source for IR-relevant marketing data.

Its principal publication is *RADAD (Radio Advertising Facts and Figures)*. This booklet, published annually, provides a source of quick reference to the radio medium. Its various sections cover future developments, the growth of IR in terms of stations and coverage, overall revenue growth, expenditure by categories, the top 25 spending brands, the role of radio in people's lives, consumer attitudes, reach and listening by demographic groups, audience share by radio service, average network adult ratings, a radio versus television seasonal tuning index, individual and combined media coverage (print), mixed media campaign comparisons, radio combined with TV network buying opportunities, station listings, maps, a glossary of terms, and details of national sales houses.

AIRC contracted for and published on behalf of member companies the earlier JICRAR (Joint Industry Committee Radio Audience Research), but this has now been replaced by the new RAJAR research described below.

ATLANTIC 252
(Radio Sales Company, 32 Bedford Row, London WC1R 4HE)

Atlantic 252, licenced by the Irish Republic rather than The Radio Authority, is not included within the present radio industry research.

Accordingly, it commissioned Continental Research to collect listening data from a representative sample of individuals aged four and over, resident within the Atlantic 252 area, estimated to cover more than 60 per cent of the UK, with a total population of 33.5 million individuals aged four-plus. The research technique is compatible with the diary studies carried out for other radio audiences. The Report provides figures for:

- Cumulative weekly audience (reach), total and average hours – Atlantic 252 and all stations. Predicted reach over four weeks – Atlantic 252
- Average audience by rate card segment – Atlantic 252
- Average half-hour audience – Monday-Friday (averaged) – Atlantic 252
- Average half-hour audience – Saturday – Atlantic 252
- Average half-hour audience – Sunday – Atlantic 252

The research splits into two main sections: total listenership figures as outlined above, with a parallel five tables showing solus listening; the audience that listens to no other commercial station.

As well as the usual tables related to age, sex and social class, the report includes some 'non-standard' demographic groups of interest to many advertisers eg 18–24 year old adults, and housewives with children aged 0–3.

BARB (BROADCASTERS' AUDIENCE RESEARCH BOARD LIMITED)
(Glenthorne House, Hammersmith Grove, London W6 OND)

Prior to 1981, the BBC and ITV used different methods of collecting television viewing data, which inevitably produced different results. To overcome this confusion, the BBC and the ITCA (now the ITV Association) set up the Broadcasters' Audience Research Board (BARB) to provide a single system for TV audience research. BARB's Board of Directors includes representatives of both partners, sitting under an independent Chairman. BARB itself employs only a few staff, and provides information using professional research suppliers to conduct and report on audience research.

BARB operates through a committee system, related to its two main areas of research – audience measurement and audience appreciation – with separate Management Committees and Technical Sub-Committees controlling each of these two activities. Various interested parties join the partner organisations on these committees. On the measurement side, the Institute of Practitioners in Advertising (IPA) represents advertising agencies, and the Incorporated Society of

British Advertisers (ISBA) represents advertisers. Both organisations, as users of television advertising, have a direct interest in how audiences are measured, and have an equal voice with shareholder committee members. The ITC is also represented on the audience appreciation committee, having an equal voice with the shareholders. Subscribers to BARB include Channel 4, the Welsh Channel 4 (S4C) and the satellite broadcasters, who are accordingly represented on the appropriate committees.

Audience measurement

Unlike many surveys, BARB does not use personal interviews to measure the size of television audiences, but relies on electronic meters fixed to television sets in a representative sample of homes throughout the UK.

The first step in selecting the sample of homes to have these meters is the Establishment Survey, based on a random sample of more than 43,000 interviews conducted continuously throughout the year. The results of this Survey, together with Government census data, are used to select a sample of homes fully representative in terms of demographics and family composition, TV equipment ownership and viewing habits, to participate in the audience measurement panel. Panel members receive a nominal incentive for their services.

BARB's audience measurement panel comprises 4,435 homes, and the Establishment Survey provides a pool of households to replace those which, for some reason or other, drop out. A sufficient reserve of homes is maintained to provide a weekly panel balanced to be representative of the ITV and BBC network. Within this total are net balanced panels in each ITV area, each representative of its own area.

The electronic meters attached to the television sets of panel households have developed considerably since the early days, as householders no longer have to remember to post computer tapes back, nor complete questionnaires. As before the meter registers when the set is switched on and off, and to which channel it is tuned but, in addition, each household now has the equivalent of a TV remote control unit with numbered buttons. Each member of the household has their own number, and presses the appropriate button when they start to view, and 'off' when they stop. Should panel members forget, a signal on the meter flashes if the television set is on but no buttons have been pressed. Guest viewers are allocated special buttons, with a facility for registering their age and sex.

The use of video recorders for viewing programmes previously recorded at home significantly affects audience measurement, so a separate meter is fitted to the VCR, with the same button-press serving to register individual viewers for both the VCR and the TV set.

If a programme is recorded, this registers on the VCR meter which imprints an electronic code (channel, date and time) on the video tape. When the tape is played back the TV meter 'reads' this code, and 'time-shift' viewing can be reported separately or added to 'live' viewing information. The contents of hired, borrowed or purchased pre-recorded tapes cannot be identified, and viewing of such tapes is registered only as 'Other playback'.

The electronic equipment can collect data from almost any number of television sets, VCRs and satellite receivers in any one home. All information is recorded by the electronic meter, retrieved overnight over the telephone line, and data automatically fed into a central computer. The meter results are then combined with details of programmes and commercial broadcasts, and the computer makes a series of calculations to arrive at estimates of audience sizes.

The data collected is compiled into a form required by BARB subscribers. The basic format comprises computer input data from the meters for those subscribers who wish to analyse it or, alternatively, calculated audience statistics showing the numbers or percentages watching particular programmes or commercials.

In the past, several bulky weekly reports were issued, but these have dwindled with the use of more efficient computer facilities. Three specialist reports are issued:

1. *The Network Report*. This shows summary information for those primarily concerned with advertising usage of research data. It summarises live and time-shift viewing figures for each of the main channels, and analyses audiences for both programmes and time segments.
2. *The Astra Report*. This summarises viewing statistics for those homes which receive Astra Channels, either by cable or by dish aerial. This information is clearly of special interest to satellite broadcasters, as well as agencies and advertisers. (Satellite data is included, but in less detail, in both the Network Report just mentioned and the BBC Report described below.)
3. *The BBC Report*. As its name suggests, this is tailored to the BBC's somewhat different needs. Although the BBC carries no advertising and most of its output is networked rather than regional, the Corporation is nevertheless interested in both live and time-shift information about programme audiences, in the performance of other channels, and in regional variations.

BARB issues weekly and monthly Press Releases. The weekly releases give the hours of viewing for each channel and list the audiences for the most popular programmes on each channel, while the monthly ones provide hours of viewing as well as regional shares, and the overall top 50 programmes for the month.

Audience measurement data is currently collected by two research companies contracted by BARB for this purpose: Audits of Great Britain (AGB) and RSMB Television Research Ltd, each company controlling separate aspects of the research operation. The contract comes up for renewal on a regular basis, and tenders are then invited from research organisations with the necessary interest and facilities.

Audience Appreciation

Measurement of audience appreciation of television programmes is carried out by the BBC Broadcasting Research Department, under contract to BARB. The system comprises a national sample of 3,000 respondents, supplemented by additional regional panels providing further samples of 500 respondents in each ITV area. Members of the national panel complete two research booklets every week; those on regional boost panels complete one booklet every four weeks. The booklets are posted to panel members before the start of each week, and posted back when completed. The panels consist of people aged 12 and over. The two booklets received by each informant comprise:

1. *The Programme Diary.* This covers a week's viewing and asks respondents to rate on a scale of one to six their opinions of every programme viewed each day. A rating of six indicates that the programme was extremely interesting or enjoyable, while a 'one' rating indicates that it was not at all interesting or enjoyable. These scores are used to produce an *Appreciation Index* (AI) for each programme, calculated as average marks out of 100, and the data is compiled into a weekly *Audience Appreciation Report*.

2. *Viewpoint.* The second booklet comprises questions asked by broadcasters about any aspect of a particular programme on a particular day. A broadcaster might wish to know, for example, what viewers think about a presenter or programme or whether a quiz game is exciting. More general questions about series or serials are also asked. Any questions can be asked about any programme, but the results remain confidential to the broadcaster asking the question.

A separate Children's Panel of 1,000 children aged 4–15 complete, once every fourth week, a similar pair of booklets specially designed for children, covering programmes up to 9.00 pm. In this case only networked programmes are covered, and there are no special regional panels as there are for measurement of adult services.

69

Videograms

BARB and AGB recently unveiled a pilot study into pre-recorded videos, in a bid to prove that not all viewers fast-foward over the advertisements. AGB's Video Trak pilot study showed that, with the co-operation of video distributors, it is now possible to inject a code into pre-recorded videos that is recognised by the BARB system.

BBP (BRITISH BUSINESS PRESS)
*(See **PPA** below)*

BRAD (BRITISH RATE & DATA)
(Maclean Hunter Ltd, Maclean Hunter House, Chalk Lane, Cockfosters Road, Barnet, Herts EN4 OBU)

The BRAD reference book is a comprehensive listing of all media which carry advertising. Published every month, it contains updated information on rates, mechanical data, circulation figures and personnel details.

The topicality of BRAD is demonstrated by the fact that every month more than a quarter of the 9,000+ media listed make changes to their rates and data.

BRAD subscribers also receive a separate supplement, *Media Mix*, which discusses important current media topics.

BRADbase

The entire BRAD database can also be held within subscribers' own PCs or computer networks, and up-dated daily using BRAD's electronic message service. The system allows unlimited viewing of data 24 hours a day.

One strength of the BRADbase system lies in its media selection capability. Users can specify an area of media interest (based on, for example, data classification, minimum circulation, frequency, or rate category) and from this produce a media list displaying comparative data on page rates, circulation and costs per thousand.

Overseas Media

Parallel volumes to BRAD are available for other countries, including Australia, Belgium, Canada, China, France, Germany, Holland,- Italy, Scandinavia, South Africa, Spain, Switzerland and the United States.

BRAD Directories & Annuals

This is a comprehensive directory of annual publications and directories in Great Britain. Covering both consumer and business publications which accept advertising, it gives full details of advertising rates and mechanical data, enabling potential advertisers to select their media and make direct contact with the relevant media-owners.

BRAD Publishing Groups Portfolio

Published each Spring, this annual guide to corporate structure in print media comprises two main sections. One gives details of Publishing Groups (an alphabetical listing of UK companies and their subsidiaries with business interests in print media), while the second provides a Publication/Company Index (listing alphabetically all publications appearing in the Portfolio, cross-referenced to their publishing company and the page on which it appears in the preceeding main section).

BRAD Advertiser & Agency List

This publication, updated four times each year, contains information about leading advertising agencies – who and where they are, their billings, recognition and status, key executives, IPA membership, and which clients and brands they handle. Similar information is given about the top national advertisers – their products or services and brands, who to contact, how much and in which media they spend, and their advertising agencies. The List also gives details of all main trade associations involved with the advertising industry.

BRAD Direct Marketing Lists, Rates & Data

This publication, updated twice yearly, features direct marketing lists covering consumer and business markets, as well as the public sector (all categorised under 'Interest' headings) giving source, profile, previous use and 'cleaning' against the Mailing Preference Service, address type (whether individuals can be mailed at home or business), rental costs and conditions. In addition, it gives the names and addresses of owners and list brokers, and also provides information about the supply and services side of the industry.

BRAD Premiums & Incentives Price Guide

Published twice a year, this guide has four sections: Consultancies & Agencies, Promotional Support Services, Incentive Travel & Corporate Hospitality, and Incentive Vouchers.

In conclusion, it is worth mentioning that BRAD not only provides an information service but is also an advertising medium in its own right, used by those whose target market is those personnel whose judgement affects media decisions.

BUSADS (BUS AUDIENCE DATA SYSTEM)
(London Transport Advertising, 10 Jamestown Road, Camden, London NW1 7BY)

London buses carry mobile advertisement sites throughout Greater London, reaching more than 200 shopping centres as well as all commercial areas. The network has been substantially restructured since 1987, with advertising available on buses running out of some 50 garages. London Transport Advertising commissioned an independent survey into the travel patterns of Londoners, to establish a database for measuring the effectiveness of bus advertising campaigns. The survey calculated:

- the audience for bus advertising campaigns in terms of net unduplicated audience coverage and repetition
- the audience profile by demographic variables
- the campaign audience in terms of campaign size, site type, duration and location.

The survey allows for updates to take account of changes in either the demographic profile of the Greater London population or changes to the bus services which carry the advertisements.

Three databases were assembled as follows:

1. Bus Network The network was recorded on detailed street maps covering all Greater London, on which the roads on which buses travel had been colour coded, in order to define the bus network as a series of links, each identified by its start and end. This information was then matched with data from the Home Interview Survey described below, to calculate campaign site encounters for each individual interviewed.

2. Home Interview Survey Interviewers recruited a sample of 1,000 individuals, representative of the Greater London population. Each respondent supplied details of all journeys made and their frequency, identified by time, purpose and mode(s) of transport, broken down into component stages. This information was then matched with the detailed maps used for the Bus Network Database, to establish the probability of each individual encountering a campaign advertisement.

3. Car Video Survey This calculated exposure to bus advertisements by car drivers and passengers. A survey car was equipped with a video camera mounted on a tripod over the front passenger seat, and driven over much of the bus network. The camera was positioned to obtain a driver's or passenger's view of the road ahead, and the car's location and travel time and distance on and off bus routes recorded. The recordings were then analysed for observations of each advertisement site, with different types separately logged. An average encounter per minute was then calculated for each site type separately (broken down between Inner and Outer London) and matched to the Home Interview Survey to establish audience coverage and repetition amongst car drivers.

A synopsis of the research methodology and results was published as *BUSADS: Bus Audience Data System*. This specifies expected pedestrian/vehicle encounters for different site types and campaign sizes, giving both coverage and frequency figures for all adults (men and women separately), businessmen, housewives, ABC1 and AB adults, and three age bands (10–14, 15–24, and 25–34 year olds).

London Transport Advertising's *BUSADS* also offers a Campaign Planning facility, advising advertisers on how to buy a bus advertising campaign which delivers optimum coverage and frequency.

CAA (CINEMA ADVERTISING ASSOCIATION)
(127 Wardour Street, London W1V 4AD)

The CAA is the trade association of cinema advertising contractors in the UK and as such is devoted to developing and maintaining high standards of practice and presentation within the medium.

Its role is partly that of watchdog, acting to ensure that professional standards are maintained by the cinema advertising industry. One aspect of this work is that it is responsible for conducting regular checks to ensure that cinema advertising bookings are screened as scheduled, and under optimum conditions, i.e. prior to the main feature film, and with the house lights down. Another aspect of its watchdog role is vetting all commercials prior to screening – a matter discussed in more detail in Chapter 16.

The other major purpose of the CAA – hence its inclusion in this chapter – is to educate and inform, and in this role it aims to provide advertisers and agencies with up-to-date information about the cinema medium and the advertising advantages it has to offer.

Gallup provides the CAA with admission figures on a weekly basis to help administer the Audience Discount Packages described earlier and these figures are accepted as the official industry source. Information about cinema screens is available from CAA under various headings: UK total by cinema seating capacity, and by Registrar General's Standard Regions. The CAA also provides information, based on NRS sources, regarding the cinema audience: composition, penetration, and cinema coverage – the coverage and frequency obtained by typical cinema campaigns. Also available, based on TGI sources (see below) are index figures of product usage by cinema-going frequency. The index figures, available for a range of product groups, give a quantitative measure of the value of the cinema audience for the product group or service in question. For example, an index of 130 means that cinema-goers are 1.30 times as likely to use a product as the average person. Five index figures are available for each product group: all cinema-goers (those who ever go to the cinema), heavy cinema-goers (go more than once a month), medium cinema-goers (go once a month or every two or three months), light cinema-goers (go less than once in three months) and non cinema-goers (those who never go to the cinema). The CAA also publishes 'Coverage and Frequency Guides', based on NRS figures, giving estimates of the levels of coverage and frequency that can be achieved by cinema campaigns. There are two such guides, one general and the other relating to school holiday weeks.

To back up the data available from other sources, the CAA commissions its own research to strengthen the case for using the cinema as an advertising medium. It is reassuring to note that, whilst a great deal of additional information is provided, the audience patterns revealed by CAA research are very much in line with those revealed by the National Readership Surveys, for example. The CAA recognises, however, that advertisers require far more detailed knowledge of whom their message is reaching and to this end commissioned and published in 1979 the first of a series of in-depth audience studies, through Carrick James Market Research. These were the forerunners of the annual CAVIAR studies described below. In addition, the CAA has conducted advertising recall studies, to test awareness of cinema as opposed to television.

A new development is that the CAA has launched its own quarterly magazine, *Projections*, carrying details of box office and audience research.

CAVIAR (CINEMA AND VIDEO INDUSTRY AUDIENCE RESEARCH COMMITTEE)
(Cinema Advertising Association, 127 Wardour Street, London W1V 4AD)

CAVIAR's annual survey researches the entire film market, from cinema to video tapes, both rented and bought, and contains information on television, satellite and cable watching, as well as newspaper and magazine readership. It is funded by the Cinema Advertising Association and a consortium of leading organisations in the cinema and video industries.

The main survey usually takes place between October and November. Carrick James Market Research (CJMR) conducts face-to-face interviews, usually in people's homes, among a representative quota sample of some 3,000 people age seven-plus, spread across 120 randomly-selected sampling points throughout Great Britain. The ninth CAVIAR study, carried out in 1991, appears in several volumes as follows.

Cinema Report

Respondents are asked about cinema-going frequency and how recently they went to the cinema, and classified along a 12-point scale.

Each annual survey analyses 36 top films on general release over the year, to give their total viewership and audience profile. In addition, the audiences of 12 selected *'art'* films are measured separately. CAVIAR has developed a classification system to identify more than 50 types of film.

Cinema-goers are asked about visits over the past two months, with the last five visits analysed in detail. Information is recorded about the film seen, name and location of cinema, and whether the screen was in a multiplex unit. Data about people accompanying respondents on cinema visits is also analysed, usually on a bi-annual basis.

Other topics are also analysed, though not always annually. These include sources of information used in relation to the last visit, how far in advance the film was chosen, method of travel to the cinema, and reasons for visiting multiplex sites.

Cinema information is now supplemented by the new *Film Monitor* studies described below.

Video Report

Respondents are asked how frequently they watch hired and bought videos, and videos they recorded themselves. Hired and bought videos are then analysed separately.

Each annual survey analyses 36 top pre-recorded video releases over the year, to provide their total viewership and audience profiles. Data is also analysed by CAVIAR's classification codes, to provide audience profiles for specific film categories. Rented and purchased tapes are considered together when determining the audiences for specific titles.

Other Media Report

This analyses the use of TV sets, including use of computers, video games, home recorded and time-shifted videos, and satellite and cable viewing.

It also covers regular reading of daily and Sunday newspapers and selected magazines. Traditionally the magazines selected are those likely to be popular with young people. CAVIAR is the only survey to cover readership of general newspapers by children aged 7–14.

Film Monitor

Since 1990 the consortium has also sponsored a cinema film monitor study, conducted on an alternative monthly basis to provide viewership and profile data more frequently than the main study. Interviewing is conducted jointly by CJMR and NOP (National Opinion Polls) with a combined sample size of more than 4,000 individuals.

Each bi-monthly survey covers 24 films, classified by CAVIAR codes, with audiences analysed by age, sex and social grade.

Report Format

Reports are available in both written and tabular form. The tabular report contains more than 100 tables, each with extensive cross-analyses detailing age, sex and social grade (certain tables contain expanded sub-groups such as frequency of cinema-going, ownership of satellite, frequency of watching hired films, and type of video bought). The written report contains pertinent trend data in addition to the survey results.

Special interest tables are also included, with analysis by:

- age, sex and social grade
- family size, siblings, marital status, age of mother/children
- terminal educational age, school/work status
- TV area
- electronic equipment in home
- length of VCR ownership
- accommodation type
- weight of media usage (TV, cinema and video)

Data tapes are also available, and further classification is possible.

CAVIAR is developed on a constant basis, to reflect current developments and has recently been expanded in a number of directions – the age range extended to cover five and six year olds, and the cinema and video sell-through sections also expanded.

CONFERENCES & EXHIBITIONS DIARY
(Themetree Ltd, 2 Prebendal Court, Oxford Road, Aylesbury, Bucks HP19 3EY)

This Diary is published quarterly and is categorised in 42 comprehensive sections. Within each, events are listed by country (the Diary now includes European events) in date order, with title, venue and location, and the address and telephone number of the organisers.

CONFERENCE AND EXHIBITION FACT FINDER
(Batiste Publications Ltd, Pembroke House, Campsbourne Road, Hornsey, London N8 7PE)

This monthly publication gives comprehensive details of Britain's major venues, events, services and suppliers, together with news, opinions and reviews, to a target circulation of management, advertising and marketing executives.

D M I S (DIRECT MAIL INFORMATION SERVICE)
(5 Carlisle Street, London W1V 5RG)

The Direct Mail Information Service is the source of official statistics on direct mail: it also provides regular reports and updates on major trends and relevant issues within the industry.

Each year DMIS undertakes several new research projects, as well as continuing its on-going programme. The work may range from gauging the volume of direct mail to more complex projects dealing with specific issues affecting the industry. Some of the most important projects provide information on consumer opinions and treatment of direct mail while, more recently, DMIS completed research into the business-to-business sector.

Run on behalf of the Royal Mail (see separate entry below) by the HBH Partnership, DMIS distributes most of its material free of charge. Recent publications include the following:

The Letterbox Factfile provides an up-to-date profile of what is received via the domestic household's letterbox and consumer attitudes towards the medium, together with new information about the business direct mail industry.

Consumer direct mail

Attitudes and Anxieties discusses consumer objections to direct mail.

The Literate Consumer examines how consumers react to receiving increasing volumes of direct mail.

Direct Mail and Consumer Personality Types segments consumers according to personality types, in relation to their treatment of direct mail.

Consumer Perceptions of Direct Mail and the Industry behind it examines how consumers feel about the direct mail industry and other types of advertising.

Direct Mail Trends Survey The 1992 report focusses on six specific areas: receipt, response, treatment, likes, dislikes and satisfaction.

Business-to-business direct mail

Business Direct Mail: Receipt and Treatment examines the sectors of industry from which business people receive direct mail, and their treatment of it.

Business Direct Mail: Perception and Reality examines the results of an in-depth study of business people's attitudes to direct mail.

DMIS also provides assistance with the planning, execution and evaluation of direct mail campaigns.

E I F (EXHIBITION INDUSTRY FEDERATION)
(PO Box 980, London SE11 5JB)

The activities of this new Federation are best illustrated by its third research report – *The UK Exhibition Industry: The Facts* – published to assist present and potential users of exhibitions in planning their marketing programmes, and to give reliable data to those who stage or service exhibitions.

The report's key findings cover data about exhibitions, visitor numbers and their spending, cost-effectiveness and auditing, and classification of exhibitions by industry sector. Further sections give details of attendance surveys, and of exhibitors' and visitors' spending, while appendices cover EIF's main board and research group, qualifying exhibition venues, audit schemes, and the classification by industry sector.

The on-going 'Attendance' and 'Spending' surveys provide a base from which trends can be projected, while the recent introduction of mandatory audits for AEO (Association of Exhibition Organisers) members' exhibitions is a significant advance in producing authoritative data. The third area of research remains the evaluation of exhibitions as a marketing tool, and their role within the total marketing plan. An independent 'Effectiveness Survey' has been commissioned, and the EIF has also supported further research initiated by a group of major UK exhibition organisers. When published, the findings will form the basis of continuing research into this important but relatively unexplored area.

The EIF's classification of exhibitions into 16 industry sectors (all sub-divided) assists those searching for a particular type of event to identify it more quickly, and also makes it possible to aggregate exhibitions into meaningful categories for statistical purposes.

EXHIBITIONS BULLETIN
(The London Bureau, 266–272 Kirkdale, Sydenham, London SE26 4RZ)

This monthly publication is a comprehensive guide to UK and worldwide exhibitions, giving information about some 2,000 events spanning 30 months, covering dates, venues, organisers and technical services. It contains a world classified industrial and trade index of fairs and exhibitions.

ITC (THE INDEPENDENT TELEVISION COMMISSION)
(70 Brompton Road, London SW3 1EY)

JICCAR (the former Joint Industry Committee for Cable Audience Research) ceased operation due to lack of funding, but the ITC now publishes quarterly bulletins. These state the number of operating franchises, and also give the overall number of homes passed and connected, together with average penetration. Two sets of figures are given: Broadband homes and All homes, the latter including Narrowband and SMATV.

The bulletins also give 'Pay/basic ratios' which are a measure of the number of subscriptions to the film channels (Sky Movies Plus, The Movie Channel and Home Video Channel) as a percentage of total subscribers. For example, if all cable homes subscribed to just one film channel and neither of the other two, the pay/basic ratio would be 100 per cent; if to all three, the ratio would be 300 per cent.

Similar figures for homes passed/connected and penetration, together with pay/basic ratios, are also given for individual broadband franchises with more than 2,500 subscribers.

The bulletins also give overall numbers for cabled homes receiving the various available channels, but do not cover the DBS dish audiences for them.

ITC cable statistics are based on returns made by every licenced cable operator, and some SMATV operators.

ITV ASSOCIATION
(Knighton House, 56 Mortimer Street, London W1N 8AN)

Incorporated as a company limited by guarantee, the ITV Association is the Association of the 16 ITV programme contractors to the Independent Television Commission. The Association provides a Central Secretariat to service the needs of the industry requiring a co-ordinated and centralised approach. The governing body is the Council, comprising all the Managing Directors of the ITV Companies, and its main task is to determine the joint policy of the Companies over a wide range of industry matters. The Association represents the Companies in dealing with Government Departments, the press and national and international bodies dealing with matters affecting broadcasting.

The Association has a Copy Clearance department which scrutinises scripts and views videotaped films of commercials for showing on ITV, breakfast TV, Channel Four and Independent Radio to ensure they comply with the ITC's Code of Advertising Standards and Practice and relevant Acts of Parliament.

The Association has recently undergone a structural analysis and, during the course of this year, will re-organise its functions to accommodate the demands of the 1990 Broadcasting Act.

JICCAR (JOINT INDUSTRY COMMITTEE FOR CABLE AUDIENCE RESEARCH)
(See ITC above)

JICNARS (JOINT INDUSTRY COMMITTEE FOR NATIONAL READERSHIP SURVEYS)
(See NRS below)

JICPAR (JOINT INDUSTRY COMMITTEE FOR POSTER AUDIENCE RESEARCH)
(c/o The Outdoor Advertising Association, 77 Newman Street, London W1A 1DX)

JICPAR comprises representatives of the Outdoor Advertising Association of Great Britain, the Incorporated Society of British Advertisers, the Institute of Practitioners in Advertising, and the Council of Outdoor Specialists.

JICPAR supervises the development and maintenance of the poster medium's audience measurement: OSCAR – Outdoor Site Classification and Audience Research. Funded by the Outdoor Advertising Association which represents some 90 per cent of the roadside poster contractors, OSCAR is based on a constantly up-dated census of all poster sites. As implied by its title, OSCAR research covers two main attributes – *Site Classification* and *Audience Research*. Individual sites are classified and rated according to location, visibility, proximity to retail outlets etc, based on data collected by NOP Market Research. These figures are then adjusted according to the figures for passages past each site (for pedestrians and people in vehicles) based on traffic counts originally undertaken by Audits of Great Britain. These combined figures thus provide a total weekly audience (or opportunities to see) for each individual panel, together with coverage and frequency.

Data is grouped by local government districts and areas, with contractor identification, and is available on-line from NOP posters or in printed form in the six-monthly OSCAR digest published every Spring/Autumn. Additional site proximity data (e.g. within 100 yards of bank, chemist etc) and quarterly competitive sheetage reports are available, and monthly competitive expenditure estimates are available from the Media Register (described below).

OSCAR also serves as a practical planning facility for advertisers and their agencies. Poster contractors in clients' areas of distribution will – given the target market, the number of opportunities-to-see sought, and the poster sizes planned – send an Availability List of Panels, together with audience estimates.

JICRAR (JOINT INDUSTRY COMMITTEE FOR RADIO AUDIENCE RESEARCH)
(See **RAJAR** *below)*

JICREG (JOINT INDUSTRY COMMITTEE FOR REGIONAL PRESS RESEARCH)
(Bloomsbury House, 74–77 Great Russell Street, London WC1B 3DA)

JICREG was launched in 1990, as a Joint Industry Committee, by the Newspaper Society, Institute of Practitioners in Advertising, and Incorporated Society of British Advertisers (and originally the former Association of Free Newspapers) to provide regional press readership figures similar to those provided by the National Readership Surveys described below. Prior to this, the regional press was the only major advertising medium without a comprehensive audience database.

Many regional newspapers undertake regular readership research on their own behalf, but any database that merely held this information centrally would have large gaps caused by titles without research. It was therefore decided, after much technical debate, to see if these gaps could be filled by mathematically modelling readership figures from circulation and demographic data. The modelled data would then be merged with the researched information, to construct a comprehensive database for the regional press. The project for modelling readership was put out to tender and the contract awarded to Telmar. Rigorous examination proved the modelled figures generally matched actual figures extremely closely, within the 95 per cent confidence levels generally acceptable as an industry standard.

JICREG now provides readership information for nearly 90 per cent of all regional titles, covering morning, evening and Sunday newspapers, and paid-for and free weeklies. There is, of course, nothing to prevent individual newspapers from commissioning research to demonstrate their particular merits, and indeed JICREG encourages this and has provision to incorporate the results within its own database. Such independent research must however be in accordance with JICREG's Survey Guidelines (which specify carefully prepared sampling procedures and precisely drafted questionnaires) to ensure it is statistically valid.

Regional and local press schedules can now be analysed against JICREG data to show reach and frequency (both discussed in Chapter 6) within any geographic area, by any combination of titles. The database is held at the Newspaper Society, and 'piggy-backed' on its *PressAd* facility (described below). Full information is also available from two authorised data-processing bureaux (Telmar and IMS), and some information is held by MediaTel (also described below). JICREG is available in printed form or on disc, while a number of active users access the data on-line.

JICTAR (JOINT INDUSTRY COMMITTEE FOR TELEVISION AUDIENCE RESEARCH)
(See **BARB** *above)*

MEAL (MEDIA EXPENDITURE ANALYSIS LTD)
(Register House, 4 Holdford Yard, Cruickshank Street, London WC1X 9HD)

The organisation is merging with The Media Register described below. The merged company will no doubt rationalise the two services, and the following details are therefore subject to change.

The main purpose of MEAL's services is to provide a continuous monitor of advertising activity as an aid to marketing management.

The monitor of consumer media is based on comprehensive coverage of display advertisements in the national press, magazines, television and selected radio contractors. It also includes national advertising in an extensive list of regional newspapers. Each month more than 250,000 individual advertisements are attributed to more than 15,000 brands. The main media groups covered by the monitoring service include:

- Television (ITV + Channel 4 + Breakfast TV)
- Eleven major radio contractors
- National daily newspapers
- National Sunday newspapers
- Weekend colour supplements
- Regional evening papers
- General weekly and monthly magazines
- Women's weekly and monthly magazines
- Special interest magazines
- Juvenile magazines

The results of the monitoring service are available in a wide range of reports and services to meet individual requirements.

MEAL regularly publishes *Product Group Reports* relating to 350 product groups which, in turn, are classified by 22 categories.

A	Agricultural & horticultural	F	Food
B	Charity, education & societies	G	Government, development
C	Drink		corporations & service
D	Entertainment		recruitment
E	Financial	H	Holidays, travel and transport

J	Household appliances	R	Pharmaceutical
K	Household equipment	S	Publishing
L	Household stores	T	Retail & mail order
M	Institutional & industrial	U	Tobacco
N	Leisure equipment	V	Toiletries & cosmetics
P	Motors	W	Wearing apparel
Q	Office equipment	X	Local advertisers

The categories may be re-classified but the overall product/service coverage will remain the same.

There are various regular services relating to these product groups and categories, including:

1 Advertisement Analysis A detailed description of advertising activity giving a record of each television and press advertisement placed during the month. The details for each advertisement are: date, station or publication, duration or size, time-on or special position, and rate-card cost.

2 Brand Expenditure by Medium This report shows television, radio and press expenditure during each of the last 12 months and in total for the period. A percentage profile is also included to give the distribution of expenditure during the period.

3 Brand Expenditure by Media Groups The report shows the allocation of brand expenditure when the main interest is in the press. For each brand the expenditure is shown during the last month and the last 12 months. Total expenditure is split between television, radio and the press. Expenditure is also shown for 13 press groups.

4 Brand Expenditure by Television Regions This service gives a detailed analysis of total television expenditure during the previous month and the latest 12 months. This is shown in total and for both channels (ITV and Channel 4) in each region.

5 Brand Expenditure on Radio 'Key Region Radio' is a continuous monitor of brand expenditure on radio. The results are compiled from ten major radio contractors in six primary marketing areas. Expenditure is shown in £000's for each contractor and in total.

6 Brand Expenditure by Area This report shows expenditure in nine main marketing areas for television and press. It is a guide to the amount of advertising weight in each area. The nine areas are defined by TV regions and the allocation of press expenditure is according to NRS readership profiles.

7 Brand Advertising by Selected Titles MEAL also provides a flexible tabulation service to meet individual requirements. There are the following options when specifying an analysis:

a) Up to 17 columns may be specified and each of these may be an individual publication or television contractor. The specified media may be taken from any of those which are regularly monitored.
b) The expenditure or advertisement volume information shown for each brand may be either monthly or quarterly together with either year to date or moving annual total.
c) The percentage profiling of expenditure across the specified media is completely flexible, and may be produced with sub-totals profiled on the grand total; individual media profiled on the sub-total or the brand total, etc.

8 Tri-media Digest of Brands and Advertisers This report shows the advertising expenditure of individual brands in total for the latest quarter, each month in the quarter, and the last 12 months. The report also gives the proportion of expenditure in television, radio and the press for each brand and product group. Each issue includes a special index showing advertisers and their brands. The Tri-media digest is also published electronically, and available through various on-line computer data-base services.

Special Reports

In addition to its monthly services, MEAL also produces special annual reports. For example, *Ten Year Trends* shows product group expenditure information in total, in the press and on television for each of ten consecutive years, summarised with all information shown in £000's. Other special reports cover *Top 1,000 Brands* spending £1M or more, and *Top 500 Advertisers* who account for 75 per cent of all display advertising.

These established analyses are available for all MEAL product groups as follows:

Annual subscription Results are produced monthly and despatched within a week from the end of the month.

Ad hoc requests Complete results are held by Client Service and readily available for current or past data within 24 hours of request.

Direct access MEAL's data base is available 'on line' to provide *ad hoc* analyses. These services may be accessed directly from most terminals or by contacting Client Service.

MEDIA AUDITS LTD
(16 Dufours Place, London W1V 1FE)

This company provides consultancy services in the measurement and use of advertising media. Media Audits neither buys nor sells space or time, and is thus objective in its analysis and interpretation. The company works for advertisers, agencies and media-owners, and in particular provides an evaluation service for major advertisers using television and press media.

For television, each advertiser provides Media Audits with a detailed campaign schedule together with actual costs paid and, as a BARB subscriber, Media Audits validates the audience ratings achieved by each schedule. This data is then pooled by target group eg adults, housewives, men etc, and these data pools serve as a common base or Cost Rating Index (CRI), from which comparisons can be made. These norms provide the basis for comparing individual campaigns, enabling advertisers to evaluate their performance against that of similar advertisers over the same period.

Both terrestrial and satellite TV channels are monitored. Full analysis can be made of the contribution of any or all channels, down to particular time segments and specific programmes. The CRI service now accounts for some 33 per cent of all TV advertising in the UK, and thus offers a realistic measure of costs paid by advertisers.

Media Audits also provides a Press Buying Index (PBI), offering a parallel service to advertisers in national newspapers and magazines. Subscribers provide full press schedules giving details of all insertions bought, again including actual rather than rate-card costs. Data is then pooled by publication and publishing group, and individual insertions and campaigns compared with the experience of the pool. Measures include discounts, positions obtained, and prices paid for the same space during the same period. In 1990, the PBI covered some 12 per cent of all display advertising.

Additional services offered by Media Audits include its Quantitative Advertising Division (QUAD) which links advertising exposure and the effects of that communication eg awareness and recall, or postal and telephone responses etc.

Retail Locations, a Media Audits subsidiary, holds up-to-date retail outlet information by postcode, allowing analyses of retail strengths/weaknesses in micro regions (such as those covered by local newspapers) or in macro regions (such as TV regions, or the UK as a whole). Proximity analysis can match particular poster sites with individual retail outlets, or larger areas can be geo-demographically analysed and matched to available retail outlets, thus tightening poster campaign targetting.

Recent developments include media training courses for clients, tackling current media issues, and 1991 saw the launch of Media Audits Holland, extending Media Audits' services into the Netherlands.

THE MEDIA REGISTER
(Register House, 4 Holdford Yard, Cruickshank Street, London WC1X 9HD)

This organization is merging with MEAL, described above. The merged company will no doubt rationalise the two services, and the following details are therefore subject to change.

The Media Register publishes regular information on TV, press and poster and cinema expenditure, to assist advertisers and their agencies in monitoring competitors' advertising expenditure.

Television expenditure

Television advertising expenditure is notoriously difficult to estimate, since most TV rate cards are based on a 'ladder' of increasing spot rates – the 'pre-empt' system described earlier. The Media Register technique is therefore linked to what is actually happening in the TV air-time market place.

Each month the total net revenue of the independent television companies is published through the ITV Association. Individual contractors' shares of homes are known, and each contractor's revenue may thus be calculated. Additionally, the audiences for every spot and every contractor are measured by BARB.

Consequently, an average cost-per-thousand may be calculated for each contractor by dividing revenue by impacts (in thousands), and meaningful data can be calculated for three broad target audience subgroups: housewives, adults and men.

Thus, TV expenditure estimates may be made for a brand by multiplying the total impacts achieved by a brand within an area by the most appropriate cost-per-thousand, and consolidating across all advertising areas. However, these estimates are not yet sufficiently accurate – there is a degree of 'slippage' that takes place as some times of day, days of week or types of programme etc offer above-average value for advertisers seeking a particular target audience. Consequently, costs-per-thousand are adjusted by The Media Register to generate more accurate costs-per-thousand, such that the multiplication of all impacts within a month within an area by the most relevant cost-per-thousand is exactly equal to the (gross) contractor revenue.

This technique yields an expected expenditure for all TV advertised brands (although some brands will spend slightly more and some slightly less than this expectation, depending on various marketplace factors).

Press Expenditure

No scientific method has yet been developed to calculate actual, up-to-date press expenditure, so the Media Register applies correct rate-card value to each advertisement monitored. The Media Register monitors more than 500 titles, examining them and recording the information in detail – not only display advertising but also all classifieds, even in regional publications, and large advertisers are credited with their individual share.

Poster Expenditure

The Media Register publishes monthly brand expenditure estimates for roadside poster advertising, using data provided by the Outdoor Advertising Association described below.

Product Classification

The Media Register has developed a classification system listing 480 product groups, attributed to 34 product categories:

Agricultural	Household Furnishings
Business to Business	Household Stores
Charities	Houseware
Classified	Industrial
Clothing	Leisure Equipment
Confectionery	Luxury Goods
Corporate	Mail Order
Cosmetics & Toiletries	Motors
Do It Yourself	Office Automation
Drink	Pharmaceutical
Education	Public Utilities
Entertainment	Publishing and Broadcasting
Financial	Retail
Food	Small Electrical Appliances
Gardening	Sport
Government	Tobacco
Household Durables	Travel

Media Register Reports

Information is available from the Media Register in various forms – a *Monthly Summary*, and *Selected Product Group Reports* (complete advertisement listings for TV & Press, or analysed by selected media titles, TV area, or advertising agency) to any frequency or to cover any time period required. Reports covering all product groups are available both on microfiche and in printed form, and will shortly be available on-line.

The Future

Although The Media Register is merging with MEAL, during 1992 the two companies will operate independently (although at the same address) with MEAL continuing to publish its Quarterly Digest, and Media Register its Monthly Summary.

From 1993 the merged company, Media Register/Meal, will publish a quarterly summary covering the following five media:

- Press
- Terrestrial and satellite television
- Radio
- Cinema
- Posters

MEDIATEL
(52 Poland Street, London W1V 3DF)

MediaTel is an on-line database of media information, news and developments specially designed for media buyers and sellers. To access MediaTel, subscribers need a PC, modem and suitable communications software. Once connected to the MediaTel computer, subscribers can then call up information covering all the major consumer and business-to-business media detailed below. If subscribers want a copy of any information on their display screens, it is immediately available through a print-out facility.

MediaTel's database covers all the cost and audience details normally used as a basis for media planning, and all information is edited and up-dated every day. Data available covers the following main media markets (each sub-divided): national newspapers, magazines (consumer and business), television, outdoor, cinema, radio, regional media and sponsorship. The *Newsline* service reports media events as they happen, and is the most heavily accessed section of the data base. *Encyclomedia* compiles useful media statistics on expenditure and revenues. The *Miscellaneous* section includes, among other items, a useful 'Minefield' warning (a chronological list by month of irregular events that may affect audience deliveries).

MediaTel's facilities include a keyword search system. Via this system, the media opportunities in any town, for example, can be accessed by keying in the name of the town, or information on a particular publication by keying in its title.

Various standard media calculations (cost/coverage ranking for press, and a coverage and frequency guide for radio, as examples) can now be performed on MediaTel's interactive services.

MediaTel also offers media-owners the opportunity to set up and edit their own pages within the overall database. In this way, media-owners can make available to MediaTel subscribers the latest research or marketing data about their own medium. MediaTel also serves as an advertising medium in its own right, with solus advertising space.

MediaTel's *Press Planner* facility extends and improves access to data held on newspapers and magazines. The database now incorporates full rate-cards for more than 3,000 titles, including details of regional editions, inserts, and contacts. Rates data can be integrated with circulation and readership data to produce costs-per-thousand for any list of titles. In addition, more than 20 different reports, ranging from readership and circulation trends through to editorial assessments, can be viewed on screen or printed out.

MediaTel's new *Mediaplan* press schedule analysis system supplements the data provided by the *Press Planner* service. The former helps with the initial stages of press planning, deciding candidate media for a press campaign, and gives cost/coverage rankings based on one insertion in each publication.

Mediaplan extends this by using BMRC, NRS and TGI data (described elsewhere) to provide detailed analysis of full press schedules featuring multiple insertions in a number of publications. *Mediaplan* calculates their net coverage, total and average opportunities-to-see (OTS) and frequency distribution (explained in Chapter 15). *Mediaplan* also cross-tabulates any one variable with any other.

M M S (MEDIA MONITORING SERVICES LTD)
(Madison House, High Street, Sunninghill, Ascot, Berkshire SL5 9NP)

This company monitors more than a thousand journal titles each month, ranging from the business-to-business press and national consumer magazines, through to Sunday and daily newspapers. MMS's system is flexible, so each report covers individual subscribers' particular needs. Each client selects the list of journals to be monitored, and reports are then provided in magnetic tape, disc or printed format. The system was originally designed by publishers for publishers, but has since been extended to cater for advertising agencies and their clients. The database can provide reports on a one-off or regular basis, in the following media categories:

Business-to-Business Press

MMS monitors over 800 titles in more than 90 markets, and its reporting service encompasses display, recruitment and classified advertising.

Reported in volume and/or expenditure terms, MMS data provides everything from 'Management Summaries' down to detailed schedules of advertiser activity by product, publication and month.

Performances can be tracked by total market, product category, individual advertiser and defined geographical area, and new business opportunities identified through 'Absent Advertiser' reports.

Printed reports can be complemented by a PC system which allows users to analyse data further in a variety of ways. The system can, in addition, create 'Prospect Lists' and includes an 'Address List' mailing facility.

Consumer Magazines and National Newspapers

MMS's *Medialog* Consumer Magazine database contains detailed advertising information across more than 150 publications and in excess of 36,000 products.

A PC system allows users to analyse raw data flexibly, to create customised reports and graphics, as well as detailed advertising schedules.

These analyses enable clients to track advertising within their defined magazine markets by product category, advertiser, agency, brand and publication.

MMS has extended its press media coverage into the national daily newspapers, thus offering a comprehensive national 'Print monitoring service'.

Recruitment

MMS measures all Recruitment Advertising across national newspapers and selected trade markets.

Detailed reports allow clients to track performance by job category and title and by individual advertiser, as well as identifying new business opportunities by reporting on 'absent advertisers' not using the client's publications.

This service will also be available in a PC system.

Classified

MMS coverage of Classified Advertising allows detailed reporting down to category and advertiser level within national newspapers, consumer magazines and selected trade publications. Users can track performance in their total sector, by category within each sector, and by advertiser, as well as identify new business opportunities.

Editorial

MMS currently measures editorial content in more than 200 consumer magazines, in the national quality press and in a growing number of trade publications.

Editorial references are measured by category within each publication, with detailed reports available showing coverage volumes, editorial/advertising ratios, category breakdowns by publication, and profiles by category.

Television

Television expenditure analysis will soon be included within the MMS database, completing a comprehensive monitoring service to meet the individual needs of publishers, advertising agencies and advertisers.

NRS (NATIONAL READERSHIP SURVEYS)
(Garden Studios, 11-15 Betterton Street, Covent Garden, London WC2H 9BP)

NRS Ltd was formed by the Newspaper Publishers Association, the Periodical Publishers Association, and the Institute of Practitioners in Advertising, together with the Incorporated Society of British Advertisers. It took over responsibility for the National Readership Surveys from JICNARS in 1992.

Currently the NRS publishes the results of 35,000 interviews a year. About 250 publications (national and Sunday newspapers and a number of national magazines) are included. The research is currently undertaken on behalf of NRS by Research Services Ltd.

Since the NRS research began (as long ago as 1956) there has been a consistent procedure for classifying informants into grades A, B, C1, C2, D and E. This system of social grading (explained in Chapter 6) has been widely adopted throughout the advertising industry. In addition to readership data, the NRS provides information on other matters, as follows.

Volume 1 This is based on fieldwork for the period July to the following June, and contains information on

- Average issue readership of all major publications analysed by sex (men, women and housewives), age, six social grades, survey region and Incorporated Society of British Advertisers (ISBA) area
- Profile tables showing the readership composition of each publication in terms of sex, age, social grade and region, and weight of ITV viewing
- Tables showing ILR listening and cinema-going, analysed by sex, age, social grade and ISBA region
- Readership of each publication by weight of ITV viewing and radio listening, and frequency of cinema-going
- Readership of each publication among special interest groups such as housewives with children, members of car-owning households, owners of consumer durables, etc. There are also sections on readership by male heads of household/chief wage-earner and heads of household/housewives
- Group readership figures
- Frequency of reading each publication plus group probabilities for informants claiming each reading frequency. Cumulative readership tables are included.

The NRS incorporates ACORN (A Classification Of Residential Neighbourhoods, described in Chapter 6) as well as Pinpoint, Mosaic and Superprofiles (described in Chaper 12).

Volume 2 This further report has the same contents as Volume 1, but is based on the calendar year's fieldwork: January to December.

Volume 3 This contains duplication tables showing the extent to which readers of one publication also read other publications.

NRS Bulletins Subscribers to the NRS also receive various bulletins, including:

- Early monthly estimates of readership for national newspapers

- Total readership figures in advance of the main reports
- Additional information including early monthly estimates for some publications that have undergone major change or relaunch, or are newly launched publications
- A regular quarterly bulletin giving results for the four quarters ending with the latest period, and for the four previous 12 months' moving averages, and the three latest six-month periods.

Additional services

Although the published reports contain several hundred tabulations, the amount of data stored on tapes is very much larger, and facilities are provided for the extraction of such additional information as may be required by subscribers:

Tapes Subscribers can buy tapes relating to each quarter's or half-year's fieldwork period.

Post-survey information service The post-survey information service provides tabulations not contained in the reports. In addition, a number of companies have been authorised to provide post-survey information services. The services offered by these companies are extensive in terms of individual methods of schedule analysis and schedule construction services, apart from the production of simple additional tabulations. The authorisation of a company is not a reflection of NRS approval or disapproval of any particular model or system, but is based on the belief that the company can offer a competent and efficient service, and on agreement by the company to pay a royalty to NRS to assist financing the survey. The cost of extra analysis by authorised companies is a matter for individual negotiation.

OAA (OUTDOOR ADVERTISING ASSOCIATION)
(77 Newman Street, London W1A 1DX)

The Outdoor Advertising Association's activities include:

1 OSCAR The Outdoor Site Classification and Audience Research described earlier is the audience measurement for posters. Based on individual site fieldwork it provides, through statistical modelling, an objective method of net audience evaluation. All OSCAR data is the copyright of the OAA, and is developed and maintained by NOP Posters, a subsidiary of MAI.

2 *Competitive Data Reports* From the Spring of 1992, Key Systems are publishing monthly reports, using data supplied by Outdoor specialists and the OAA, listing the sectors/advertisers/brands that have used roadside advertising, and the numbers/sizes of panels used. A split by ISBA television areas is also available.

The Media Register described earlier publishes monthly brand expenditure estimates for roadside poster advertising, using data from the *Competitive Data Reports*.

OSCAR (OUTDOOR SITE CLASSIFICATION AUDIENCE RESEARCH)
(See **JICPAR**, *above)*

PETAR (PAN EUROPEAN TELEVISION AUDIENCE RESEARCH)
(Nielsen Media, Nielsen House, Headington, Oxford OX3 9RX)

The 1991 PETAR study was on a smaller scale than in previous years, and covered only six countries: Belgium (Flanders only), Denmark, Germany, Netherlands, Norway and Sweden. 2,341 individuals aged four-plus in homes with cable TV kept diaries over a four-week period in November, to record their viewing of some 100 satellite channels, covering all major channels across Europe. In Germany, there was a boosted sample of 250 individuals who are dish owners.

The PETAR report provides the following information, reviewed by each country and network in turn:

- Demographic descriptions – both households and individuals
- Universes – total and by channel with key demographics
- Reach, total hours viewed, channel hours viewed and channel share percentage for all individuals within each channel's own universe based on a 24-hour viewing period. Then, share of audience within each channel's own transmission times and key day-parts (identified by the sponsoring channels as their own key viewing periods)
- Four tables (one each for individuals, men, women and adults 16–34) showing the same information as above, but within the total cable universe.
- Other key data such as viewing repertoire (eg number of channels sampled in one evening, and the amount of short-term switching among some demographic groups).

The data contained in the printed PETAR Marketing Book is also available in disc format for further analysis.

PPA (PERIODICAL PUBLISHERS ASSOCIATION)
(Imperial House, 15–19 Kingsway, London WC2B 6UN)

The Periodical Publishers Association represents magazine publishers in the UK. Its members publish some 1,400 titles (ranging from mass-circulation consumer magazines to highly technical business and professional journals) and generate more than 80 per cent of all magazine advertising revenue.

The PPA's activities include publishing information to support the case for magazines as an advertising medium. Recent publications include the following.

The Media Multiplier

Commissioned by the PPA, this research examined the communications benefits gained from advertising campaigns which used both television and print. Undertaken by Communications Research Ltd (CRL), the research comprised a series of hall tests in which respondents were shown the magazine advertisements and TV commercials from mixed media campaigns. Eight detailed case studies show how television and magazines working together produced full and more effective communications than either medium could achieve alone – each medium multiplying the effect of the other (hence the title of the research, which up-dated an earlier award-winning study published by PPA as 'Multiplying the Media Effect').

The Power of Magazines

This publication highlights how magazines played a leading role in effective advertising, illustrated by more than 20 campaigns which in 1990 received *Media Week* Consumer and Business Press Advertising Awards.

People love their magazines

In 1989 the PPA commissioned a review of all current research into magazine publishing, covering both consumer and business titles. 44 research studies were examined and the Media Research Director of WCRS Mathews Marcantonio, which undertook the analysis, summarised his findings in this way: *'We believe there is a research-based generic case for magazines as an advertising medium. Leaving aside their impressive coverage data, the most striking lesson from current re-*

search is that readers enjoy a very close relationship with the magazines they choose to read. It is a relationship which is impossible for other media, however remarkable their achievements, to replicate.'

Magazine News

The publication *Magazine News* was launched in 1989 and is circulated on a bi-monthly basis to selected individuals (including major advertisers and agencies, city analysts and publishers).

Magazine Handbook

The PPA has developed a comprehensive database to provide up-to-date information about the magazine industry's size, spread, development and readership. This data is the basis of the PPA *Magazine Handbook*, first published in 1991. Its various sections cover the size of the industry, circulation, advertising revenues and the part they play, readership levels in both business and consumer titles, and profitability.

Business Press

The PPA also specifically promotes business periodicals, originally through its BBP (British Business Press) association and now through its BBP Committee. The booklet *An Introduction to Business Press Research* examines the various types of research available to the business press and their uses, showing how research can improve the quality of information available to advertisers.

PRESSAD
(The Newspaper Society, Bloomsbury House, Bloomsbury Square, 74–77 Great Russell Street, London WC1B 3DA)

PressAd is the commercial wing of the Newspaper Society (the employers' organisation for the regional press). It was founded in 1988 after the demise of RNAB, the Regional Newspaper Advertising Bureau. The subsequent failure of the AFN (Association of Free Newspapers) means PressAd is now the sole promotional organisation for the regional press. As such, it provides a number of services to advertisers and agencies.

The PressAd database

The largest of its kind in the world, this covers all regional titles, giving rates, production details, key staff etc, by title. It also contains details of subscribing titles' circulation areas, by some 8,900 postcode sectors. These sectors can then be used as building blocks to cover any larger geographical area, from villages and towns, through to store/dealer catchment areas, shopping centre 'drive time' areas, counties, or television areas. Coverage can be provided by population, household and other demographic data, or by geo-demographic systems. In many cases, resultant press lists or media schedules are then analysed against the JICREG readership data described earlier.

The database is available in printed and disc format, while other users access it by telephone or even on-line. For planning and presentation purposes, PressAd provides a computerised mapping service to advertisers, agencies and publishers.

Production services

PressAd also offers facilities for advertisers or agencies who wish to centralise the task of advertisement production. On receipt of master copies of each advertisement, PressAd then sends out correct-size material to each newspaper in the schedule.

Co-operative advertising

Co-operation with distributors is a major component of many campaigns: co-operative advertising currently accounts for some £250 million each year, almost all of which appears in the regional press. PressAd works with manufacturers and suppliers in facilitating effective joint manufacturer/dealer schemes, by helping advertisers contact their local outlets. PressAd has worked with or instigated co-operative advertising schemes in 40 different categories, ranging from motors to photography and carpets to holidays.

RAB (THE RADIO ADVERTISING BUREAU)
(At time of writing, this new organisation had not yet finalised its office address)

The radio industry recently announced a new marketing initiative, the formation of the Radio Advertising Bureau, to promote radio generically and complete airtime sales deals. The Bureau is separate from the industry association AIRC, from which it has bought the *Radio Marketing Bureau* name to ensure there is no confusion. The rationale behind the establishment of RAB is to increase radio's share of the advertising cake.

RADAD – RADIO ADVERTISING FACTS AND FIGURES
(See **AIRC** *above)*

RAJAR (RADIO JOINT AUDIENCE RESEARCH)
(c/o AIRC, Radio House, 46 Westbourne Grove, London W2 5SH)

It is intended that, from September 1992, RAJAR will become the industry source of radio research: it includes representatives from the Institute of Practitioners in Advertising, the Incorporated Society of British Advertisers, the Association of Media Independents, the Association of Independent Radio Companies and the BBC.

This new organisation, set up to continue and develop the work of JICRAR (the Joint Industry Committee for Radio Audience Research) is still finalising its proposed research operation and, in consequence, the following details are subject to change.

The company was formed to agree a new specification and commission joint audience research, following agreement by the BBC and AIRC to join forces in this respect. For many years, ILR stations had commissioned and published, under the auspices of JICRAR, regular audience surveys covering all ILR stations. This research provided network audience data, as well as information about each individual ILR area.

From 1992 BBC radio broadcasting will be included in the research. Data will be collected continuously using random-location sampling, funded by all the radio broadcasters participating, from both the independent sector and the BBC. Other research features remain as before: personal placement and collection of a seven-day diary, with listening recorded on a quarter-hour basis. Appropriate ILR and BBC stations are shown in the diary, together with an 'Any other station' category. The research contract is currently out to tender.

If all goes according to plan, RAJAR will commence operations in September 1992. The final JICRAR survey is scheduled for April/June 1992, and the new research will probably contain the following tables for each station area:

- Cumulative weekly audience (reach), total and average hours – ILR
- Average audience by ILR rate-card segments
- Cumulative audience by ILR rate-card segment
- Average half-hour audience – Monday to Friday (averaged): ILR
- Average half-hour audience – Saturday: ILR
- Average half-hour audience – Sunday: ILR
- Cumulative weekly audience (reach), total and average hours: other stations
- Reach and frequency for six standard ILR packages.

Analysis will be provided in terms of age, sex and social class, the complexity of the sub-divisions depending on the sample size selected.

Network, regional, national services and large local/regional stations will probably be covered by quarterly reports, with supplementary reports every six months for most other local services. The BBC reports will not be 'published' as such, but will be available.

RAJAR will monitor the research to consider amendments and improvements and the best methods of publishing data.

RMB (RADIO MARKETING BUREAU)
(See **AIRC** *and* **RAB** *above)*

RNAB (REGIONAL NEWSPAPER ADVERTISING BUREAU)
(See **PressAd** *above)*

ROYAL MAIL STREAMLINE
(Direct Marketing Department, Streamline House, Sandy Lane West, Oxford OX4 5ZZ)

The Direct Marketing Department of the Royal Mail publishes a number of useful free booklets for the benefit of advertisers seeking advice on the direct mail medium.

The Royal Mail Guide to Successful Direct Mail gives comprehensive guidance on how to use direct mail effectively.

Response Services gives details about the Royal Mail's range of postage-paid reply services, including the Business Reply and Freepost schemes, as well as the *Admail* redirection service (described in Chapter 18) which enables you to receive orders and enquiries at an address different from that used in your promotional material.

Mailsort details the discounts business users can obtain, in return for carrying out sortation work that would otherwise be undertaken by the Royal Mail.

Household Delivery Direct mail, as defined (individually addressed and stamped material), does not include unaddressed letterbox deliveries. The Royal Mail nevertheless also offers a household delivery service, described in the booklet *Household Delivery*. This details the Royal Mail's services for unaddressed mail.

TGI (TARGET GROUP INDEX)
(Saunders House, 53 The Mall, Ealing, London W5 3TE)

The Target Group Index is a national product and media survey produced by the BMRB (British Market Research Bureau) and available on subscription to advertisers, agencies and media-owners. The TGI is entirely owned by BMRB and, unlike the usual industry media surveys, e.g. the various JICs described above, there is no guaranteed long-term contract or indeed guaranteed income.

TGI findings are based on 24,000 self-completion questionnaires received from informants who have been previously contacted by random location methods in some 5,000 sampling points in Great Britain. TGI provides an up-to-date base directly relating media and product usage.

TGI identifies heavy, medium and light users as well as non-users in a vast range of product categories and sub-categories. A full range of demographics and media usage is reported for these groups. TGI tables can explain who these people are, what they are like and which media vehicles are best to reach them.

The TGI product group information provides the foundation for assessing individual markets' major or potential users and their characteristics and media habits. It similarly provides information about brand usage, listing solus users (users of the product group who use a brand exclusively), most frequent users (including 'solus' users and those who prefer it to another brand also used) and minor users (those who are more casual in their use). These definitions establish some element of brand loyalty and the degree of involvement that users have with a given brand.

TGI reports the users of thousands of brands. As with heavy to light users of product categories, demographics and media usage are reported for brand users. By using TGI, you know who your users are and what they read, watch and listen to. You also have the same information for your competitors.

For the appliance and durables category, TGI provides a further measurement – whether the respondent had a major or equal say in the purchase.

The TGI measures the following product and media habits of the population:

Products Heavy-to-light usage for over 2,500 brands in more than 200 fast-moving consumer product fields. Additionally, usage of over 150 other 'brands' is covered in the fields of banking, building societies, airlines, holidays, cars, grocery and other retail outlets, etc. Brands with more than a million claimed users are broken down demographically and by media.

Media Audiences of 220 newspapers and magazines, weight of ITV viewing and half-hourly viewing behaviour for television, weight of listening to commercial radio and exposure to outdoor media and the cinema. The TGI is designed to be complementary to NRS, the industry's readership survey. The levels of readership are, wherever possible, weighted to equal the NRS readership figures for the corresponding period of field work. Depending upon the relative importance of men or women in the readership, TGI readership levels may be weighted so as to reconcile with the NRS for men only, for women only, or for both.

Fusion of the main TGI information with BARB data is also available. This enables media owners and agencies to directly link BARB's TV programme-viewing data with TGI's product and brand usage data.

Characteristics The full range of standard demographics including social grades, household income, together with special breakdowns such as terminal education age, working status, home ownership, length of tenure in homes, size of household and marital status.

TGI was the first major survey to offer analysis by ACORN (A Classification of Residential Neighbourhoods) described in Chapter 6. It has kept pace with developments and now offers also *Super Profiles*, *Mosaic* and *PiN*, described in Chapter 12.

Lifestyle as well as factual data is available, as respondents also provide scaled responses to 200 attitude statements related to their lifestyle, plus a measure of interest in more than 80 TV programmes. These can be cross-related with any part of the database.

The TGI reports

There are 34 separate TGI volumes summarising a vast amount of data. In outline, these cover:

Volumes	1–2	Demographics
	3–10	Food (virtually all packaged lines)
	11–14	Household goods
	15–16	Pharmaceuticals and chemist products
	17–20	Toiletries and cosmetics
	21–23	Drink (alcoholic and soft drinks)
	24–25	Confectionery
	26	Tobacco
	27	Motoring (cars and accessories)
	28–29	Clothing and shopping
	30	Leisure
	31	Holidays and travel
	32	Financial services
	33–34	Consumer durables and appliances

AB Target Group Index

The AB TGI seeks to give a higher degree of detail than the main TGI within those areas of product purchasing and lifestyle especially relevant to heads of household/housewives in the high (AB) socio-demographic status households. It also provides this information based on significantly larger sample sizes than are found in the main survey.

The survey is based on a sample of 5,500 AB adults, entirely separate from those interviewed in the main TGI. Respondents are initially interviewed by telephone in order to collect classification data, and then sent a self-completion questionnaire.

There are eight volumes, devoted to demographics; holidays and travel; sports and leisure; clothing; personal possessions, cosmetics & gifts; house, home and car; drink; and finance.

Accessing the TGI or AB TGI

While media-owners featured in the TGI or AB TGI buy the entire sets of 34 or 8 volumes, it is possible for advertisers and advertising agencies to buy individual volumes or even separate product fields.

TGI is a 'single source' measurement and all elements of the survey can be cross-referenced, eg media exposure relating to product usage.

Choices

BMRB has its own analysis system, called *CHOICES*, for conducting any special analyses on behalf of the main TGI and AB TGI subscribers. This *CHOICES* desk-top system is also available to subscribers, so that they are able to carry out their own analyses direct, without having to access a third party. Alternatively, should you require direct contact with a computer bureau, there are various companies which offer post-survey analysis on the TGI. Understandably, access to the tapes is only permitted to those who have purchased the relevant TGI volumes.

TRAC (TUBE RESEARCH AUDIENCE CLASSIFICATION)
(London Transport Advertising, 10 Jamestown Road, Camden, London, NW1 7BY)

London Transport Advertising has commissioned an independent survey into the travel patterns of Underground users, in order to establish a database for measuring the audience coverage and frequency of advertising campaigns on the medium.

Nearly five thousand respondents, recruited at Underground stations throughout the system, supplied details of all the journeys they made during a period of four consecutive weeks. By breaking down the resultant journey patterns into their component 'locations' i.e. ticket hall, corridor, escalator and platform locations, London Transport Advertising were able to calculate exposure to campaigns of different sizes and site types.

A synopsis of the research methodology and results was published as *TRAC: The Campaign Planner* and gives audience profiles and coverage of all adults, businessmen, 15–24 year olds, AB adults, and men and women.

London Transport Advertising's TRAC also offers a Campaign Planning facility, advising advertisers on how to buy an Underground campaign which delivers the optimum coverage and frequency.

VFD (VERIFIED FREE DISTRIBUTION LTD)
(Black Prince Yard, 207–209 High Street, Berkhamstead, Herts HP4 1AD)

Verified Free Distribution (VFD) is a wholly owned subsidiary of the Audit Bureau of Circulations (see separate entry) and is the independent certifying authority for all publications whose distribution is not through regular newstrade channels or by single addressed copies mailed through the Post Office.

The VFD operation

1 On application each publication's records and distribution system are subjected to a close inspection by a VFD Inspector to determine elegibility to join the system. This check confirms good record-keeping and distribution control, including agreed standards of backchecking on delivered copies on a regular and systematic basis. Further VFD inspections are carried out as a regular routine. (If the publication cannot meet VFD standards, the application is suspended until the publisher's system has been revised and checked again.)
2 Issue-by-issue records for standard six-month periods are kept by the publisher on VFD forms, and these are then audited by an approved independent firm of chartered accountants.
3 If the results are approved, VFD Certificates of Average Net Distribution are issued for each standard period, January to June and July to December. Also stated are the average number of pages achieved, and the percentage of advertising content. This information, in addition to a description of the distribution area, form the basis of the VFD Certificate for each registered title or group of publications.

4   All publishers are required to maintain lists of households checked for regular delivery, and these records are subject to random tests by a research company arranged by VFD.

The Scope of VFD

Verified Free Distribution operates in three divisions:

1   Free local newspaper-format publications and free magazines (delivered as single copies).
2   Free directories (delivered).
3   Courtesy magazines (not delivered as single copies but available for pick-up at hotels, airlines, clubs, etc.). This service is known as Bulk Verification service and has a different certificate from 1 and 2 above.

Optional services

1 Three Star. VFD operates an optional additional certification service based on a national standard of interviews with recipients of free delivered publications in designated areas, either by telephone or face-to-face interviews, which confirms the level of regular receipt of the particular free publication. Publications taking out this service successfully are granted three stars within the VFD logo as a mark of confirmation.

2 Leaflet Distribution. VFD operates an optional additional service to provide certification of systems employed by publishers in membership of VFD to control the distribution of leaflets either within their publications or solus.

OTHER SOURCES

There are other useful sources of media information, in addition to those already mentioned. Some are covered later in Chapter 5, which is devoted to the specialist services available, and necessarily overlaps with this chapter since various of the organisations just described make available services additional to the basic ones mentioned. Other data sources belong more rightly in this chapter.

Media-owners' research information

As a means of making valuable information available to potential advertisers and also to assist current advertisers in producing more effective media schedules, many media-owners subscribe to various research and other services.

Some media-owners also commission their own research. It is rare for a media-owner to undertake research to disprove the information provided centrally, although such action might be taken if he considered the findings presented an unfair picture of his medium. More usually, media-owners seek to provide additional information which might persuade advertisers and agencies to view their medium favourably.

Media-owners' own surveys can provide much useful information and often venture into fields untouched by central research. As examples, media-owners have undertaken research into the effect of advertisement size in relation to page size, into the effect of advertising on retailers, and into page traffic and the 'life' of advertisements in publications which are kept for reference rather than read and thrown away.

Media-owners who are not, for some reason or other, included in the central reports may commission research to provide comparable information to permit their medium being assessed on the same basis. Where no central research exists, media-owners may have no choice but to provide details of their medium's coverage and to undertake research to obtain this information.

Media-owners' information activities are many and varied, and this aspect of the media-owner's work is discussed again in the later chapter devoted to 'The Media-Owner'.

An interesting development in recent years has been the increasing provision of co-operative research and activities. Rather than compete with each other for larger slices of the same size advertising cake, rival media-owners have joined forces to promote the advantages of their combined media group over others to increase their share of total advertising expenditure. Most such co-operative campaigns have been reviewed within this chapter and, viewed as a whole, these combined activities have made valuable contributions to the provision of media research data.

A major difference between central research and media-owner's own information is that whereas the former is provided on a regular basis, media-owners undertake research activities often on a more *ad hoc* basis, from time to time whenever they wish to prove a point about their medium. Another difference is that, somewhat understandably, advertisers and agencies are likely to suspect it of being biased in favour of the medium sponsoring it. In this respect it is worth noting that the Media Appraisal Committee of the Institute of Practitioners in Advertising provides a service for member agencies in appraising such published surveys and sends out its report in the form of an appraisals bulletin. The IPA has published a booklet 'Producing useful

Media Research' by Guy Consterdine, and also welcomes advance consultation in regard to any surveys proposed by media-owners.

Some media-owners undertake a great deal and do so frequently, whereas others provide very little information. This makes it difficult to include within this book any formal list of the additional research information available from this source. Nevertheless, any executive concerned with the effective use of media should be aware that some extremely valuable research has been undertaken and should certainly check out this source of information.

Agency- and client-sponsored research

This field of research is comparable in many ways with media-sponsored research, in that it is aimed at providing additional information. It may suffer from the same drawbacks: failure to cover all the media in the group, or being carried out at irregular intervals. A further disadvantage (other than to those directly concerned) is that the information may not be freely available, which is understandable since the advertiser or agency incurred considerable research expense to gain a competitive advantage. Such research is, in fact, a business investment and is rightly regarded as confidential information.

Other information sources

In addition to the wealth of useful information contained in reference publications, it would be wrong to leave this section without mentioning that some media-owners and trade and professional bodies have their own publications which they use to communicate items of interest and that, in addition to these special interest publications, articles of specific interest appear from time to time in a host of other publications, both newspapers and magazines.

In conclusion, it is worth mentioning that some of the organisations mentioned are not just sources of media information, but powerful influences on the way media will develop in the future.

Chapter 5

Further Information and Additional Information Sources

FURTHER INFORMATION

Although the published reports just discussed contain many tabulations, the amount of data stored on tapes is very much larger, and there are often facilities for obtaining further information (at a fee appropriate to the cost of providing the additional tabulations required). These can be provided by the organisations which commissioned the original research, by obtaining on-line access, by purchasing your own copies of the tapes, or by specialist data-processing firms having authorised access to the research data.

ADDITIONAL INFORMATION SOURCES

A number of readership surveys were not included in the previous chapter because they relate to specialist areas. Some extend their coverage beyond readership figures, to include what are called 'U & A' studies covering *Usage* (read regularly, read half or more etc) and *Attitudes* (best source of new ideas, usefulness of advertising etc) as well as other media (direct mail, exhibitions, seminars, television etc). Specialist surveys include the following:

- Agridata Readership and Media
- Architects
- Asian Businessman Readership
- Building Centre Readership
- Businessman Readership
- Captains of Industry
- Computer Readership

- Computer Industry
- Construction Industry Readership
- Design Engineering
- Electronics Readership
- Electronic Times
- Engineering Industries Readership
- Eurofood Readership
- European Businessman Readership
- European Institutional Investors Research
- Farmedia
- Hospital Media
- International Financial Managers
- Investment Intermediaries Readership
- Managing Directors Readership
- Medical Advertising Readership
- Pan European
- Transport Week
- Travel Agents Readership
- Travelmeter.

All these specialist surveys are discussed in my other publication *Business-to-Business Marketing and Promotion* (Century Business, 1989).

Specialist surveys are not restricted to press media, nor to business-to-business markets. The Exhibition Marketing Group, for example, commissioned research into Exhibition Effectiveness, covering both visitors and exhibitors. There are also specialist consumer surveys covering, for example, the baby market (that is, among mothers with babies 0–2 years old).

A problem that arises with some specialist surveys is that, unlike the general surveys mentioned in the previous chapter, the research is not always undertaken on a regular basis. Some are in fact 'one off' exercises, mounted and published, but never repeated.

There is, of course, no sharp dividing line between general and specialist surveys – some of the general databases discussed in the previous chapter also provide 'specialist' information, while advertisers seeking to reach general markets such as 'business executives' would find a wealth of information in the specialist surveys listed above.

Furthermore, the list is not exhaustive, in that there is a steady flow of new media information as new research material becomes available.

Chapter 6

Media Evaluation – Criteria for Comparison

To use media to full advantage, it is clearly essential to evaluate them to select those most suitable, and many criteria exist by which you can compare one medium with another. There are various factors you must take into account when making decisions. Part 3 will review criteria for evaluating complete advertising schedules, but this chapter looks first at how you can compare individual media.

A first step in establishing criteria for media comparison is to differentiate between *quantitative* and *qualitative* aspects. Quantitative data refer to the *numbers* of copies sold or read or viewers reached, while when reviewing qualitative criteria media planners must express *opinions* as to the value of, for example, sound or movement or high quality colour reproduction. The difference between quantitative and qualitative criteria is essentially a simple one: particularly interesting, however, are the recent attempts to quantify qualitative aspects through the 'U&A' studies already mentioned, which measure Usage (number of pick-ups, proportion read, etc) and Attitudes (most/least useful source of new information, helpfulness of advertisements, etc). These quantitative and quantitative factors can vary in priority according to each advertiser's marketing objective and so, in reviewing them below, they are not necessarily in your order of importance.

QUANTITATIVE CRITERIA

These include:

Who will your advertising message reach?

One major consideration is the market covered by the medium in question. Market investigations have a high priority in the work of advertiser and agency alike, both of whom will make a straight cross-check between the market covered by the medium and the market they wish to reach. Clearly the closer the approximation, the more effective the medium.

The term used here is *demographics*, commonly defined as a means of analysing an audience by sex, age and social status or other classifications. Information about age is usually given in fairly broad groupings, e.g. 15–24, 25–34 and so on. The social grades commonly used are those pioneered in the National Readership Surveys and are normally based on the occupation of the head of the household. There are six such grades:

Social grade	Social status	Head of Household's occupation
A	Upper middle class	Higher managerial, administrative or professional
B	Middle class	Intermediate managerial, administrative or professional
C1	Lower middle class	Supervisory or clerical and junior managerial, administrative or professional
C2	Skilled working class	Skilled manual workers
D	Working class	Semi and unskilled manual workers
E	Those at lowest levels of subsistence	State pensioners or widows (no other earner), casual or lowest grade workers

Many of the data sources described in Chapter 4 include a wide range of other demographic classifications (such as terminal education age, or ownership of consumer durables) but in some cases, e.g. with industrial or technical products, your interest may be in the job description of the people your advertising message will reach, the industry in which they are employed, or their special interests, rather than their personal attributes. In other instances, your interest may be in product-related data. Are they heavy or light users of your product? Or in their attitudes. Are they conservative in their buying habits, or are they likely to respond favourably to new products? Are they in need of your product and *ready* to buy? Whatever the categories, the fundamental question is a basic one. Who do you wish to reach, and to whom will the medium in question deliver your advertising message?

Where?

This cross-checking procedure applies equally to geographical location, since this aspect of the media audience is just as important as its composition. This information may be available in terms of the Registrar-General's Standard Regions, or perhaps by television area. Marketing areas vary, and there must be strong correlation between your own marketing area and the area to which the medium would deliver your advertising message. For local advertisers the two areas should coincide as closely as possible. Even so-called 'national' media vary in intensity of coverage across the country and you should clearly take account of these variations.

Another way of asking the 'Where?' question overlaps with 'Who?' when we look at the residential areas in which individuals live and, to use more precise terminology, classify your markets *geodemographically*. ACORN (CACI's A Classification of Residential Neighbourhoods) has been introduced to some of the important surveys, e.g. NRS and TGI, discussed earlier. This classification into some 39 neighbourhood types, e.g. inner city terraced, retirement areas, affluent areas, can add a more meaningful dimension for marketing analysis and planning than the conventional socio-economic classification alone, since it provides a discriminator between life-styles, different patterns of expenditure and different levels of exposure to advertising media. To the marketing and advertising executive its importance lies in its ability to show clear life-style differences between neighbourhoods leading to many differences in consumer behaviour. Being area-based, ACORN leads to a more scientific answer to the marketing question '*Where* should I . . .?'

Other ways of classifying media coverage geodemographically are described in Chapter 12.

How many?

In evaluating media you need to know not only the composition and location of the media audience covered but also its size, together with the number of individuals in each of the various categories. How many of each type and in each area? Breakdowns may be required for several categories simultaneously, to show how many people of a given sex, age and socio-economic group receive your advertising message within a defined area.

There may be different stages of answer to this 'how many?' question. With press media, for example, you may have at your disposal circulation figures and also readership – but much depends on definitions and research methods. To illustrate this point, contrast the differences in the data available about television audiences and press readership.

For television advertising, measurements can be made at the time of viewing, and numbers may be quoted to you in terms of TVRs or Television Rating Points. A homes television rating is the percentage of ITV homes tuned to a particular transmission, and can refer to commercial breaks or to programmes. The term can apply to any time period, such as one minute or an individual commercial, or to average coverage of a commercial break, or quarter-hour, or rate-card segment or even a complete programme. TVRs may also be expressed in terms of individuals viewing rather than homes with sets switched on, so that one TVR represents one per cent of the potential TV audience. A viewer is defined as someone who is present in the room with a set switched on. Viewing starts from the moment the person records their presence, provided that the viewing to a channel persists for a minimum of 15 seconds. Viewing figures are processed and reported on a minute-by-minute basis. You should note that the term 'in the room' covers anything from attentive watching to a casual glance while undertaking some other activity. The Newspaper Publishers Association, in its advertising campaign promoting the merits of national newspapers, cited research which showed that 'viewers' might in fact be engaged in a range of other activities – or not even in the same room as the switched-on TV!

With press media, by way of contrast, advertising contact can be made over a considerable period, and the definition of a 'reader' is equally important. With the National Readership Surveys, a key concept is the *issue period*. Average Issue Readership (AIR) is the number of people who claim to have read or looked at one or more copies of a given publication for at least two minutes during a period dating back from the date of interviewing equal to the interval at which the publication appears – a daily newspaper is thus held to have an issue period of one day, a weekly publication has an issue period of seven days, a monthly publication between 28 and 31 days and so on.

You should note that the term 'reading or looking' covers anything from thorough reading to a casual flip through, and that it does not matter *which* issue – any issue will do. Readership may also be affected by other problems of definition:

(a) *Parallel readership* This refers to people who read more than one issue within the issue period prior to interview. No matter how many back issues had been read, it would still be counted as reading one issue, and average issue readership would thus tend to be deflated.

(b) *Replication* This refers to cases where the respondent reads the same issue of a publication (perhaps a 'special' which may have been kept for reference) across two or more publication periods. This would inflate average issue readership, since it does not truly represent additional readers.

(c) Page exposure The counter-argument to replication is that some publications will be 'read or looked at' more frequently than others, thus increasing the numbers likely to receive your advertising message. Hence the increasing importance of the 'U&A' studies.

You should also bear in mind that any figures are necessarily dated in themselves: readership surveys, for example, are sometimes 6–12 months old before new data is published. This, ironically, benefits media in decline (unless you arbitrarily reduce readership pro-rata according to the latest available circulation figures which, for national newspapers, are published with greater frequency). When considering the number of people your advertising message will reach, you should therefore always remember that whilst numbers are important, the research methods which produce them are by no means perfect. This statement is not made with a fault-finding attitude, but simply to set matters in context. Furthermore, it is always comforting to reflect that in many countries of the world even authentic circulation figures are not available, let alone readership (or viewing or listening) figures. Under such circumstances, we must be grateful for the wealth of data at our disposal, and not cavil at any minor imperfections. Furthermore, we should remember that with television and press the research needed to provide such information is well established but, as earlier chapters made clear, with a number of other media you will not have all the data you need.

Penetration versus profile

In discussing the number of people your advertising message reaches, you need to know the degree of penetration or coverage represented by the number reached. In simplest terms, penetration means the *proportion* of the total market covered. If you seek to reach housewives, for example, it will interest you to know that by using a certain medium you can reach 20 per cent, 50 per cent, or some other proportion of *all* housewives.

Later, when considering advertising planning, we will consider the cumulative coverage or 'reach' achieved by a full media schedule, but within this chapter the term 'penetration' is restricted to the proportion of the total market to which any given medium will deliver your advertising message.

A medium's 'profile' typifies the categories of people reached. Profiles differ from penetration in always adding up to 100 per cent. A simple example which illustrates the difference between the two terms is that of women's magazines. A women's magazine read by half the women in the country has a 50 per cent penetration. If you look at the magazine's profile, however, this will be 100 per cent women. (In point of fact, the profile might well be 95 per cent women and five per cent men, since even women's magazines have some male readers). This is of course an over-simplification since profile information may be broken down in numerous different age-group, socio-economic, area or product usage categories but, whichever sub-groups are detailed, the total profile always adds up to 100 per cent.

A 'trick' question which illustrates the difference between penetration and profile is 'Which newspaper will give you the highest coverage of AB business executives – *The Sun*, or *The Financial Times?*'

The answer is not in fact *The Financial Times*. While *The Sun*'s profile includes only a relatively small percentage of AB business-people, a small proportion of a very large readership gives a larger number than a high percentage of a relatively small readership. Those wishing to reach AB businesspeople might not consider *The Sun* the ideal medium, however, for various reasons. One might be wastage, discussed next, while others concern qualitative considerations discussed later.

Wastage

It is unlikely that any advertising medium will give you perfect coverage of your market. Some potential purchasers will not be covered and so you will not achieve 100 per cent penetration. Equally, some of the people you *do* reach will not be in the market for your product. Since you nevertheless have to pay a charge based on the medium's total circulation, readership or viewership, you will clearly want to assess what proportion of its audience is likely to constitute less valuable coverage. Such considerations will clearly influence your choice of media, but should not lead you to undervalue that part of the total coverage which *is* of your target group. If coverage of the people you want to reach is properly evaluated, then coverage of others can be considered as a bonus rather than 'wastage'.

There is one further quantitative criterion: Cost. This will be discussed later, since media planners must consider whether or not the qualitative criteria which follow are worth the money.

QUALITATIVE CRITERIA

These include:

The medium

A factor of prime importance in media selection is the means by which your advertising message is delivered. What form does it take – do people read it, watch it or listen to it? Television gives you the benefit of movement to demonstrate your product in use, together with sound in the form of music, and the human voice to speak the advertising message. Cinema advertisements, too, have movement and sound. Both can have the advantage of colour. Posters have colour and size but not movement. Many newspaper advertisements are printed in black and white. In magazines, colour is more frequently available, to attract attention and show your products in their natural colours as they appear on retailers' shelves. Colour availability is not enough in itself, however, for quality can vary considerably, and this will influence selection within the range of colour media.

When selecting media, you should therefore make more than a superficial study of the actual means by which your advertising message will be delivered to your target audience. Changes in technology are not restricted to press, and have equally important implications for other media.

Mood/Environment

Your prospective customer's state of mind when receiving your advertising message can directly enhance or weaken your campaign effectiveness, so this consideration should be well to the fore when you contrast the media available to you. In this respect you should distinguish between media where advertising is an intrusive element and others where it is acceptable or, better still, has positive interest value. By advertising in women's publications, for example, your advertising message will reach women – the 'Who?' question tells you this – but you know that it will reach women when they are in a receptive state of mind. They will be relaxed and seeking information about homes, beauty, fashion or food, and thus receptive to advertising messages about merchandise in these product fields. Special interest publications similarly offer you the double benefit of reaching a selected group of likely purchasers and of delivering your message when they are in a receptive mood, and the same is true of many exhibitions. This principle can be extended to specific positions within a medium: an advertisement on the gardening page of a newspaper selects gardeners out of the total readership and delivers the advertising message when they are mentally 'tuned in' to the subject of gardening.

In that editorial reflects readers' interests, any advertiser is advised to check previous issues to see how frequently there has been editorial relating to his particular product area, since this should give a further indication of whether readers are likely to be in the market for his product.

A medium's editorial content may influence mood in another way by lending an atmosphere of authority or expert knowledge of a subject, with consequent benefit to the advertiser and his product.

In preparing advertising campaigns, many people make the mistake of concentrating on their own activities, rather than thinking in the terms of their potential buyers. An extension of the mood question can place the emphasis where it should be – on the consumer. Rather than asking 'What will my advertisement do to people?' you should ask 'What will people do to my advertisement?' The answer to this question depends not only on the creativity of your advertising campaign (which is of course beyond the immediate scope of this book) but, equally, on the state of mind they are in when they receive your advertising message. This question thus links back with the 'Who?' question – if a medium reaches people ready to buy your product, and delivers your advertising message when they are likely to respond favourably to it, the medium is likely to be highly effective. Usage and Attitude studies, when available, clearly provide highly relevant information about your target market's mood when receiving your advertising message.

The extreme example of mood/environment is advertising in certain directories or works of reference, the very nature of which indicates that those people consulting them are not only potential customers but are in the market *now* and thus ready and eager to buy – why else should they be consulting the directory?

When?

Timing your advertising message is a vital consideration. For some advertisers this is a question of seasons: promoting summer goods in the summer and winter goods in the winter. Others may need to be more precise, and deliver their advertising messages on a given day of the week. Some media, such as point-of-sale displays, deliver your message seconds before the purchase is made. Again, this is a straight cross-checking procedure – when is the most effective time for your advertising message to be received, and when will the various media deliver it?

Frequency

A second aspect of timing concerns repetition: the regularity with which your advertising message can be delivered. Some media permit you to stimulate your market only once a month, while others enable you to give weekly or even daily reminders. Consumer buying habits – day and frequency of repeat purchases – thus directly influence your use of media.

Speed

A third aspect of timing relates to speed of operation rather than when and how often your advertising message is delivered, since some media must receive advertising material far in advance of publication date. Should you need to deliver an urgent sales message such as a price reduction, you would choose the medium with the shortest copy date in order to make your announcement as speedily as possible. Similarly, if your future plans are subject to constant change, you might be averse to using media with long copy dates (perhaps months in advance of actual delivery of your advertising message) since this means you have to decide your mesage on a long-term basis, whereas immediate short-term considerations are of major importance. You might equally be wary of using media that demand notice of cancellation long in advance of publication date, and thus do not permit flexibility in planning.

This is another area where, yet again, changes in technology are of vital importance: copy dates are being reduced, thereby making media attractive to new potential advertisers, and more flexible for those already appearing.

Flexibility

Speed is not the only factor affecting flexibility in media usage. Direct mail is perhaps the ultimate example – not only do you control timing and frequency but also *quantitative* aspects – you can turn the tap on or off as you wish to increase, decrease (or stop) stimulating your target group as market conditions dictate.

Span of attention

The attention that prospective purchasers pay to your advertising must be considered from two aspects: the duration of your message and the amount of time for which it will receive attention.

Some advertising messages have a very brief existence: a ten-second television or radio commercial, for example, clearly cannot receive attention for more than ten seconds and, once transmitted, the prospective purchaser cannot refer back to it (unless and until it is broadcast again). Newspaper and magazine advertisements exist for a longer period, and so can be studied at leisure.

Equally important is the amount of time prospective purchasers will devote to your advertisement. Posters exist 24 hours a day, seven days a week (even if they are not at work all that time) and thus have a longer life than most media. Nevertheless, your advertising message must usually be kept short, since most posters are only glanced at by people hurrying past. Posters on stations or in buses and trains, where there is a 'captive audience', may be studied for longer periods.

These two aspects of attention must be considered from the communications standpoint, for brief duration is neither good nor bad until related to a specific advertising task. Hence, you must consider how much information you need to convey. Is your message brief enough for a ten-second commercial or poster, or do you need to convey details about prices and sizes and so on?

A balance must be struck between the amount of time needed to convey your message and the duration of interest the message will receive. The decision you reach has direct media implications.

Life

Some media repay their use within a very few days, while others give you full value for money only over a much longer period. From the advertisers' point of view this means you may receive results in one short burst or spread over weeks, months, or even years. Since this affects the period for which the market for your product is stimulated, the life of any medium is an important consideration. A television or radio commercial, for example, delivers its full impact at the time of transmission, whereas a magazine printed on high quality paper may go on bringing results until it literally falls to pieces. Here you should distinguish between publications that are read once and thrown away, those that are passed to others (thus providing 'pass-on' or secondary readership), and those that are kept for reference.

This consideration affects not only evaluation of media, but also of campaign results – it would clearly be unwise to evaluate the results of any advertisement before the medium has had full time to deliver its message.

Indirect influence

Some media bring results through their effect on important groups other than the main media audience. Such influence frequently bears on retailers, who stock and display merchandise in the belief that advertisements in a given medium will stimulate consumer demand from which they can profit. Manufacturers place tremendous importance on obtaining good distribution and display, and any medium that helps in achieving this has a marked advantage over others. The example most frequently quoted is television, which exerts a strong influence on retailers as well as the main media audience. Co-operative press campaigns, where your stockists' names and addresses are featured in advertisements, can be equally effective in influencing retailers. Where this is the case, you should clearly take account of it in reaching media decisions.

Availability

This heading in fact covers three criteria for media selection. One is fundamental and governed by the rules and regulations relating to certain media, which might categorise certain types of advertising as unacceptable. Products or services that are not acceptable for advertising on television, for example, include cigarettes and cigarette tobacco; and also gun clubs, soothsayers, private detectives, and breath-testing machines! Television as a medium is thus not available to such advertisers. Bear in mind, however, that such restrictions may vary over time, as circumstances change. The ITC changes its rules from time to time, and the same applies to other media.

A second availability criterion that links with the question of *how* the medium will deliver your advertising messages, relates to creative scope and thus could be asked under either heading – what colours are available (specials or publisher's choice only)? More directly under this heading of availability, however, what precise sizes and positions does the media-owner accept? Is it possible to have your printed material included, either as a bound-in inset or as a loose insert? It is beyond the scope of this book to list all the standard transport sizes and positions, for example, or to detail the various sizes and positions available in newspapers and magazines, and you would of course want to study these when making a more detailed review of those media of interest to you. In making this review, the fundamental question is a simple one. What advertisement 'units' – or choice of units – must you think in terms of when preparing your creative proposals? To give an extreme example, there would be little point in preparing a campaign based on diagonal half-pages, only to find this size totally unacceptable when you attempt to make your bookings.

Clearly your creative proposals must be put in hand in a practical manner, in a form acceptable to media-owners. The range of units is considerable and most media-owners are keen to co-operate, so this need be no creative straightjacket. And it is always worth asking the media-owner if odd shapes will be accepted.

Thirdly, under this general criterion of availability, you will most certainly need to know what advertising spaces or positions are actually available. Should all the best positions be already booked, or only a limited number of spaces available, you have little choice but to consider spending the balance in other media.

Constraints

Some media-owners impose house-rules about the types of advertising they will accept, and reject any offending advertisements. It is therefore clearly advisable to know if there are any limits on type size, for instance, or restrictions on white-on-black advertisements, since this would perhaps constrain creative content.

Reliability

How certain can you be that your advertising message will in fact be delivered? Any advertiser who has based his selling efforts on the belief that his market will be stimulated at a particular time will naturally be wary of any medium that omits his advertisement for some reason or other. Equally important, how reliable will the delivery *quality* be – in terms of, for example, colour? And, if your advertising message is not delivered to your satisfaction, what compensation can you expect?

Competitive activity

This overall heading covers various criteria for media selection. First, before booking with any medium it is advisable to check if rival manufacturers appear regularly, and in what sizes and positions and with what frequency.

Secondly, you should also consider the general weight of advertising, and in a publication carrying a vast amount of advertising you may think it necessary to book a larger advertisement or a special position, to ensure that your advertising message receives attention.

Thirdly, there is the matter of the company you will be keeping: the fact that a medium carries (or does *not* carry) well prepared advertisements for leading firms can, in itself, influence the mood of the media audience.

Facilities

The range of facilities offered by media is wide. However, they can all be grouped together under the general theme of what the media-owner will do in addition to delivering your advertising message.

Some magazines, for example, include reply-cards which readers use to obtain further information about the products advertised. One television contractor's rate-card, selected at random, featured telephone-answering and reply-handling facilities, supporting press advertisements, promotional 'trailers' to stimulate viewer action, a retail sales force available to help sell-in to stockists, a 'Merchandiser' circulated to grocers giving the trade advanced details of major advertising activity on TV, direct mail facilities for advertisers to promote their campaigns to distributors, sales conference assistance, research facilities and help with production of television commercials.

The provision of valuable research data by media has already been mentioned. This can extend to provision of computer runs and help with media scheduling. Less ambitious, but nonetheless vitally important, is the assistance given to inexperienced advertisers by media respresentatives in preparing and producing effective press or radio advertisements.

Some of these facilities may be provided free as part of the media-owner's normal service, whilst there may be an 'at cost' charge for others. Such facilities can be most useful and you should most certainly check them out and use them as necessary. You should, however, beware of 'letting the tail wag the dog'. Media-owners, quite understandably, want repeat orders: hence the range of additional facilities to help you achieve a successful campaign. The prime reason for using any advertising medium is, however, to deliver your message and, in evaluating media, the answers to the questions listed above are of greater importance than any secondary facilities that the media-owner might offer. Of even greater importance is the answer to the next question: cost.

QUALITATIVE AND QUANTITATIVE:

Cost

The factor deliberately left until last, though it is of course a prime consideration in media selection, is cost. Much depends on the size of your appropriation, for some media call for large expenditures and may thus be out of the question for advertisers with small budgets. Cost is basically a straightforward question but nevertheless presents considerable problems in terms of booking unit, size, position, amount of advertising booked and other considerations discussed below.

Booking unit

The complication here is that advertising is sold in different units, making straight comparisons impossible. Newspapers, for example, are usually sold by the 'single column centimetre': one centimetre in one column costs £X and space is sold in multiples of this. A 20 cm × 2 cols advertisement simply means 20 centimetres taken in two adjacent columns, or 40 cm, and the cost of this advertisement is thus 40 times the basic unit cost. Similarly, a 25 × 4 cols advertisement is charged at 100 times the unit cost. Media planners often make cost comparisons of charges for the same-size advertisement in two publications, but a straight comparison is not possible. Even when advertisements in two media are the same size, they may appear in publications of different page sizes. It is argued, for example, that a given-size advertisement in a tabloid newspaper is more effective than in a broadsheet, because it is more dominant in the smaller page than the larger and will thus attract higher readership.

Research can overcome this problem, but comparison of media on a straight cost basis is still difficult to achieve, especially when the basic unit differs. Magazines, for example, are usually sold not by the single column centimetre, but by the page or fractions of a page: half-page, quarter-page, eighth-page, etc., and posters sold by number of sheets, whereas cinema and television and radio advertising is sold by time – 10, 20, 30, 40, 50 or 60 seconds and so on.

The problem of contrasting media that sell advertising in different units is further complicated by the fact that cost varies with three factors: size, position and amount of advertising booked.

Size

There are three obvious advantages to large advertisements - more people see them, there is scope to include more information and better creative work, and the advertisements themselves usually have greater impact. The bigger your advertisement the higher the cost, but the complication arises that cost does not always vary 'pro rata' in *direct* proportion to size, when calculated on the unit rate. Some media offer large advertisements at a 'bargain' rate to encourage you to take such sizes: other media, where larger sizes are in heavy demand, may charge higher premium rates so that, for example, a 25 cm × 5 cols advertisement costs more than 125 times the single-column centimetre rate. This is a straightforward matter of supply and demand for the media-owner, but for the advertiser and his agency it makes more complex the already difficult problem of comparing competitive media.

Position

The cost of an advertisement also depends on its position. An advertisement on the front page is seen by more people than one inside the publication: similarly, a 'solus' advertisement may receive more attention than one that has to compete with other advertisements. A poster on a main road is seen by more people than one in a side street, and the same is true of a television commercial transmitted at peak viewing time rather than in the afternoon. Good position results in high coverage of the total potential audience and there is accordingly a higher charge, which advertisers try to evaluate in relation to what they are getting for their money.

If you do not book a special position, your order will be at a less expensive 'run of paper' (ROP) rate which permits the media-owner to place your advertisement anywhere within the issue.

Your advertisement's position affects not only the number but also the type of people who see it. An advertisement on the motoring page is more likely to be seen by motorists, and a similar argument applies to advertisements on sports pages, fashion pages, home hints pages and so on, which select likely customers for betting shops or football pools, fashion houses and food products. The editorial content of such pages also influences the mood of the media audience, who will be more receptive to the advertising message. With other media, position can equally well influence the type and mood of the media audience.

Size and position

Size and position may be fixed jointly by some media-owners, so that no choice is offered. The position on the front page of a newspaper, for example, may be guaranteed to be solus, but the publisher restricts it to a certain size and may, in effect, be offering a 20 cm × 2 cols front-page solus. Similarly, the publisher might offer a 25 cm × 2 cols, facing TV programme page. Both these advertisements would be charged at special rates, since they are important sizes and positions. With other media, the same reasoning may apply.

The effect of size and position

Size and composition of the media audience directly affect media selection, yet surprisingly there is, for some media, very little information available about the different audiences that will be reached by varying sizes and positions. The National Readership Surveys, for example, give only overall readership figures for publications. Common sense tells you that more people see large advertisements or a front-page solus, and that an advertisement on the women's page selects women out of the total readership, but this is by no means precise enough: you need to know exactly the size and composition of the audience you will achieve with a given advertisement on a certain page, rather than a general picture of the medium's average issue readership.

Similarly, with television, you do not know what difference it will make to your audience if you have a 20 or 30 second or some other length of commercial, but the television audience surveys do indicate, on the other hand, both the size and composition of the media audience you are likely to achieve if your commercial is transmitted in a particular time segment. Similar information could be made generally available for press media, but some practitioners have questioned the research techniques used to measure page traffic and the effect of advertisement size and, in addition, there are the usual problems of agreeing, organising, supervising and – above all – financing such research.

Amount of advertising booked

Cost varies not only with size and position but also with a third factor – the total amount of advertising booked. This is because most media-owners, in order to encourage repeat bookings, offer some form of discount to advertisers who support them regularly.

Series orders bring direct advantage to the media-owner, since it is most helpful to know what bookings are in hand for future issues. Furthermore, there is a considerable economy in time, salary and selling expenses if, say, 12 orders are achieved through a single call instead of the representative having to make 12 separate calls to achieve the same results.

Newspapers and magazines frequently offer a 'series' discount if the booking is for a minimum number of insertions. There is a similar 'volume' discount for television, and other media usually decrease their rates as the size of the total booking increases.

Special discounts

Cost varies with size, position and total booking, and most variations appear on published rate cards, but other types of discount may also be featured. A rate card selected at random included a 'first-time' discount to encourage new advertisers to use the medium, test market discounts, expenditure investment discounts, limited expenditure investment discounts, limited expenditure discounts, limited expenditure development discounts and cash-with-order rates. These and many other variations may be featured on standard rate cards, which clearly merit detailed study.

From time to time, however, media-owners often find it expedient to extend other special offers to boost sales in otherwise slack periods. These offers are many and varied but divide into two basic groups – a discount offer to sell the same amount of advertising at a reduced charge, or alternatively a bonus offer of more advertising at no additional cost. These offers may be made known by special mailings and sometimes, when the offer applies for an extended period, special rate cards may be issued.

Another type of discount relates to 'packages' of advertising: if you help media-owners overcome possible selling problems, they in turn help you by giving lower rates. Most media-owners, seeking to balance supply and demand, offer financial incentives to advertisers who are flexible in their requirements regarding both timing and/or geographic location. If, however, you want precise control of when your commercials are to appear, which precise sites feature your posters, or which specified cinemas show your commercial and in which weeks, you must book at the full price in the normal way.

Some or all of these offers may be linked with the other question raised above – how many? – in that the advertising offer is linked with a guaranteed minimum audience, as revealed by research. With television advertising, for example, you may encounter GHIs – Guaranteed Home Impressions – when the contractor guarantees to transmit a given number of impressions. This is defined as the gross number of homes receiving exposures. As these packages usually consist of more than one spot and many homes receive your commercial more than once, consequently the *net* coverage of homes is likely to be less. Similar guaranteed audience 'packages' are frequently available for other media, such as radio and cinema.

Many advertisers employ both methods – their media plan includes a carefully-targetted component to ensure a minimum number of advertising messages are delivered to the right people in the right place at the right time. This planned component is then backed up by the purchase of 'bargain packages' which offer good value for money when delivering additional messages.

Finally, media-owners may find themselves called upon to negotiate special arrangements at top level, particularly where big advertising expenditures are involved. Basically, this amounts to hard bargaining between the media-owner and the advertiser or his agency, both sides seeking to conclude arrangements to their own best advantage. The advertiser and agency seek lower rates or, what amounts to the same thing, premium positions without paying a higher rate. The media-owner, naturally enough, seeks the maximum amount of revenue he can secure. Before undertaking any bargaining, you should of course consider the media-owner's relative strength in the marketplace, since this will influence the flexibility of his attitude. Some media-owners see discounting as anathema: a signal that a publication is in trouble.

Cost and value for money

1 Cost per thousand Cost is frequently considered together with quantity, and one medium compared with another, by what is termed CPT or 'cost per thousand' – the cost of reaching each thousand of the target universe (homes, housewives, adults, etc). It is usually expressed in pence, and is used as a general yardstick of media cost and efficiency. Cost per thousand is calculated by dividing, for example, the single-column centimetre rate of a publication by its circulation. To illustrate this with simple hypothetical figures, a newspaper charging £1 per s.c.c. and with a circulation of 20,000 thus has a cost of £1.00/20 = 5p per thousand circulation. Another newspaper might charge £10 per s.c.c. and have 500,000 circulation and here the cost per thousand circulation is only 2p. The second paper costs more in outlay – £10 instead of £1 per s.c.c. – but the circulation is larger, and so in this respect you get more for your money.

The cost per thousand concept is frequently used in evaluating different media and is, therefore, one with which you must be thoroughly familiar. It is also perhaps the most misused: it can be treated as a precise measuring instrument but in many cases it is used much too loosely. To quote 'cost per thousand' is meaningless unless it is made clear just what is being measured. Before accepting any cost per thousand figure for one medium in comparison with its rivals, you should ask a very basic question – 'Cost of *what* per thousand *what?*' Costs per thousand are most frequently quoted per s.c.c. for newspapers (or per page for magazines) per thousand circulation, but very few advertisers are interested in total circulation, and few (if any) plan in terms of single-column centimetres. Their interest lies in the advertisement size required, and only that part of the total media audience likely to buy their product. For this reason, cost per thousand calculations are frequently extended to compare actual advertisement costs – the cost per thousand of a 20 cm × 2 cols insertion or of a solus position in one publication rather than another. Equally, it may be calculated not for circulation but for readership, or for readership of a particular category – cost per thousand housewife readers in the 16–24 age group and in a stated socio-economic category. Similarly, television cost per thousand is sometimes based on numbers of homes and the cost of a 30-second commercial: many advertisers, however, use commercials of a different length and calculate costs per thousand for specified target audience groups, rather than the number of sets switched on.

2 *Weighted values* Cost per thousand calculations are useful in comparing one medium with another as regards value for money in terms of the audience numbers you are likely to reach, but the approach is sometimes extended to allow for qualitative as well as statistical values, through including 'media weights' in your calculations. A media weight is necessarily subjective and reflects the importance you place on intangible factors. If you think colour or high-quality printing of particular importance to your advertising, or feel that the mood of the potential customer receiving your message through a magazine is of greater or lesser value in comparison with the same message received through a newspaper, you may wish to allow for this in your calculations since this would provide a more relevant measure of cost effectiveness than cost per thousand alone.

The concept to be used under such circumstances is called Valued Impressions per Pound, or VIPs:

$$\text{VIP} = (\text{Media audience} \times \text{Media weight})/\text{Cost}$$

The media weight is the value you place on intangible factors such as colour, expressed in numerical terms.

Quite apart from allowing for subjective views as well as statistical information, there is another important difference between VIPs and cost per thousand. One calculation is the inverse of the other, i.e. the *higher* the VIP index then the *more efficient* the medium, whereas with cost per thousand calculations you seek the lowest possible figure. The two different methods, nevertheless, have the same underlying aim – they are simply alternative methods you can use in assessing value for money.

Production costs

Another factor that indirectly affects media planning is production costs, as distinct from the charges levied by media-owners. With some media, production costs constitute only a small proportion of total costs, while in others they are important enough to demand major consideration. In some cases, such as direct mail or display material, production charges are of course inseparable from media costs. The importance of keeping up-to-date with changes in technology is again apparent.

OVERALL MEDIA COMPARISON

Bearing in mind the wide range of comparison criteria, it is clear that there can be no such thing as the *best* medium. All media have their respective advantages (and drawbacks) and your task is to assess the contribution they can make to achieving your advertising objective. This task, together with the problem of balancing conflicting demands for impact versus frequency versus coverage, is considered in Part 3.

Part 2
THE ORGANISATION OF MEDIA

Having considered the range of media, this Part turns attention to those organisations and individuals responsible for their use. You cannot separate media planning principles from the people applying them or the firms in which they work: the first chapter in this Part therefore covers the media-owners and subsequent chapters concentrate on the advertisers and their agencies. The fourth chapter in this Part describes the role of the media independents, and a fifth outlines some of the specialist services available.

Any media representative must fully understand how advertisers and their agencies operate if he hopes to gain an order, and it is equally essential for advertisers and agencies respectively to appreciate the working of the other two parties to the advertising contract, if they hope to use media to best advantage.

Any reader who wishes to skip the chapter describing that part of the industry in which he is employed – on the premise that he knows its contents from everyday working experience – is welcome to do so.

Chapter 7

Role of the Media-Owner

THE MEDIA-OWNER'S STRUCTURE

All media-owners differ in their precise organisational pattern, but it is nevertheless possible to describe a basic structure around which individual media-owners make those variations best suited to their particular operation. This chapter discusses the media-owner's various departments, the inter-relationship of their activities and how they can best work with advertiser and agency respectively for more effective advertising.

The financial circle

Before examining the component activities of any media-owner's various departments, it is important to realise their inter-relationship. If a medium is of a quality which attracts a large audience, it not only gets considerable cover revenue but can also sell space to advertisers wishing to reach that audience. High cover and advertisement revenue enable the media-owner to maintain, or even improve, the already high quality and to promote the medium's sales effectively. This will increase the audience even further, and so the financial circle is complete: in this case in a beneficial upward spiral.

Conversely a medium of poor quality will not attract many purchasers. Without a worthwhile audience, the media-owner will find it difficult to sell advertising space. Poor sales of space means poor advertisement revenue as well as poor cover revenue. The media-owner thus has insufficient funds to produce a medium which consumers wish to buy, and no funds to promote it to them. In this case, the financial link is a vicious circle, with a downward spiral.

There are of course other factors – such as the state of advertisers' markets and the relative efficiency of other media – but the financial circle should be borne firmly in mind when reading the following review of the media-owner's various departments and their relationship. The review is mainly in terms of press, since this is still the largest medium in terms of advertisement revenue. The principles apply to other media, however, where the financial circle is equally applicable.

The editorial department

With most media, advertising is not their reason for existence but only a means of helping them exist. Newspapers and magazines are read for their editorial content and television watched largely for news and entertainment, and it is editorial skill in interpreting and satisfying target audience taste that determines the size and type of media audience. This in turn influences the possibilities for using these media as effective means of advertising.

The editorial side is frequently sub-divided, with special sections appealing to particular groups within the overall media audience. Newspapers, for example, have special gardening or motoring features, or pages written expressly for women readers. On television and radio, there are similar specialist programmes. Some features appear regularly (whether daily, weekly or monthly) while others appear only on particular occasions. The latter category could include features giving special coverage to, for example, the Boat Show or the Royal Academy Summer Exhibition.

Editorial is not always the reason for the existence of an advertising medium, however. Outdoor advertising, for example, has no editorial content and justifies itself solely as a publicity medium. With some media, advertising also serves as 'editorial': the 'editorial' of an exhibition for example, is of course the advertisers' stands. It is worth bearing in mind that advertising serves the media audience just as much as the advertisers and media-owners. Exhibitions provide a clear example of this but the same point applies equally to press media. Fashion advertisements in women's magazines are – at least to the male eye – virtually indistinguishable from editorial pages.

The production department

The writings of the editorial staff together with relevant illustrations must be put into print, and readership depends not only on the editorial being of interest but also on it being well printed. Printing quality also affects advertising effectiveness and is one of the factors that advertisers and agencies should consider when selecting media. Those using media should therefore keep themselves up-to-date with changes in printing technology, since these directly influence the efficiency with which your advertising message will be delivered to your target market.

Similarly, television and radio programmes must be produced and transmitted. Poster sites must be constructed and the posters themselves pasted up. For some media, such as point-of-sale display material, production is of major importance and constitutes the main part of the advertising: the same applies to direct mail and to exhibitions. Technological changes are equally relevant to these media.

The circulation department

There is more to successful publishing than writing and printing alone, for printed copies are of little use until they are delivered to actual readers. This is the task of the circulation department and the sheer physical work is often under-estimated. The flow of printed copies coming from the press must be bundled and addressed, and special transport is frequently necessary: fleets of delivery vans, special trains, or even aircraft. A few minutes' delay in the delivery chain may lead to missing a vital connection, and thus to loss of sale of thousands of copies. A whole network of wholesalers and newsagents is involved and the media-owner must ensure that his publication is available in sufficient quantities and well displayed. In this respect, the work of the circulation representative is similar to that of most consumer goods salesmen. In addition to the routine circulation operation, complex enough as it is, the circulation department may often arrange special distribution facilities for extra sales at important events or exhibitions. Some media-owners, rather than undertake this complex work in-house, prefer to sub-contract the task to an external service organisation.

Changes in printing technology are having their effect here also. No longer is it necessary to print in one location, and for the circulation department to then physically transport heavy bulk supplies to other parts of the country. New printing technology means that material can be written and typeset in one location but actual printing take place at another (perhaps where there is spare printing capacity) thus speeding up the circulation process at the same time as cutting distribution costs.

With a number of publications, magazines particularly, a considerable proportion of copies are not distributed through newsagents, but posted direct to readers on a subscription basis. Free newspapers, on the other hand, omit the wholesaler/newsagent/subscription link, and the media-owners achieve circulation by direct delivery to the home. By contrast, with some media there is no 'circulation' in the sense of a separate physical activity. With direct mail, for example, circulation is really only an extension of production work and, with television and radio, building of audiences depends not only on production and transmission of the programmes but equally on their promotion. To this end, many media-owners develop promotion departments. Circulation, subscriptions and promotion departments may operate as separate units, or may be joined to form an overall publishing department.

The subscription department

Many publications rely to a great extent on subscriptions for their distribution. Subscription circulation is important not only as a source of revenue, but also because it implies regular readership, which is of prime importance to potential advertisers. Indeed, analysis of subscriptions, as a form of research, can provide valuable information about the type and location of readers. With magazines on controlled circulation, where copies are sent (free of charge) addressed by name to individuals in certain defined categories, this research aspect is dominant, and the subscription revenue foregone. Publishers of controlled-circulation journals count on the assurance they can give potential advertisers about circulation and thus readership to bring them an advertising revenue which more than compensates for the loss of subscription income, so that in this respect the readership aspect is all important. The same applies to specialist journals received by members of various professional bodies, as part of the service they receive in return for their membership subscription. The research is becoming increasingly sophisticated as the relevant databases become computerised.

The promotion department

With subscription copies of publications, or those sold through newsagents or booksellers, the promotion department plays a key role. Other media, which do not have the equivalent of circulation or subscription departments, rely equally on the promotion department. The size of audience that views a television programme, for example, or attends an exhibition, turns on the skill of the promotion department. This department may also sponsor special events such as sporting and arts events or exhibitions, as part of the medium's overall promotional programme. In recent years, some promotions have become increasingly lavish, with rival media-owners competing for readers by offering bingo cards or other forms of promotion with 'Free Houses', 'Free Holidays' or 'Pay Off Your Mortgage' prizes.

In considering the promotion department's activities, any media-owner should be considered a manufacturer in his own right, with merchandise to sell, who must plan his advertising with as much care as other producers. It is not unknown for a media-owner to have an advertising manager (responsible for promoting the medium) as well as an advertisement manager (responsible for advertising revenue).

The advertising manager may plan a number of distinct campaigns. There may be a promotional campaign aimed at the public, persuading them to buy a publication, to watch a television series or attend an exhibition. Just as manufacturers usually have a second campaign aimed at retailers or wholesalers, so the media-owner will mount promotional campaigns aimed at wholesale and retail newsagents, with the object of persuading them to stock up and display his publication. Media-owners differ from other producers in needing a third campaign to potential advertisers and their agencies, to bring in advertisement revenue. Most media-owners undertake a great amount of promotional activity, to back up the efforts of their media representatives. These campaigns include a whole range of material: direct mail shots, trade press advertisements and sales aids for media representatives to use in their presentations. The promotion department will also devote considerable attention to making known the work of ancillary services such as the research department.

The research department

Much research is undertaken centrally: the readership surveys and television audience reports described in Part 1, for example, provide information about reading and viewing habits which is readily available to all advertisers and agencies, and serves as an important tool in media evaluation. Given the existence of this central research information, you may wonder why a media-owner should run his own research department. Quite simply, the main purpose is to provide additional information not contained in the central research, which might persuade advertisers and agencies to view the medium more favourably.

In describing the data available, Part 1 pointed out that much valuable information was available from media-owners' own surveys, and such work is the province of the research department which may also subscribe to the various research services available: all this activity has the common aim of providing information that might be useful to you in your planning. This information might well be provided by the media-owner undertaking special computer runs of the central surveys, to present additional tabulations not available in the surveys' standard formats. Much of this information will equally be of assistance to the media representatives in their selling tasks, but there is however a major problem underlying such research activities by media-owners.

The surveys commissioned centrally and those sponsored by media-owners complement rather than duplicate each other. There may be areas of overlap and differences may arise through use of varying research methods, but these problems are of minor importance in comparison with the underlying question of whose responsibility it is to undertake and finance the research.

Advertisers and agencies can justifiably claim that the media-owner has a responsibility to provide information about the coverage of his medium. No difficulties arise when a medium is included in the central research, but where the media-owner starts to provide additional information a fundamental problem does occur.

An overall review of media-owners' research shows that much of it is at one of two levels. The first level of research provides information about the medium's coverage, to enable media planners to judge the medium's power to reach that market. But should the market not be worthwhile, no amount of research will persuade manufacturers to use the medium. Hence some media-owners tend to provide 'second stage' research information to show the value of a market – and thus persuade manufacturers to mount a campaign in that market, in which case the media-owner should get his share of the advertising expenditure, and can use his first-level research to ensure inclusion in the schedule. Some media-owners go even further, into what can be termed 'stage three' research, by checking the sales in their market of particular groups of products, to show manufacturers of these products the desirability of mounting a campaign in the area. In short, the media-owner researches the market he serves, rather than the medium itself.

Such research is really aimed at providing marketing information and this is where the controversy arises. Why should it fall to media-owners to provide costly marketing information which advertisers or their agencies should have collected themselves, if they are to mount successful marketing campaigns? And, again, to *whom* should the media-owner make the information available? The marketing information was collected to influence marketing policy, and it is only *after* this is decided that media planners make their contribution – selecting media to reach the market that is the target of the campaign. Yet many marketing surveys are sent to media planners, to whom they are not of immediate *media* interest. The same problem arises where media-owners promote their areas as ideal for test marketing. The decision to mount a test campaign is a marketing decision and not a media one, yet media planners are frequently bombarded with such information, just as they are mailed about merchandising services. Media-owners thus have the problem of distinguishing between the tasks of selling the market and that of selling the medium, since these call for selling activity directed to different individuals. This problem, however, is relatively easily resolved in comparison with the more controversial one of who is to finance the research, and the answer to this has yet to be agreed.

Returning to less controversial but perhaps more interesting matters, it is worth noting that some media-owners are moving into 'stage four' research – providing 'Usage and Attitude' or 'Advertisement Recall' information about the ability of their media to *communicate* and whether the same message received through Medium A is more effective than if received through Medium B.

'Stage five' research occurs when rival media-owners, rather than fight each other for an increased share of a static market, work alongside their immediate competitors to mount co-operative research about their media group and its advantages over other media. Part 1 described the many interesting developments in this type of research, undertaken for cinema and video, direct mail, business press, national newspapers and general magazines, posters, radio and the regional press.

The need for marketing information has resulted in some media-owners' research departments operating to an entirely different end, acting as an internal service organisation for the advertisement department. The research role here is to assemble facts and figures that advertisement representatives will find helpful in their contacts with advertisers and agencies. In addition, research staff may analyse current advertising to predict future trends. Where research is entirely devoted to securing additional business, the department may be known by another name, such as 'Sales Research', 'Marketing Services' or 'Business Development', and operate independently of the research department, which devotes itself to field research.

Marketing and merchandising departments

In many cases, a research department marketing survey is linked with an outline of the various merchandising services provided by the media-owner to assist advertisers in ensuring the success of their campaigns. The one 'Marketing and Merchandising' document thus includes details of activities such as trade mailings, conference facilities, reprints, display material and many other aids which, when criteria for media comparison were discussed in Part 1, were grouped under the general heading of 'Facilities'.

The advertisement department

The advertisement department has the vital task of obtaining maximum advertisement revenue. For some media such as television, radio or posters, where there is no income from sales or subscriptions, advertising is the sole source of revenue on which the medium depends for its existence. (There may, of course, be income from sale of editorial or programme material to other media-owners, or from sponsorship, but our concern here is with sale of advertising.) Even where a medium does not wholly rely on advertisement revenue, such as a publication sent to association members in return for their subscriptions, advertisement revenue is still of importance in that it permits publication of larger issues with better quality printing. Never forget, also, that the advertisements communicate information and are thus a service to readers.

The individual who controls sales of advertising within a medium is usually known as the advertisement manager or director (a very different individual from the advertising manager, whose responsibility is to buy advertising). Before starting to sell, the advertisement manager – and his representatives – must know exactly what is available to sell. For press media, the advertisement manager must negotiate with editorial and production staff, and agree precisely what advertising space he can sell. He must then decide the units into which the total advertising space can best be broken down, and obtain agreement on precise sizes and positions. The advertising rates at which these spaces and positions will be charged must also be decided.

This exercise, which must be performed for every issue of the medium, is not a one-way process with the advertisement manager asking what is available. The degree of advertising support achieved by the advertisement side directly influences the size of the issue and the number of pages of editorial that can be included. With other media, a similar process will apply. Television and radio representatives must know how many minutes of advertising time are available, in what units, and the precise positioning of the commercial breaks. Exhibitions organisers must know what stand space can be accommodated within the exhibition area, and the location and size of individual stands. Once advertising availability is known, the advertisement manager can set about achieving sales.

The advertisement manager as head of a department The advertisement manager is head of a department in just the same way as the editor, the production manager, the circulation manager, or a manufacturer's advertising manager. He must evaluate the amount of selling to be done, the number of calls to be made, their geographical location, and the level at which contact must be made, since some selling jobs call for representatives with special experience and skill.

Assessing the market and division of work A list of potential advertisers must be built up, and a careful analysis made of each. Once the list of potential advertisers and – if appropriate – their agencies is built up, the advertisement manager's next task is to divide it among his various representatives and provide each with a call list. There are various ways in which this can be done and the advertisement manager must decide the most suitable division for his medium. It may be a straightforward sharing of work, each representative having a list of advertisers and agencies on whom to call. Alternatively the division may be by type of advertising, some representatives being responsible for classified advertising, for example, and others for display. There may be further specialisation within each division, with one representative having special responsibility for, say, car or fashion advertising. Again, calls may be split by area, each representative being responsible for all advertising within his defined territory.

Where division is by area, this reflects the advertisement manager's responsibility for predicting levels of activity, for such division assumes that there is adequate potential within each area and sufficient work to support, say, a Northern representative. Should there not be sufficient work to justify full-time employment, the advertisement manager may arrange for his representatives to make field trips from time to time to various areas. A final point is that some media-owners find it preferable to contract out of advertisement selling altogether, and to appoint space-selling agencies to undertake the work. For certain mainly local media, representation by national sales houses accounts for a significant proportion of advertising revenue. Naturally, these methods of dividing the work are not mutually exclusive, but frequently overlap.

The advertisement manager must also bear in mind possible future expansion and increase his staff in good time to meet it. For even when the new man arrives he cannot be put to work immediately and, however experienced, will still need training to acquaint him fully with the new medium he is selling. The advertisement manager thus has a major responsibility in the selection and training of representatives, as well as their control. Some media-owners now pay more than lip-service to this matter and have appointed training officers, but the advertisement manager still remains directly concerned, as the type of training given will depend upon his view of future requirements.

Staff training This activity is an important and also a controversial one, since there has been considerable criticism of the calibre of representatives employed by certain media (some media-owners have been equally critical of client and agency staff!). It might be helpful to review briefly the knowledge required if a representative is to make a positive contribution to effective use of the medium. This knowledge reflects the tasks of the advertiser and agency described in Part 3 of this book, on the effective use of media:

1 *The product* The representative must be fully acquainted with the physical means by which the medium delivers your advertising message, advertisement sizes and positions and rates, copy dates, and all the mechanical production data regarding the advertisement material required.

2 *Editorial policy* Though the physical format remains the same, editorial content changes with each issue and may open up prospects of attracting advertisers previously not interested. Hence the representatives must be fully conversant with overall editorial policy, and with all future details: in this respect, training is a never-ending task.

3 *Media audience* Potential advertisers are directly concerned as to the audience they can reach through the medium. One of the first tasks of advertiser and agency is to define their market and, in evaluating media, they make a straight cross-check – with what certainty will the medium reach the defined target market? Accordingly, the representatives must have at their command readership or viewership figures, or other research information.

4 *Potential advertisers* Representatives must understand thoroughly the marketing and advertising problems of the advertisers and agencies on whom they are to call. What type of advertising do they undertake, in what sizes, with what frequency, and on what dates? What are their marketing objectives? When does their season start? Which groups constitute their market, and what coverage of these groups does the medium offer? Which agencies are employed, and how is the work shared with the advertising department? Who plans the media schedule, and when? Part 3 discusses these investigations in more detail but here it is sufficient to point out that if media representatives are to be of service to potential advertisers and their agencies – and thus obtain the orders they seek – they must have this knowledge at their fingertips.

5 *Competition* Since the media-representative is selling against rival media, a knowledge of the competition is important under each of the headings listed above. This applies to indirect as well as direct competition: specialist publications, for example, compete not only with rival journals but also with alternative media such as direct mail or exhibitions.

6 *Media selection and planning* Understanding the potential advertiser's objective, and the principles by which media are evaluated and schedules planned, the advertisement representatives can then

help ensure that their particular medium makes its maximum possible contribution to the success of the overall campaign.

7 *Creative skills and constraints* With some media, it is not sufficient for the representative to merely sell space. Where advertisers are inexperienced, it may be necessary to create and produce advertisements for them to use, for without this help it would be impossible for them to use the medium. This aspect of the advertisement department's work is discussed in more detail below, as are the legal and voluntary constraints affecting creative content.

8 *Selling techniques* Even when representatives have full knowledge of the physical format of their medium, its editorial policy, the market covered, the potential advertisers and the contribution which the medium could make to achieving their advertising objectives, there still remains the basic task of selling. While 'salesmanship' is important, it must be based on sound knowledge and reasoning, for all the sales talk in the world cannot compensate for lack of basic reasons for advertising in the medium. This is stressed because there are still a few media representatives who believe that string-pulling will bring orders.

A well-stocked wardrobe and superficial charm will not alone induce a media planner to include a medium in an advertising schedule. The same applies to lavish entertainment. Advertisers and media planners are busy people, with better use for their time than wasting it on unwanted hospitality, and are unlikely to accept invitations from media which do not merit serious consideration.

Supervision and control While the representatives are making calls, the advertisement manager must keep himself informed of their progress. Some media representatives, like their colleagues on the manufacturing side, are required to submit regular call reports, so that the advertisement manager knows what orders have been received or are pending, and can maintain up-to-date records.

The direction of selling The advertisement manager and his representatives must decide the best direction for selling. Should their sales effort be directed to the advertiser or advertising agency or both, and which individuals in these organisations should they contact? Here the detailed structure of the advertiser and agency, described in the following chapters, becomes significant.

The direction of selling is affected by client/agency relationships. Deciding which individual should be the target for sales effort may be a problem as sometimes more than one individual, or even a committee, is concerned. Advertisers employ agencies for their expert advice and experience, but this generalisation masks numerous possible variations. Division of the budget into 'above the line' expenditure handled by the agency and a 'below the line' budget handled by the client can vary from case to case, depending on each client's expertise and inclination, and the expertise of his agency. Even with 'above the line' expenditure by agency planners on the more conventional advertising media, client/agency relationships can vary, thus influencing the media-owner's selling activity.

Much depends on the relative dominance of the advertising department and agency. In some relationships the agency is the dominant partner, planning and executing the campaign, the client playing the more passive role of briefing the agency on the problem, and checking and approving the proposals. With a number of companies, however, particularly those with strong marketing orientation, the tendency is for the advertiser to adopt the more dominant role. Where a company's marketing manager is responsible for the full range of marketing activities (including advertising, selling, merchandising and sales promotion, research and even product policy and pricing) it follows that the client/agency relationship must differ from cases where the advertising manager is responsible for advertising alone.

Marketing-orientated companies are not necessarily dominant in every aspect of advertising and marketing: all depends on the relative strength and expertise of the individuals in both advertising department and agency. Furthermore, a change in staffing on either side could result in a shift in this pattern of dominance: another reason why it is so vital for media-owners to keep up-to-date with staff changes.

The background and experience of the individuals concerned influences the approach as well as the direction of media selling. When calling on an advertising manager, for example, much depends on his specialist expertise (or any weaknesses in his knowledge). By definition, an advertising manager should have an all-round knowledge of advertising matters, but clearly any individual must be more expert on some topics than others, and will therefore be more searching in his questions on his special advertising interest. An advertising manager who trained originally as a copywriter or visualiser is bound to have a different outlook from one whose background is research or media. One will be influenced by the creative possibilities of the medium, while the other will make a far more statistical assessment. Clearly the approach made by the media representative must vary accordingly, and for this reason a thorough personal knowledge of prospects is essential. The same is true when calling on an agency account executive.

On contacting a manufacturer's advertising manager, the media representative will frequently be referred to the agency. The key figure through whom the client makes contact with all the agency specialists is the account executive and so, naturally enough, his is the name mentioned when referring representatives to the agency. Many representatives make the understandable mistake of insisting on speaking only to the named executive, and virtually refusing to accede to his request to contact the agency's media department. This practice is likely to upset both parties: the executive wants the expert advice of his media department and not constant phonecalls from the media representative, however well-meaning he may be; and equally the media planners are unlikely to view favourably any media representative unwilling to speak to them initially, and then doing so only with an attitude of 'second best'. By all means media representatives should maintain contact with the account executive, but they should remember that he relies on the advice of his media department and directs their selling efforts accordingly.

When contacting the agency's media department, many representatives find themselves unable to decide *who* to speak to – group heads, media planners, media buyers, media assessors, media researchers or any of the other titles that abound in agencies. The various media department structures and the wide variety of organisation patterns described in Chapter 9 make it difficult to give general advice, but many media-owners have found it helpful to extend their central records to include information about advertisers and agencies. Thorough and continuous investigation into which people are influential in media decisions can build up a 'structure chart' for advertiser and/or agency. In this way, the record can show the names of the advertising manager, the account executive, media planners or buyers and so on. More important, 'weights' can be allocated to each (just as media planners often assess media) according to the relative influence each has on media decisions. Where different representatives from the same medium call on the same agency, media-owners often build up a structure chart for each agency in the same way, based on the combined view of all the representatives concerned. The structure chart can then be up-dated as necessary, to take account of staff changes.

Media/agency/client contacts

There are occasions when the representative may feel that his medium has not received the attention it merits in the client's media schedule, and he therefore seriously considers that his case could not have been adequately presented to the client, or was insufficiently considered by the agency. It is usually advisable for the representative to be open with his views, rather than go to the client 'behind the agency's back' or to try to play off client against agency (or account executive against media department). A clear statement of his case to the agency, with adequate reasoning as to why the schedule should be revised to include his medium, will have more effect than complaining to the client, quite apart from any ill-will that may be caused. Agencies do not often make mistakes, but they do occur from time to time, and an agency would naturally prefer to correct its own error, rather than have it pointed out by their client at a media-owner's prompting. If, after requesting the agency to review the position, the media-owner feels that his case has not received due consideration, the representative should most certainly go direct to the client, but should pay the agency media staff the courtesy of notifying them of his intention to do so. And the media representative should make sure he *has* got a case to present – many representatives are, understandably, over-enthusiastic and biased towards their own medium, perhaps in excess of its merits. Advertising managers do not like to have their time taken up reviewing situations that have already been considered by their agency. The media representative may see the advertising manager the first time but, unless he feels the visit was justified, the chances are that the media representative will not be so lucky on the next occasion. All being well, however, this selling activity will result in an order being placed, and attention should now be focused on the media-owner's next task.

Confirming the orders

Most media-owners keep some form of 'space register', or 'flat plan', showing the amount of advertising space available for sale in future issues. This shows the total amount and sub-divides it into run-of-paper and special positions (or their equivalent for other media). The register must be kept up-to-date so that the advertisement manager and his representatives can see at any moment what space has already been sold and what is still available. Leaving space unsold, through oversight rather than through lack of effort, means loss of potential advertising revenue.

Immediately an order is received it must be checked carefully for accuracy of vital facts such as size, position, cost, discounts, etc., and to ensure that the order has been duly signed and is correct in every way. This done, the order must be checked against the register to see if the space requested is in fact available. For run-of-paper insertions this is a straightforward operation, a simple check that total bookings do not exceed the amount of space available. For special positions, however, the operation is more complex since it means placing a named advertiser in a particular position in the medium. Such positions can be sold only once, and considerable ill-will would result if the same space were promised to two advertisers. It might even lead to future business from one advertiser going to another medium, perhaps less suitable, but where it was certain to appear as promised. Reliability was one of the criteria for comparison discussed in Part 1.

The space register is of vital importance even before an order is received, for its accuracy may determine whether or not the order is placed. With many media the space register is used by representatives who telephone in during discussions with advertiser and agency, and make immediate bookings based on the information given. Under such circumstances, information must be literally up-to-the-minute.

Space registers are maintained by publishers, and owners of other media have similar systems. Television and radio contractors, for example, have 'time registers' showing the booking position for commercial breaks between programmes. Poster contractors must know their site bookings, and be able to say which will become available and when. Even where the medium has a high production and service content, such as direct mail, and there is no top limit to the amount of advertising that can be sold, the direct mail houses must know when their various machines are fully occupied, and when they have capacity to accept further work.

Immediately the order has been checked against the register, an appropriate entry must be made and the order duly acknowledged, either by returning the tear-off slip which may be incorporated in the order, or by sending the media-owner's own acknowledgement form. Some media-owners have put the detailed record-keeping aspect of their work on to computers and, in this general area, most media have administrative and 'paperwork' systems just as thorough as those in advertising departments or agencies, which will be described later. Two actions then follow: the production staff must obtain the necessary material, and the advertisement department must consider where best to place each advertisement, and decide upon the most suitable 'make-up'.

Production and creative services

Advertising material must be obtained from the advertiser or his agency. Even when this is received well in advance of copy date, the prudent media-owner checks all material immediately it arrives: is it of the right size and type, and does the advertisement conform to the various voluntary codes and legal restrictions, and to any rules that the media-owner himself imposes? Advertisers and agencies have thorough administrative systems but the possibility of errors still exists, so material must be checked without delay. Should the material be at fault, prompt notification enables the client or his agency to rectify the mistake and supply correct material. It will be too late to check at the last minute, as there would then not be time for errors to be corrected. For other media, similar action is involved, according to the production process.

Even where the advertiser or his agency supplies a complete advertisement, its appearance in the medium still involves some production work. With press media, for example, the advertisement must be inserted in the appropriate place in the medium and correctly printed. For other media, similarly straightforward production work is involved.

Frequently, however, additional services are called for, particularly by smaller advertisers. Where a complete advertisement is not supplied, but only typed or even hand-written copy, the media-owner must undertake typesetting and is thus involved in more production work. Indeed, without this production work it would be impossible to accept the advertisement.

The service may extend to creative work and some media employ special staff to prepare creative suggestions for prospective advertisers, so that their representatives can submit copy and design proposals. Alternatively the representatives themselves may prepare these creative suggestions.

Creative and production services may equally be provided by other media. Many television and radio contractors offer facilities for special 'budget' commercials, quoting special low all-inclusive rates covering scripting, actors, studio and production. The same applies to the cinema, where stock films may be available which local advertisers can purchase at much less expense than they would incur in producing a film for themselves, and which they can personalise by including their own name and address. Direct mail houses similarly extend their services beyond production alone, and offer creative advice to those using their medium.

It is not only for inexperienced advertisers, who for lack of expert staff might be precluded from advertising, that media-owners provide these creative and production services. In other cases, media-owners have virtually been forced into such activity to safeguard their own interest. Some media-owners, for example, have encountered advertisers who do not take full advantage of the creative possibilities of the medium and, in extreme cases, produce advertisements that are actually *negative* in effect. Clearly the advertiser would receive little or no benefit from his campaign in such circumstances and would decide, wrongly, that there was no point in using the medium, since it had 'proved' itself ineffective. Incredible though it may seem, this was the case in the early days of television, when many advertisers withdrew from the medium for this very reason. Direct mail houses still find the same thing today. Some media-owners therefore extend their facilities, taking the more positive attitude of ensuring that their advertisers produce effective advertisements, and no longer take the more passive role of providing help only when asked. Action such as this is, of course, self-defence for the media-owner since if the advertisements do not bring results he will not get repeat orders.

Preparing the make-up

Where advertisers have booked special positions the problem of make-up does not arise, since the location of such advertisements is determined by the booking. Many advertisements, on the other hand, are booked on a 'run of paper' basis and it is left to the advertisement department to place these in the most suitable position. And to do so is in the advertisement department's own interest as well as being a service the advertiser expects, for a well-placed advertisement results in better response, and thus greater likelihood of a repeat order. Clearly an advertisement for a garden product is better placed on the gardening page and a car on the motoring page, than *vice versa*. Such obvious cases speak for themselves but, in practice, positioning is usually more difficult and the advertisement department finds it a problem to satisfy all the conflicting calls for right-hand page, top of column, outside edge, front half of publication, and similar requests. Once the detailed make-up is decided, however, the media-owner can then proceed to the next stage.

Final proofs

The production staff proceed simultaneously with two separate tasks – editorial and advertising. The advertisement department's make-up, placing advertisements next to the most favourable editorial, serves as production's guide in placing the advertisments in position. Further proofs are usually produced but not circulated to advertisers, since they are for internal use only. Their purpose is to ensure that all is in order and that no mistake has slipped through the previous careful checks. The advertisement department may, for example, have sold space in the belief that a 25 cm × 2 cols advertisement is to appear on a given page, while the editorial staff have designed on the assumption that space was needed only for a 20 cm × 2 cols advertisement. Or perhaps, through a production slip by advertiser and agency, an advertisement of the wrong column width was sent in error and, through an equally unfortunate error, this was not noticed on receipt. Again, page proofs may reveal that two advertisements containing coupons have been placed back to back: under such circumstances neither advertiser could get maximum results and the advertisement department would lose revenue by having to give both advertisers a rebate.

Page proofs may also bring to light unfortunate positioning which may have to be corrected: the advertisement department's make-up may have placed an advertisement for holidays abroad on a general news page, but if the news of the day happens to describe riots or some other unfortunate event in the country concerned, the travel agent would not be at all happy to see his advertisement next to news that must inevitably reduce response to his offer. Events or mistakes such as these are rare, but the possibility that they may occur nevertheless exists; hence the rule for the media-owner – just as much as for the advertiser and agency – is meticulous checking and double-checking to remove all possibility of error. If all goes well, no last-minute changes will be necessary and publication can proceed.

Publication

Copies must be printed and physically distributed to newsagents or subscribers. Television and radio programmes and commercials must be transmitted, and cinema films screened. Although the advertisement department is not directly concerned with this side of affairs, its activities still depend on the successful completion of this vital stage: the actual communication of advertisements to the media audience. Immediately the advertisements appear, the accounts department must be given all the information they need to invoice advertisers correctly.

Invoicing and voucher copies

The advertisers or their agencies must be invoiced before they will pay, and the invoicing task is to ensure that every advertiser is charged at the correct rate for each appearance of his advertisement. A smoothly operating accounts department avoids any loss of advertisement revenue through failure to invoice, and directly affects the speed of payment. Invoice queries by advertisers or agencies often cause ill-will or frayed tempers, and hold up payment. Delayed settlement can cost money in bank charges, and if settlement of many invoices is held up the consequent shortage of funds could place the media-owner in a difficult financial position.

Equally important is an efficient voucher service, for before the advertiser or agency will settle the invoice they will want to check that their advertising appeared as booked. The voucher may sometimes take the form of a 'tear sheet' rather than a full copy of the publications. With some media it may not be possible to provide a voucher copy or physical proof of appearance, in which case the media-owner may send a 'certificate of transmission (or of posting)' or some other assurance that the advertising has appeared. Failure to send the necessary voucher copy or certificate means that payment of the invoice is delayed until this omission is rectified. The smooth functioning of the voucher section is just as important as an efficient accounts department: the purpose of all this activity is receipt of advertisement revenue.

Follow-up

Once the advertisements have been invoiced, do not imagine that the operation is complete and the way now clear for further selling. Adequate follow-up of the issue just published is essential. The representatives who obtained each advertisement should check them with as much attention as the advertisers and their agencies will devote to them. Did the advertisements print well? What ratings did the television commercials receive? Did the exhibitor have an attractive stand? Evaluation of results, with a view to improving future performance, is of major importance to both advertiser and agency, and advertisement representatives, in selling future issues, must be equally concerned with the advertisement which has just appeared. This also provides them with the ideal opportunity to seek repeat orders.

The new issue

The financial circle mentioned at the start of this chapter has now been completed. All being well, this should be a beneficial upward spiral. Every new issue presents opportunities to follow-up previous advertising and affords scope for new sales, which means we are now considering the operation of the advertisement department from the same point at which we started.

Chapter 8

Role of the Advertiser

The actual tasks of the advertising manager which, overall, make for good advertising, are:

1 *Research and investigation* Gathering the company, product and market data essential for effective planning.
2 *Advertising strategy* Deciding your campaign objective, which directly effects both media selection and the creative approach to be featured.
3 *Budgeting* Fixing the advertising appropriation, so that you spend the right amount in achieving your chosen objective.
4 *Preparation of advertising proposals* Planning an advertising campaign, creating advertisements and selecting media, to achieve your determined objective.
5 *Approval of proposals* Checking, prior to executing the campaign, that your proposals are likely to be successful.
6 *Execution of these proposals* Putting your plan into effect.
7 *Follow through* Ensuring that the company is geared up to cope with the response generated by your advertising.
8 *Evaluation of results* Checking that you received value for money, and seeing what lessons can be learned for the future.

This process is a closed loop, and evaluation of the results of this year's campaign should provide additional information on which to base next year's planning. All these tasks will be examined in detail in Part 3. This chapter, however, reviews the role of the advertising manager and how he can best tackle them.

ADVERTISING IN PERSPECTIVE

Before examining how the advertising manager sets about his tasks, consider for a moment the goods or services to be sold. Advertising will *not* sell poor merchandise: if it does, buyers will soon realise that the goods are of poor quality, there will be no repeat purchases and the harm done goes beyond your initial sales. Advertising should therefore never be used to sell 'mistakes'. If customers will not buy goods when they see them on the shelves, why on earth should they buy them just because they are advertised? This point is stressed because manufacturers or retailers do sometimes try to clear dead stock through advertising, and then blame advertising when no sales result. Clearance items can be featured with profit from time to time, at attractive bargain prices, but these are special cases. For advertising to be effective, it must offer customers a benefit, such as a new or improved product, lower prices, or newly arrived stocks. Thus a first essential for effective advertising is a good product.

The second essential is that your products must be made known to the right people. This is, perhaps, obvious, but there is no point in telling people about goods which are of no use to them, however much of a bargain is offered. So careful consideration of your 'market' is another essential. If potential purchasers do not know of your merchandise they will not buy it, hence effective advertising means telling the right people about the right goods.

With the right merchandise and the right people to inform, a third consideration is the right means of conveying information to these people. There are many ways to reach prospective customers with your advertising message (and this book concentrates on how to use them effectively). There is no *one* medium that is best – they all reach different markets by different methods. So it is vital for you to select the advertising medium that reaches the people you want, and which will deliver your advertising message most effectively. Correct media selection is therefore vital to effective advertising.

A fourth essential in planning advertising is to get the right message. If you have the right goods, know who your prospective purchasers are and have the means of contacting them, then for successful advertising your message must attract their attention and convey your product's benefits. Hence great care must be paid to the wording of your advertisement, the choice of illustration and the overall layout.

Fifthly, but of equal importance, is timing. Advertisements that appear too early or too late, before your customer is in a position to think about buying or after the purchase has been made, are wasteful.

Finally, your goods must be readily available in the shops when the customers go to buy. Any weakness in distribution will result in your advertising merely increasing your *competitor's* sales, for the retailer – rather than lose his profit – will recommend an alternative brand.

In short, for your advertising to be effective, careful planning must ensure that several factors are right:

Right products – which people would buy if they knew about them.
Right people – to whom your product is of interest.
Right media – which reach these people effectively.
Right message – which conveys your product's benefits.
Right time – when your potential customers are likely to buy.
Right distribution – when your goods are available in the shops.

A Jewish colleague once illustrated this by remarking that there was no point in trying to sell bacon to Jews by advertising in the Catholic Herald on a Friday! Amusing though this anecdote is, it does not cover *all* the essential 'rights' – it stresses wrong product to wrong market in wrong medium at wrong time, but ignores the vital matter of message. This omission nevertheless only reinforces the importance of right product and right market, for *no* advertising message, however brilliantly created, could ever persuade people to buy a product that is forbidden them. Another omission is right budget, so you do not spend too much or too little on achieving your objective.

This planning of 'rights' is an over-simplification, but it does make clear the need for planning. It is vital that your advertising is carefully planned. Advertising is not a separate operation unconnected with your company's other marketing activities: advertising, sales and display effort must all be co-ordinated. With careful planning, advertising expenditure is controlled and spent to best advantage, and ensures results that bring profits which more than pay for the advertising. Part 3 describes how this planned advertising can best be achieved.

THE CHANGING STRUCTURE OF THE ADVERTISING DEPARTMENT

The structure of the advertising department will vary with the firm and with circumstances, and the background to such changes must now be considered. Advertising is no longer treated in isolation: advertising and marketing activities now play an important role in influencing overall policy rather than merely reflecting it. Advertising and marketing executives are found on Boards of Directors and the status of their departments has changed accordingly.

Another aspect of change relates to the range of work carried out by the advertising department, whose manager may find himself with responsibilities such as public relations, merchandising, marketing, sales promotion and market research. Again the structure varies: in some firms, one individual controls all these activities and his title (and that of his department) changes accordingly, while in others they are divided among two or more executives, each the head of his own department.

Whatever the structure, it is essential that all these activities interlock: unless advertising ties in with merchandising, sales promotion and public relations in aiming to achieve the identical marketing objective, it is impossible for advertising media to be used to maximum effect. For this reason, we should examine these allied activities.

Public Relations

The chapter on Other Media stressed the importance of giving attention to both editorial and advertising columns. Press relations is an important part of PR. The Institute of Public Relations defines PR as 'the deliberate, planned and sustained effort to establish and maintain mutual understanding between an organisation and its publics'. Advertising is one of the tools used to achieve mutual understanding, but public relations is another far broader one which covers every contact made by the organisation in every field.

To illustrate its wide scope, take the launch of a new product by your company. Certainly you would need to inform the public and forewarn retailers, and public and trade press advertising would play a key role in ensuring public and retailer acceptance of your new product. Public relations activities, however, operate on a much wider front, for the new product is also 'news' and the editors of consumer and trade publications need information to keep their readers up-to-date. The same applies to other media such as television and radio.

It would be a great mistake, however, to regard editorial mentions as 'free advertising' and to set about public relations work with the intention of 'getting something for nothing'. Instead, you must consider the special requirements of each editor and what will interest his readers. The art of good press relations is knowing just what is of news value to different media, and so presenting the editors with the information *they* want, in the form they want it, and in good time for them to use it. Sending out extra copies of a News Release to all and sundry publications in the belief that 'they may use it, and it only costs a stamp' will, in fact, do your firm a disservice. Editors who repeatedly receive useless News Releases from the same source will, before long, no longer bother to read them. Then, when something occurs which is of genuine interest, your Release will not get the attention it would otherwise have received. Editors are busy people, working under pressure against the clock, and cannot be expected to waste their time reading releases in the hope that one in a hundred will be of interest.

Public relations activity does not end with the issue of News Releases but covers any contact, on any topics of interest, with the different sections of your public. Many people will be personally affected by the new development, and should be told directly of its implications rather than being left to read about it by chance. Those on the factory floor will want to know about the new product and the sales staff will be equally interested. Many other staff divisions – such as warehouse, despatch and accounts – will want to know how the new product affects their work and, even outside the firm itself, there will be many sections of the community affected by or interested in your new product. Retailers and wholesalers, for example, will be directly interested, as will be the suppliers of raw materials or machinery, while your company's shareholders will most certainly want to know how their money is being spent. In each of these cases there is need for public relations activity to ensure a flow of clear information – a flow which, in the Institute's definition, is deliberate, planned and sustained. Failing this there could be lack of mutual understanding and, in extreme cases, even ill-will, all of which could have been avoided had you taken the trouble to inform people of what was going on, rather than leaving them to find out for themselves.

Public relations activity covers *every* contact, and not only those made as a result of paid-for advertising. Playing a vital part in your firm's operations, it demands top-level attention and in some organisations public relations work is linked with that of the advertising manager. In others, it is developed to such a scale that a full-time public relations officer is necessary, often with his own department. Alternatively public relations consultants may be employed, or the advertising agency's PR service used. Clearly then there is a variety of ways in which your company's public relations can be safeguarded and promoted: the important thing is that this must never be neglected and must interlock with other activities, if advertising media are to make their full contribution to achieving your business objective.

Merchandising and Sales Promotion

The advertising manager's responsibilities may also extend to merchandising and sales promotion, since an advertising campaign's success depends as much on your goods being in the shops at the right time, or on potential purchasers actually *trying* the product, as on the effectiveness of the creative work and media schedule. Many companies ensure that their advertising is backed up by extensive merchandising and sales promotion campaigns. These tasks may be undertaken by the advertising manager as an additional responsibility, separate merchandising and sales promotion managers may be appointed, or the work may be shared with the appropriate section of the company's advertising agency or with outside services.

Sales promotion is defined in *The British Code of Sales Promotion Practice* as 'Those marketing techniques which are used, usually on a temporary basis, to make goods and services more attractive to the consumer by providing some additional benefits in cash or kind.' The Code also applies to sales and trade incentive promotions, to editorial promotional offers, and to some aspects of sponsorship.

For planning purposes, however, it is better to separate what has been grouped together under the single heading of 'sales promotion' since this does not distinguish between two very different objectives. In consequence, I offer an alternative definition: 'Activities which pull people towards products, or which push products towards people.'

Sales Promotion

To stimulate trial by potential new purchasers, or to encourage brand loyalty among existing customers, manufacturers often mount sales promotions such as coupons redeemable for gifts, cut-price banded packs, free samples, gifts with purchase, in-pack premiums, in-store demonstrations, offers of informative booklets, short-term price reductions, or any of a host of other incentives which can serve as useful devices for pulling potential customers towards your products.

Having stimulated the market through advertising (supplemented by appropriate public relations and sales promotion campaigns) what a waste of time if potential customers then find that retailers know nothing about your new product or free trial offer, or are not prepared to redeem your coupons! So, in addition to your public campaign, there should be a second campaign aimed at your distributors.

Merchandising

Before retailers will stock or display new merchandise they must be convinced that the line will sell. This means stimulating their enthusiasm by telling them of your forthcoming advertising and the demand it will create, and persuading them to stock and display the new product.

To secure maximum distributor co-operation in pushing your products, your 'dealer campaign' might include trade press advertisements, sales letters telling of future consumer advertising, and the provision of display material. There may also be arrangements for 'co-operative advertising' in which retailers join your firm in local media advertising, perhaps on a shared-cost basis, to announce that they stock the advertised brand. For retailers unskilled in display, you may provide a special window-dressing service. In addition, there might be competitions for best performance, dealer conferences, and 'stocking-up bonuses' or other financial incentives. All these activities can be grouped under the heading of merchandising, in that they aim to make sure your products have wide distribution and are well displayed in the shops when your advertising campaign breaks on the public.

Merchandising can also help your company's salesforce in persuading retailers to stock and display the goods. Accordingly, for effective marketing, your salesforce must be kept fully informed.

Sales force activity

The vital links with distributors, or indeed with customers direct, are your sales representatives, so merchandising activities should extend to them: they then push products towards distributors, who in turn push them towards ultimate purchasers. Many of the same merchandising techniques apply, but this time aimed at sales staff rather than wholesalers or retailers.

Promotion plans may include a sales conference at which your production manager explains the new product range, the sales manager talks about sales targets, and the advertising manager – aided perhaps by the agency – outlines the advertising campaign. The advertisements and media schedule are shown to the sales staff and the thinking behind your advertising explained. The purpose is to make sure that all representatives know of and understand the advertising support that will back up their sales efforts. And it is of vital importance that representatives *do* understand the campaign, for even when a product is widely advertised it cannot be bought until it is in the shops, and shopkeepers will not stock it unless the sales staff have convinced them it will sell.

The consumer advertising campaign can thus serve as an effective means of persuading retailers to stock and display your lines, and each representative may be provided with a portfolio containing specimen advertisements and details of your media schedule, for use as a sales aid when making presentations to potential stockists.

Although separated for ease of analysis, advertising, merchandising, public relations and sales promotion are not watertight compartments, and there is no hard and fast line between one activity and another. Advertising might be the means of announcing a sales promotion incentive (which also achieves editorial mention through effective press relations). Response to the offer may in turn serve a merchandising function, by providing leads for sales representatives. These many activities also clearly influence mutual understanding, and thus have public relations implications. The important thing is for your company to consider all aspects of marketing communications: this in turn has direct implications for the role of the advertising manager.

Marketing

The Chartered Institute of Marketing has adopted the following definition:

'Marketing is the management process responsible for identifying, anticipating and satisfying customer requirements profitably.'

Marketing thus directly influences the work of the advertising manager. Sometimes his work is linked with that of the marketing manager, or both functions might be united in a single post – perhaps with the added responsibilities of public relations, merchandising and sales promotion, and market research.

The modern concept of marketing has in fact revolutionised production and selling. In the early days of large-scale production, a firm manufactured a product, the sales manager sold it and the advertising manager devised a suitable campaign. Their joint effort was aimed at achieving sales of a product already in production. Salesmen perhaps passed back any comments they received from retailers regarding public reaction to the product or, more recently, there may have been some research to define the market and to learn consumer attitudes to the product. Then, on the basis of this somewhat meagre information, the company or its agency designed the pack and planned the advertising campaign. In essence, however, all this activity was aimed at selling a product already produced: in other words, the product came first and was followed by the selling and advertising decisions.

This brief description over-simplifies the process, but serves to illustrate how the modern concept of marketing has meant a complete reversal of this attitude. Instead of manufacturing a product and then selling it, marketing now attempts to locate and define a need and to ascertain in advance in what size, shape, colour, packaging and at what price consumers would most want the product. Only then does marketing assess how best to produce, distribute and promote the product itself. Thus, long before any production facilities exist, and when the idea is still at concept stage, marketing plans the complete production and selling operation. Research ascertains the form and quantity that will best suit the market: an obvious prerequisite to production, for how else can management decide what facilities are necessary to manufacture the product in the right quantities, and in the packaging and at the price required? Marketing also considers distribution of the product, the type of retail outlets, trade discount and sales force structure, and the degree of emphasis to be placed on advertising and personal selling.

Today, most marketing plans go even further: they look to the future by attempting to predict your product's life cycle (introduction, growth, maturity and decline), and also include research and development activity to improve existing products as well as providing new products for your company to market in the future.

Marketing unites advertising, selling, market research and many other activities. None of these is new: the only new concept is linking these various activities under the common heading of marketing. The marketing man must have a full appreciation of the parts played by market research, production, packaging, price, advertising, personal selling, merchandising, sales promotion, and distribution in successfully producing and selling his company's lines and in planning future products. In many companies marketing has become the hub of all activity. Sales and advertising departments have always been complementary, but the new concept of marketing is leading to these 'separate' activities being united under a single marketing director, who controls a number of executives responsible for various aspects of the marketing mix, or brand managers responsible for individual products within the range. Even in companies where sales and advertising remain separate, the concept of marketing implies that the staff in both departments must work in close co-operation, fully 'market-orientated' and conscious that the all-important factor is not what they wish to sell but what the customer wants to buy. The two are not necessarily the same and, where there is a difference, it is increasingly rare for the manufacturer to regard his view as the dominant one. The consumer is sovereign and has freedom of choice: maximum profitability for the company must be balanced by a corresponding satisfaction for its customers.

Direct and Database Marketing

Marketing itself is changing: direct marketing has increased partly through increased use of direct mail. Direct mail, a formerly static medium, has undergone major changes in the light of new technology, particularly the computerisation of mailing lists. This situation is very much chicken-and-egg – has use of direct mail grown because of increased direct marketing, or has direct marketing increased because of improved direct mail technology?

Direct marketing has been described as *'any activity which creates and profitably exploits a direct relationship between seller and prospect.'* Its two essential requirements are recording names and addresses, and measurement of results – both of which directly affect advertising planning, and in particular the use of direct mail.

The new concept of database marketing is rooted in an old philosophy – that of getting closer to your customers. An organisation which identifies its customers, understands and meets their needs, and treats these customers well, will do well even in the most competitive environment – and database marketing is basically a sophisticated new means of serving this old philosophy. Its principles apply particularly to direct mail advertising but are equally relevant to other aspects of marketing: the same approach can increase salesforce or telemarketing effectiveness, with results fed back into the same database.

A mailing list should be more than a collection of names and addresses; it should be a complete database of your target markets. Information is usually stored on computer, and arranged so that:

- Your records contain purchasing history as well as names and addresses and other customer details
- Different sections of your list are readily identifiable, by purchasing patterns or other criteria
- The database includes promotional history – which customers were targetted, what messages were delivered through which media, who responded, when and how?
- It is regularly up-dated – lapsed customers identified and removed, and new enquiries/purchases or address changes etc entered as soon as possible
- Addresses are postcoded, for efficiency of mailing – as the earlier reference to *Mailsort* on page 100 made clear, there are valuable discounts for those who carry out sortation work that would otherwise be undertaken by the Royal Mail. Database marketing can thus help stretch your advertising budget even further, quite apart from improving campaign effectiveness.

The final stage of advertising planning, evaluation of results, applies particularly to database marketing. Your advertising campaign can result in off-the-page sales or enquiries which serve as sales leads, which in turn permit a tracking system far more sophisticated than simply recording cash sales or enquiries, and enquiries converted into orders. The database should not only specify goods sold but should also analyse purchases in 'Recency, Frequency and Value' terms, as well as including conventional data such as age, sex, socio-economic group, and geodemographic classification or location. These details, fed back into your database, then serve as an integrated information system.

An effective database enables you to maximise customer potential, and to:

- select individual customers whose records indicate they are ripe for possible repeat purchases
- select those whose purchase patterns suggest that they are prospects for other products/services in your range
- apply regional or timing controls to your direct mail activities
- send these selected customers a personalised message, related to their individual needs
- select specific market segments for further advertising attention.

With conventional marketing, market segmentation is often achieved by 'desegregating' large market groups into smaller target categories, whereas database marketing achieves accurate segmentation in the opposite way – by aggregating individual customer records.

This information can help target 'cold' mailings to potential customers with whom you have had no previous contact. Such new lists should of course be merged and purged against those names already on your records, the response to mailings evaluated, and your database adjusted accordingly.

Database marketing can help you move these potential new customers up a five-rung 'ladder of loyalty', leading them through five market stages:

1. *Suspects* – potential customers who have not yet indicated interest in your product or service, but who merit a 'cold' mailing
2. *Prospects* – those recipients who have indicated interest, but not yet purchased
3. *Customers* – those who have purchased
4. *Loyal customers* – those who buy regularly
5. *Advocates* – those beyond passive brand loyalty, who actively recommend your product or service to others.

Apart from these advertising applications, database marketing also improves salesforce effectiveness, as it can:

- assist with call and journey planning
- produce pre-call briefing documents for sales representatives
- standardise post-call reporting.

The database approach can also be applied to telemarketing, with equally beneficial results.

Database marketing is thus not just a means of communicating with customers, but rather a new way of defining supplier/customer/advertising relationships. It is also a new way of doing business that provides marketing and management information: database marketing could eventually replace conventional market research through advertising campaigns planned to provide all necessary information by seeking and measuring customer response. By mapping market trends, database marketing helps ensure opportunities and threats are swiftly identified, and speeds up the process of capturing these market opportunities and neutralising any threats. The system can also provide management ratios, such as advertising expenditure to enquiries, enquiries converted to actual sales, and average order value. It can further help evaluate both media and messages.

The database approach thus serves as a functional basis for management and marketing planning, salesforce control and telemarketing, just as much as for direct mail and other advertising. It can also help you to co-ordinate these separate activities so that they all interlock to maximum effect.

A final but extremely important point relates to external constraints on your direct marketing activities. A later chapter discusses the *Code of Advertising Practice* in general terms, but the Advertising Standards Authority recently added to its scope through new *'Rules for Direct Marketing, including Lists and Database Management'*. These came into effect in January 1992, thus proving a point repeatedly made throughout this book: the vital need to keep up-to-date with new developments.

Marketing Research

When database marketing is not applicable, the purpose of market research is to provide information which will help manufacturers anticipate consumer needs so that they can decide how to satisfy these needs in a profitable way, and the need to adopt a marketing approach has already made clear the vital role of research in locating and defining consumer needs. The many different applications of marketing research, and the various ways in which information can be obtained, call for major attention and cannot be covered within the scope of this book. All that need be said here is that research may be an additional task for the advertising manager, or it may be the responsibility of the marketing manager, perhaps through a specialist market research manager, through the research department of the advertising agency, or through an independent market research company.

ADMINISTRATION OF THE ADVERTISING DEPARTMENT

The advertising manager as head of a department

The advertising manager is head of a department just as much as the head of production, sales, transport or any other section: he thus has responsibility for staffing his department, and its size depends to a great extent on whether or not any advertising agency is employed.

Where the firm does not use an advertising agency, the advertising manager must have in his department creative staff to prepare the advertisements, or be in touch with freelance workers on whom he can call. Similarly he must be able to deal with the work of media selection, planning and booking, and the physical production of advertisements.

Even where this work is undertaken by an advertising agency (or by the creative workshops and media independents described in later chapters), it does not follow that there is no staffing problem for the manufacturer's advertising department. Careful control must still be kept of schedules, accurate records maintained of the company's advertising, and voucher copies and invoices checked. Perhaps the advertisements call for readers to fill in a coupon. This simple request involves a vast amount of work in sending out booklets, sorting out the coupons and perhaps passing them on to the firm's representatives as sales leads, and analysing the response to the campaign. Responsibility for advertising involves a great deal of executive, creative and purely routine administrative work, even when an agency is employed. Division of work between advertiser and agency varies but, whatever the circumstances, the advertising manager must ensure he has staff to cope with whatever work he accepts as his responsibility.

Agency selection and liaison

The advantages and disadvantages of using an agency will be covered in the next chapter, but clearly the decision whether or not to employ an agency rests largely with the advertising manager and he will be called upon to advise his Board of Directors accordingly. If it is decided to do so he will be responsible for selecting a suitable agency, negotiating arrangements for handling his advertising, and for briefing the agency on his company's requirements. After this briefing he will throughout the campaign work closely with the agency team in the preparation and execution of proposals, and the evaluation of their results.

The importance of agency liaison must never be under-estimated and, in fact, it largely depends on the client's advertising manager whether or not the agency produces a good scheme. There is no question of the advertising manager sitting back and leaving everything to the agency, for even the finest agency, staffed by experts in every specialist branch of advertising, can give of its best only if it receives full backing and co-operation from the client.

Division of work

Some advertisers rely on their agency for the full range of advertising media, while others undertake part of the work themselves. More usually press, television, radio, cinema and outdoor advertising come within the agency's orbit, while control of other media may rest with either party. Exhibitions, direct mail and display material are frequently retained under the advertising department's direct control, even when an agency is employed. Some advertisers adopt a policy of dividing their appropriation into two parts: an 'above the line' budget to be spent by the agency and a 'below the line' budget which is retained by the advertising department. There is no uniformity about where the client's work ends and the agency's starts, and much depends on the staffing arrangements the advertising manager considers most effective under the circumstances in which his firm operates.

The size and structure of the advertising department

There is no limit to the variety of structures within different companies' advertising departments. A firm may or may not employ an advertising agency and, either way, the advertising manager may rely on only a few staff or alternatively he may have a large department containing numbers of expert staff, equivalent to a fully-equipped agency. The advertising manager may in fact have in his department a number of specialists who are the counterparts of the agency experts. In such circumstances, agency media proposals will be checked by the advertising manager's own media expert, creative proposals by his creative staff, research by research specialists and so on, with the advertising manager in overall control and taking an overall view. Alternatively, these experts may undertake the full advertising task without outside assistance.

Where a company has several different divisions or products, there may well be separate advertising departments, each under its own advertising manager and co-ordinated by an advertising director. Each of these departments may produce its part of the company's advertising without agency assistance, but in other cases the advertising departments may employ one or more advertising agencies.

In some cases, this structure may be extended to include the media independents. One company used four separate advertising agencies for its four separate divisions. Since all four advertised heavily on television, the company then employed a media independent to co-ordinate their activities and to prevent any possibility of the divisions wasting valuable resources in pre-empting each other's television spots.

There is thus a wide variety of organisational patterns, but there is certainly no question of one business structure being 'better' than others: each firm adopts the organisational pattern most suited to its circumstances and adapts itself as the business world, and the firm itself, changes. The advertising manager must consider future expansion, perhaps caused by additional products to be marketed and, reverting to his role as head of a department, must recruit and train new staff and/or review his agency arrangement accordingly.

In-house or agency?

There are, as always, advantages and drawbacks to both in-house and agency operations. What is not always immediately apparent is that one is the converse of the other: the advantages of agency service, reviewed in the next chapter, are the drawbacks of undertaking the work yourself. Conversely, the advantages of in-house work are the drawbacks of agency service.

There is, however, one further factor: added flexibility. Should you take on additional staff in anticipation of additional work, there may be redundancy costs involved if the anticipated work does not materialise. Using an agency means that they, rather than you, have the work-load problem. Much the same applies to quality of work: it is relatively easier to change agencies than the staff of a department, should the advertising they produce not match up to the standard required.

Who represents advertisers generally?

ISBA (the Incorporated Society of British Advertisers) represents advertisers' interests, across the full range of industry and commerce. As such, it is their main point of contact with the media and government, on *all* issues related to marketing communications. Its main area of expertise is advertising, but its advice and activities extend into related fields including direct marketing, exhibitions, research, sales promotion, and sponsorship. The benefits of ISBA membership are best summarised by a quotation from its own literature, which points out that it: '*provides a constant service of up-to-date information; provides an invaluable consultancy service; helps protect your company's interests, at home and abroad, by acting as the advertiser's collective voice; and enables your company to improve its marketing communication skills.*'

ISBA has working committees devoted to different aspects of advertising, including direct marketing, exhibitions, industrial, international, outdoor, press, radio, research, sales promotion, self-regulation and legislation.

The Society publishes a monthly newsletter, including industrial and exhibition supplements, and numerous informative booklets. Recent titles include *Advertising Briefing Procedure, Business-to-Business Advertising, International Marketing Communications*, a *Guide to Sales Promotion and Sponsorship* and a *Best Practice Guide* aimed at ending the problems experienced between advertisers and their agencies.

Chapter 9

Role of the Advertising Agency

Whether undertaken by advertiser or agency or shared between them, the various component tasks which overall make for good advertising remain the same. These tasks were listed at the start of the last chapter. The aim of this chapter is not to consider these tasks as such, but to review how the agency sets about them in partnership with its client.

It is interesting to recall that agencies were originally media-owners' service departments, not independent organisations. In the early days of advertising, agencies acted as representatives for newspapers and sold space in them to advertisers. At first, the agencies bought space in quantity, and made their profit by selling it in smaller units for as much as they could get. Later still, agencies started to sell space on a commission basis, and a commission system is still the current basis for agency remuneration, agencies taking their profit from commissions granted by media-owners rather than from advertisers.

Finding it easier to sell space if they suggested how it should be used, the agencies started a copywriting service, and soon afterwards design and art services were added. By this time, agencies were really working more for the advertisers than for the newspaper proprietors, and before long they became fully-fledged service organisations giving their clients a complete range of advertising services. They also became independent, and bought space in whichever newspapers or other advertising media they thought best served their clients' interests. Today, the term 'agency' no longer applies in the legal sense, since the agency makes contracts in its own right – with its clients on the one hand and with media-owners on the other – and remains a party to the advertisement contract, which it would not were it an 'agency' in the legal sense of the word. Agencies are thus liable in law for debts to media, even though they made the bookings on their client's behalf. To minimise the risk factor, many agencies take out indemnity insurance, to ensure they can settle their accounts with media-owners, should any client unfortunately fail to meet financial commitments.

Media-owners, in their turn, also take action to protect themselves, to prevent a situation in which an agency might be unable to meet its financial obligations. Often this defensive action is taken on a collective basis through the appropriate trade organisation, which may operate an agency-monitoring system. One such system calls for audited accounts from all recognised agencies. Those companies which do not comply, those whose accounts fail to meet minimum financial criteria, and those which consistently demonstrate poor payment performance, are placed in 'intensive care' and member media-owners alerted to the danger. Such agencies would then be invited for interview in order to provide an explanation and, if necessary, some form of guarantee. In extreme cases, the agency's recognition for commission could be withdrawn.

THE ADVANTAGES OF USING AN ADVERTISING AGENCY

There are a number of reasons why a manufacturer employs the services of an advertising agency instead of relying on his own advertising department.

1 A team of experts Primarily, agencies exist to provide a team of experts to work in closest co-operation with the client's own advertising staff. The team includes specialists in all the many aspects of advertising practice including, of course, media. There are, however, many other advantages to agency service.

2 The work load problem The advertiser could no doubt recruit experts on his own staff, but there might be insufficient work to keep an expert on, say, media, fully occupied. The agency, on the other hand, can afford to employ the specialist, since he will be working full-time for a number of clients, according to their varying needs for his expert advice. Alternatively, the client might himself employ a number of independent consultants but they would not be accustomed to working together, whereas the agency has the experts immediately available and already working as a team.

Points 1 and 2 viewed together mean that perhaps an advertiser who cannot offer adequate scope and challenge (quite apart from remuneration) may fail to attract staff of the right calibre.

3 A new approach A further advantage of employing an agency is that it brings a fresh approach to a problem, since its staff are detached from the company's day-to-day operations, whereas an advertiser's own staff often become so involved in detailed work that they no longer see the wood for the trees.

4 Experience in allied fields Again, since they are handling different products for a number of clients, agencies have wider experience and their personnel, not being restricted to any one company's problems, are unlikely to take a narrow view. Besides, the knowledge and experience gained from one marketing problem can frequently be adapted to meet another, and in this way each client derives benefit from the agency's experience in other fields – an advantage of particular importance today when markets and trading patterns are changing so rapidly. An agency keeps abreast of new developments through direct contact with the marketing problems of a number of advertisers, and can advise its clients in the light of its wider knowledge and experience. Advertisers, of course, also keep themselves up-to-date but, because they operate in only one product field, their experience is inevitably limited.

5 Buying power The advertising agency's total expenditure must necessarily be larger than any one client's individual budget. Accordingly, when buying on its clients' behalf, it can bring considerable pressure to bear on suppliers and media-owners – far more pressure than most advertisers can exert on their own. This buying 'muscle' can be exerted by the agency not only on media purchases but on all other items, such as print or artwork, that the agency buys on its clients' behalf. Added to expert knowledge of the market climate and of which suppliers to approach, this can result in considerable savings for the agency's clients.

6 Reduced cost A further advantage of agency service arises directly from the commission granted by the media-owners, which helps reduce the costs of using the agency's team of experts. Media-owners grant commission, usually ranging from ten to 15 per cent, to recognised advertising agencies, and agencies get commission on almost everything they buy on a client's behalf. If an advertisement costs £1,000, that is the amount the client spends whether he makes the booking direct or through his advertising agency. But by booking it through his advertising agency, though it still costs him £1,000, the agency receives 15 per cent commission, or £150. Where the commission granted by media-owners is less than 15 per cent, the agency may 'round up' the charge made to clients, at +17.65 per cent of the net cost, to recoup the difference in income from that advertisement.

For some clients, where the commission is enough to cover costs and provide a sufficient profit, the agency will work on commission alone, and the advertiser then reaps the benefit of agency service without charge. Should the client consider that the commission received from his account is more than sufficient to cover the agency's work on his behalf, he may – when negotiating arrangements – call for the commission level to be reduced. On the other hand, if an agency finds its expenses in handling the client's advertising exceed the commission received, or leave an insufficient margin of profit, it will charge a 'service fee' to obtain the additional income necessary. Even where the advertiser pays a service fee, however, this is usually still less expensive than taking all the experts into his own staff.

For many years there has been talk of the commission system breaking down but, despite much controversy and discussion of alternatives, it still survives – even if in changing form.

Commission was originally granted only to 'recognised' advertising agencies, and the financial vetting of applicant agencies was usually undertaken by the appropriate media-owners' trade organisation, as a central service for its members. Following the extension of restrictive practices legislation to services, however, the recognition system came under review.

After discussion with the Office of Fair Trading, it was agreed that joint financial vetting of applicant agencies was an essential area for continuation of collective action, and thus acceptable within the terms of the legislation.

Other matters formerly incorporated in the joint recognition system have however now been excluded: these are the agreement to pay commission, the former ruling about non-rebating of commission to clients, and the granting of recognition to certain categories of agency only (with requirements as to their equipment/staffing and ownership). It is now considered that these areas primarily concern the individual relationships between media-owner and agency and between agency and advertiser, and should therefore not be covered by the revised recognition system.

All matters relating to payment of commission are thus now for the individual decision of each media-owner. Accordingly, under the new arrangements, recognition no longer carries with it any entitlement or conditions regarding the payment of commission. Recognised agencies do, however, benefit from the central trade body's recommendation to its members that such agencies should receive credit terms.

Further legislation or new rulings by the Office of Fair Trading may lead to other modifications. Alternatively, internal business pressure within the advertising industry may still lead to the commission system breaking down, or perhaps being amended to allow for two or more commission levels, on a decreasing scale as advertising expenditure increases. A further possibility is payment on a straight-fee basis. Accordingly, the other – and main – benefits of agency service should be the prime considerations, rather than possible savings on commission.

7 Other savings Other benefits of agency service, though of less importance, can nevertheless result in considerable administrative savings. Any company placing its advertising direct receives individual invoices from all media on the schedule, as well as accounts for artwork, production of press advertisements, and for making television, cinema or radio commercials. When an agency is employed, however, the advertiser receives comprehensive accounts covering all these many and varied items, which he can then settle with a single payment. In addition, there are clerical savings in that typed copies of media schedules and other documents are provided as a normal part of the agency's service.

A final note

As pointed out in the previous chapter, the advantages of agency service are the drawbacks of the client undertaking the work within his own organisation. Conversely, the disadvantages of agency service listed below are the advantages of in-house work.

THE DRAWBACKS OF AGENCY SERVICE

Employing an advertising agency is not without its drawbacks, though in most cases these are outweighed by the advantages.

1 Divided attention One disadvantage is that agency personnel work on several different accounts at the same time (thus helping to overcome the workload problem) and clearly cannot give their undivided attention to all of them simultaneously. If something urgent crops up with one client, agency personnel may be prevented by other commitments from devoting all their time to dealing with it, whereas a manufacturer employing his own advertising staff knows that his problems receive undivided attention all the time.

2 The time lag Again, agency service is not always as speedy as direct working, and a manufacturer whose advertising is constantly subject to unexpected changes might prefer to do the job himself. If the content of the advertising campaign is under continual review, this could well apply: a mail order firm, for example, might wish to drop one item from an advertisement immediately stocks were exhausted and replace it with another line. Similarly, a travel agent might wish to stop advertising his Italian holiday tours just as soon as all places were booked, and to substitute another country where he still has vacancies.

3 Cost A further drawback arises from the commissions received by the agency, the service fee charged, and the amount of work involved. For some types of advertising, the commission may be so small and the service fee so high that it becomes more economical for the advertiser to engage his own experts and to set up an advertising department which amounts to a small agency. Much depends on the nature of the advertising, for where media costs are low the agency receives little income from commission. On the other hand, it takes just as much effort to prepare an advertisement for a technical journal as for a national newspaper, yet the former task will bring the agency far less revenue than the second, simply because it receives commission on a smaller sum.

4 Built-in 'inertia' The income *versus* workload problem can be extended, since the agency receives roughly the same commission on £50,000, whether it is spent on a single advertisement or on hundreds, but its costs will vary considerably. A travel agent, for example, might get far better results from classified insertions than from display advertisements and would consequently want to advertise in this way. From the agency standpoint, however, this could be extremely uneconomic – imagine how many classified or semi-display advertisements you could buy for £50,000 – each one would necessitate typing an order, preparing copy and type mark-up, checking proofs and vouchers, and paying an invoice. The administrative costs would leave little or no profit from the commission. The commission system thus has a 'built-in' temptation for agencies to achieve maximum income with minimum effort.

The same argument can be applied to changes in advertisement content. The agency incurs lower staff costs by preparing one advertisement and letting it run week after week for a year than if it changes the content each month. The income from commission remains the same, yet monthly changes of copy mean 12 times as much work, with consequent higher staff costs and lower profits.

Agencies need to make a profit, and to some extent this can be achieved by charging a higher service fee to recoup the additional staff costs involved. The higher the service fee, however, the more attractive it becomes for the advertiser to run his own advertising department, or to transfer to an agency charging a lower fee.

Agency directors are of course more than aware of all these drawbacks, and take the necessary steps to overcome them. Agency management is thus of great importance in ensuring that advertising skills are used to maximum effect, on behalf of the agency's clients. Equally, responsibility for the disadvantages rests to some degree with the advertiser: drawbacks should ideally have been ironed out at agency selection stage, and client/agency relationships be compatible.

AGENCIES AND MEDIA-OWNERS

Employment of an advertising agency should bring benefits to media-owners as well as to advertisers. Ideally, it means that a media representative presents his sales argument to an advertising expert who will appreciate his medium's various selling points, evaluate them in terms of the client's marketing strategy and prepare a schedule in which all the media dovetail in a carefully planned campaign.

With companies which have little experience of advertising – particularly small firms – media representatives often find selling a difficult task, because before they can present the case for their medium, they must devote considerable time to selling the need to advertise. With some inexperienced advertisers the media representative has to go even further, even to the extent of writing copy and suggesting layouts. This point brings to light another benefit that media-owners receive from agency service: when an agency is employed, there are expert staff to create advertisements and the media-owner's production staff can expect to receive the necessary material in good time. In many cases, media-owners receive from agencies complete advertisements, and are not involved in any typesetting expenses. Furthermore, when proofs are submitted, they are returned promptly with alterations indicated with the accepted proof correction marks instead of the crossings-out and arrows used by the inexperienced layman.

As every media-owner knows, there are times when the agency does not deliver as promptly as it should (perhaps because of pressure caused by rush campaigns for a number of clients simultaneously) and the media representatives find themselves chasing the agency for material or the return of corrected proofs. For the most part, however, the media-owner's life is made easier by the smooth function of agency procedure.

There can also be financial benefits, since the media-owner is dealing with an advertising agency he recognises (either directly or through his trade association) rather than a number of perhaps little-known clients into whose creditworthiness he would otherwise have to make individual and time-consuming investigations. The agency is liable in law for space or time booked on its clients' behalf, and the media-owner can thus look to the agency direct for payment, hence the importance of the central media trade organisation's recommendation that the agency be recognised as creditworthy.

AGENCY PROCEDURE

When a company appoints an agency, the first task of the agency personnel is to find out all about their client's activities and problems. The agency's investigations, discussed in detail in Part 3, necessarily duplicate those undertaken by the advertising manager when he was first appointed, since the agency staff need an equally clear understanding of the client's company background and marketing objectives. The agency will spend considerable time making a thorough investigation, for not until the advertiser's requirements have been accurately defined can the agency attempt to meet them. The size of the appropriation and the period to be covered are also important to the agency, as are precise instructions on what the appropriation covers. Are production charges included or only media costs? Is the client undertaking part of the campaign himself and keeping back a 'below the line' budget for this purpose? Practice varies with the firm, as we have seen, and there are no hard and fast rules. Obviously, however, the agency must know what money is available and what it has to cover.

Ideally, the client will give the agency *all* the information it needs when he gives his advertising 'brief': the quality of work produced by the agency to a considerable extent depends on the client's skill in giving his agency all the information it needs in order to prepare advertising proposals on his behalf.

Once the agency is confident that it has a correct understanding of the situation, it can start the vital work of preparing an advertising campaign to help its client achieve his marketing objectives. In many cases, to ensure that its understanding of the problem is correct, the agency will prepare a 'facts book' detailing the marketing situation, which the client will double-check for accuracy.

Planning the campaign

An important person in defining and solving the advertising and marketing problem is the agency's account executive. This title is rather misleading, since the executive has little to do with accounting as such, although he certainly bears responsibility for expenditure of the appropriation. The account executive is, in fact, responsible for *all* aspects of handling the client or 'account'. He is usually selected soon after the agency is appointed and attends the meeting at which the agency is briefed on the problem. It is true to say that no client, however well-intentioned, ever gives a 100 per cent perfect briefing and it is up to the executive to ensure, by asking the right questions, that his agency has all the facts it needs to solve the problem. In some cases, inexperience may prevent a new advertiser from giving a proper briefing. In such circumstances it is up to the account executive, through relevant questioning, to get one.

The account executive has a two-way role, in that he represents the agency to the client and the client to the agency. He is the individual to whom the agency staff in all departments turn for information: equally, it is through him that the client's problems are channelled to the appropriate agency specialists, and their work co-ordinated. Frequently you may encounter different levels of account executive. Some larger agencies have account executives backed by assistant executives who handle the day-to-day work on each account. At a higher level, there may be account supervisors, each responsible for a number of account executives handling a similar number of accounts. Again, there may be account directors at a still higher level, with overall responsibility for the campaigns handled by their account supervisors. Another variation is that an individual on the executive side may be responsible for a number of accounts rather than just one. For greater cross-fertilisation of ideas, and to prevent them getting into a rut, many agencies deliberately give their executives varied responsibilities. This practice also helps the agency overcome the workload problem discussed earlier. You may also meet agencies where the term 'account executive' is not used, executive staff being referred to as 'representatives' or 'managers'. For the sake of simplicity, however, the term 'account executive' is used from this point on, to identify the executive function.

Once the problem is clearly defined, the agency staff can start to solve it, and here the account executive plays a key role. He may start by calling a meeting of a 'Plans Board' (formal or informal) on which will be representatives of all the important agency departments. Creative staff are present to consider the theme to be featured in the advertising, and the media department to advise on whether the prospective customers could best be reached by press, posters, television or some other medium. Both media and creative departments *must* be represented on the plans board, since the decision of one department directly affects the other.

Use of any medium also involves *production* considerations, for there is obviously no point in booking space if the advertisement cannot be prepared in time to meet the media-owner's copy date or if the medium's ability to *deliver* your advertising message is not utilised to full advantage. Production costs, too, are important and can influence media selection. The agency production staff are thus directly concerned in media decisions, and will give their views at plans board meetings. Others beside creative, media and production staff may also be represented on the plans board, including any experts in the agency's team who can contribute to solving the particular problem. The plans board may also include other account executives, in addition to the one handling the particular client, for the benefit of their experience and advice. Similarly, other senior members of the various departments may sit on the plans board, even though they are not involved in the day-to-day running of the account. Thus the client gains maximum benefit from the combined talents of the agency.

The plans board discusses the client's overall marketing problem from every angle and finally agrees on a basic solution. Since any advertising campaign represents a combination of interlocking decisions regarding marketing, media, creative, production and other aspects of advertising, clearly broad agreement must be reached by the board as a whole.

Account planning

Some agencies set about solving their clients' advertising and marketing problems in a different way, by separating out the account-planning function. Drafting advertising strategy is considered too important and too time-consuming to be undertaken by busy account executives on a 'part-time' basis. This task is therefore made the primary full-time responsibility of an account planner, whose aim is to bring a stronger discipline to the essential first stage in creating effective advertising campaigns - developing the advertising strategy on which creative and media proposals are based, and by which they are evaluated and justified.

The planner's initial role is to collate and analyse relevant available data, and to propose any new research required to supplement this information. In the light of these findings, the planner then drafts the advertising strategy document for discussion and agreement by the account team or plans board, before it is presented to the client. In due course, the account planner will interpret any research feedback about consumer reactions, to see whether the advertising objectives are being achieved, and recommend any necessary modifications to strategy in the light of this new information. Account planners also think beyond the current campaign, assessing long-term market trends in order to develop long-term strategies. Their multi-skill function is one of increasing importance, and formally recognised as such in the departmental structure of more and more agencies.

The research department

When agency staff attempt to define their client's marketing problems they may decide that they lack sufficient information to reach a sound and reasoned judgement and will call in the research department. This department may already have a representative on the plans board, for the benefit of his general advice, but when more detailed information is required the research department starts to function in its own right.

A tremendous amount of information is readily available in published form, so before any 'field' research is undertaken there is always 'desk' research, which involves checking through existing sources of information. In some agencies desk research staff form a separate department and may be known by another title such as 'Information' or 'Library', while a second department – usually with the formal title of 'Research Department' – looks after field research.

Desk research is carried out before field research, as a matter of form, but if some vital questions remain unanswered, or if some of the information available was published some time ago and is thus out-of-date, then field research becomes essential and the agency research department takes action. Its task lies in planning the operation rather than undertaking the actual 'fieldwork', which is usually carried out by a specialist market research organisation. The agency selects and works with the most suitable market research company in planning the research and supervising the fieldwork. Equally, it gives much thought to interpreting the results and making recommendations for action.

Some 'research departments' have converted into account planning sections, as described above. Many research staff found that restricting their activities to gathering data did not give them job satisfaction: they wanted to be directly involved in the practical application of the valuable information they had gathered. This feeling coincided with the management view that drafting advertising strategy could not be undertaken by busy account executives on a spare-time basis.

As soon as the information collected has been carefully checked and interpreted, there are further meetings of the plans board to consider the advertising and marketing campaign. Once the overall campaign strategy has been agreed, the individual departments set to work to crystallise their ideas and to produce detailed proposals in accordance with the agreed broad plan.

The media department

The media department is represented when the overall campaign is discussed at plans board level. Once the general strategy is agreed, it is then up to the media department to get down to detailed planning with the aim of spending the client's appropriation in such a way that his advertising message reaches prospective buyers as effectively and economically as possible. The media planners are experts on the full range of media and have at their command all the relevant statistics about press, posters, cinema, television, radio and other media.

There is often considerable specialisation within the media department. At its head there may be a media director who represents the media viewpoint on the plans board and agrees the overall strategy. Immediately responsible to him may be media planners whose task is to take the broad strategy and go into the detail of specific media, size, position, number of insertions, dates and so on. Once this stage is agreed, specialist media buyers may take over to put the plan into operation. For example, specialist television time-buyers may negotiate with the programme contractors for the best possible implementation of the media planners' proposal and decide in exactly which breaks, at what times and on which days the client's television commercials will appear. The time-buyers keep this schedule under constant review, adjusting it in the light of changes in rival BBC or commercial programmes, statistics on audience size and composition, or any additional information likely to influence the schedule's effectiveness.

The time-buyers may also be responsible for radio and cinema advertising, or these two media may be the province of separate specialists. Even in the field of press media, specialisation may occur, one space-buyer concentrating on national newspapers, a second on the regional press, and another on, say, women's magazines. In some agencies outdoor advertising might be the responsibility of specialist staff, as might be exhibitions. These different experts have, however, a common aim: to communicate the client's advertising message as effectively as possible through the media which are their own particular responsibility. Other agencies find it more effective to avoid over-specialisation and require their staff, at all levels, to handle the full range of media, and to be responsible for both planning and buying.

Some agencies have specialist media research staff, sometimes called 'media assessors'. Media-owners issue a great deal of useful research material and the flow of information is such that some agencies appoint staff whose main task is to evaluate these documents, thus leaving others free for their main function of planning and buying.

In larger agencies there may be many experts and the media department may operate on a 'group' system, each group containing both planners and buyers, with the media director exercising general control over all groups.

Whatever the agency structure, the experts' skill lies not so much in their detailed knowledge of media (although this may call for years of experience) but in applying this knowledge to their client's advertising problems. If the media specialists are to match the advantages (or drawbacks) of the wide range of advertising media with the requirements of each client's individual marketing problem, they must fully understand that problem. A full briefing of the media department is, therefore, essential if it is to come up with the right answers.

Given this efficient briefing, the media department can then evaluate the range of media, select those most suitable in the light of the client's requirements and prepare detailed proposals. This work is complex and merits more attention than can be given in one chapter dealing with an advertising agency's overall operation. Media evaluation, selection and planning are, therefore, the subjects of later discussion in Part 3.

The creative department

While the media department interprets in detail the broad approach agreed at plans board level, the creative staff take their work to a more advanced level. Copy is written for press advertisements or printed material, and layouts prepared. For posters or display material, roughs or dummies are made, and storyboards drawn up for television or cinema commercials. Detailed discussion of these activities is outside the scope of any book on media, although clearly the creative content of advertisements is vital: there is little point in spending hours on devising a complex media plan only to have it deliver the wrong message. The reverse is just as true – even a superb advertisement cannot work to best advantage if delivered to the wrong audience. Creative and media aspects of campaign planning are of equal importance if you are to use advertising media effectively. In larger agencies there may be several creative as well as media groups.

Review of proposals

As soon as detailed media and creative proposals are ready, the plans board meets again to review the work. Possibly there may now be a formal change of title, and the committee becomes known as the 'Review Board'. In some agencies, the review board comprises precisely the same individuals as the plans board and would therefore probably continue under the same name. In others, the individuals as well as the name are changed. Whatever the practice, the purpose is to check meticulously, point by point, the proposals to be submitted to the client to ensure that there are no discrepancies in the work of the individual departments, that all the various aspects of the campaign interlock, that the proposals conform to the basic strategy agreed by the earlier plans board, and that the quality of the work matches up to the agency's standards.

This, then, is the pattern of agency work – investigation, analysis of the problem, agreement on a basic solution, working out a detailed plan, and careful checking to ensure that the proposals are faultless. The various stages involved are an indication of the care which agencies take in their work, even though the procedure may not always be on a formal basis. Indeed, a plans board meeting may sometimes be completely informal, with the account executive talking over the problem with individual members of the various departments, after normal office hours and away from the interruptions of the telephone and other distractions. Some practitioners argue strongly against formal plans or review boards on the grounds that they stifle individuals and impose an agency style on all clients regardless of their requirements. For this reason, meetings may sometimes be completely informal.

Presentation of proposals

Once the detailed proposals have been approved by the review board, they are made ready for presentation to the client. The media schedule is typed out in its final form, as is the advertisement copy, and finished versions of designs are prepared by the creative staff. These are then presented to the client, and the inter-relationship between copy, design and media explained. It is essential that these three are presented together, for the client would be unable to approve a media schedule without knowing the advertisements to be featured, nor could he approve creative work without knowing the media in which it was to appear. Creative and media proposals are accordingly presented together, with other parts of the plan.

The presentation of campaign proposals is of major importance and should not be viewed as 'selling' the proposals to the client but rather as careful explanation of the individual parts of a complex plan and how they are related. Presentation of proposals is, in fact, the very reverse of the agency's first task. When the problem was first discussed, it was broken down into individual components for detailed work by the various departments, whereas in the formal presentation the specialist proposals are joined together and presented as a co-ordinated plan.

At the presentation, the account executive usually outlines the market situation and the agency's approach to the client's problem. He then introduces individual members of the agency team who, in turn, present their own sections of the campaign and explain the reasoning behind them. The research staff outline how prospective customers were defined; the media planner in his turn presents the schedule designed to reach the market defined by research; and the creative staff show and discuss the proposed advertisements. Experts from other departments may also be called on to clarify their particular part of the plan. Finally, the account executive concludes the presentation by summarising the major points made and the reasoning behind them.

An effective presentation is of major importance, because the client's acceptance of an agency's proposals depends on a clear understanding of the many complex and interlocking sections of the campaign plan. Cases are not unknown where a campaign has been rejected, not because the plan was a bad one but because the agency failed to explain adequately the thinking behind it. For this reason, agencies often go to considerable lengths to ensure that the client has a clear understanding of the proposals. On the media side, charts are prepared (some often very elaborate) to present visually the proposed schedule and further charts are used to clarify the reasons why this particular media pattern has been selected. Some agencies even have 'charting departments', set up solely to prepare the visual aids necessary for perfect presentation of their proposals.

Where the presentation is on a major campaign, the agency may call on all those concerned to make a 'dry run' beforehand, amounting almost to a rehearsal, and may go to the extent of preparing scripts for the entire proceedings, showing the order of speaking, the words to be spoken by each individual, and the charts, slides or other visual aids to be used. Some agencies even put the entire presentation on film or video and screen this to the client, rather than risk the possibility of error that is always present in a 'live' presentation. Presentation techniques have become increasingly sophisticated, with agencies using computerised and electronic systems rather than the standard visual aids. This sounds an elaborate procedure, as indeed it is, but it could be well worth while in ensuring that the campaign is faultlessly presented. It is all too easy when speaking to overlook some point or fail to express it clearly, or to take points out of order and so destroy the logic of an argument. The more complex the scheme, the greater the need for the details and the reasoning behind them to be made completely clear. As marketing problems and advertising planning become more complex, so the need for lucid presentation becomes even more vital.

Execution of proposals

Before giving the agency formal approval to proceed, the client checks the proposals to ensure that they are sound and that they dovetail with his company's marketing activities. Once the agency has the client's agreement, the advertising proposals can be put into effect: the media schedule must be converted into actual orders to media-owners and parallel action must be taken by creative staff and other departments to bring their proposals to finished form. The detail of this work is described in Part 3.

The control department

The control department is often described, and with justification, as the nerve centre of an agency. Its function is evident from the various titles by which it may be described – 'progress', 'traffic', 'control', or 'copy detail'. It controls the progress or traffic of detailed work, and the smooth functioning of the agency turns to a great extent on the efficiency of this department.

Copies of media orders come to the traffic department and set in motion the complex procedure of producing an advertisement. Take, for example, the task of handling a straightforward insertion in a Christmas issue. The booking may be made many months in advance, but it would be foolish to wait until the last minute and then do a rush job, since this rarely results in effective advertising. The control department, therefore, undertakes the complicated arithmetic of routing the advertisement through the agency. The copy detail staff must prepare a detailed time schedule, working back from the media-owner's copy date, which may be weeks or even months in advance of publication date. Time must be allowed for typesetting and production and for correction of proofs by both client and agency. Account must also be taken of the time needed to produce artwork, and to mark up copy for typesetting. Before this work can be done, the copy must be written and a visual prepared, and adequate time must be allowed for these to be submitted to the client and approved. Even before the creative team can start work, the account executive must contact the advertising manager, to see if there are any special requirements for this Christmas advertisement, and this, too, must be allowed for in the time schedule.

The control department must anticipate the time needed for each of these stages and build in a safety margin to allow for unexpected delays and, if necessary, the revision of copy, visuals, or proofs. A time-schedule must be prepared, allowing so many days for each stage, and careful watch must be kept to ensure that no delays occur anywhere along the line. If there is delay on the part of someone early in the chain, some other unfortunate individual will, later on, have to race against time. Too much haste seldom produces good work, as well as greatly increasing the possibility of error – and mistakes in advertising tend to be *very* expensive. A good control department thus makes for efficiency and prevents costly errors, as well as directly affecting the quality of the agency's work.

In addition to press advertisements, the control department is frequently responsible for the progress of television and radio commercials, printed material, exhibition stands – in fact all agency work, whatever the medium. With a major campaign, where media and creative proposals are submitted together for approval, the work of the department even extends to ensuring that the proposals are ready in good time for submission (and prior checking by the review board). Once the proposals are approved, the control department also supervises their execution.

Vouchers and accounts

Just as the advertising manager checks to see that his company receives value for money spent on advertising, so does the agency. The voucher section checks that the correct advertisement appeared on the appointed day, in the position booked and that the printing quality was up to the required standard. Not until the voucher copy has been checked is the media-owner's invoice passed through for payment. The location of the voucher section varies: in some agencies it is part of the media department, in others it is attached to the production or control departments or is an extension of the accounts department.

Other departments

The general pattern of agency operations remains the same whatever the variations in size and agency structure: problem analysis, preparation of media and creative proposals to solve that problem, and execution of the approved proposals. The proposals are based on the three functions of advertisement creation, media selection and production work, and these three form the essence of agency service.

In the course of time, however, and reflecting the increasing complexity of marketing problems, many agencies have extended the scope of their services by developing other departments, staffed with experts capable of solving specialist sections of their client's marketing problem. Some agencies, for example, have a special research department, and other activities such as television, marketing, merchandising, sales promotion, below-the-line media, public relations and international operations may also merit the status of separate departments, each under its own director. Some agencies develop these activities in another way, by establishing subsidiary or associated companies which operate on a commercial basis, and offer their services to all, rather than restricting them to the agency's immediate clients. As well as being profitable in their own right, such companies can also play an important part in attracting new clients to an agency.

Television The specialist nature of television advertising once led some agencies to group the various specialists together in a working unit, rather than leave them in the various departments that would normally house them. Production of television commercials calls for different expertise than for printed media; the agencies therefore include specialist television producers on their staff. Similarly, on the creative side, the agency's staff may include specialist storyboard artists and scriptwriters, who think in terms of moving rather than still pictures, and the spoken rather than the printed word. On the media side, as we have seen, specialist time-buyers may be employed.

Whatever the agency structure, the aim is to create effective television commercials and to screen them to best advantage. It is now rare to concentrate all television staff in a single department and, where separate television departments do still exist, they tend to concentrate on the production side, and to leave time-buying to the media department.

Merchandising In reviewing the advertising manager's work the point was made that, as well as stimulating public demand for his company's products, he must also ensure that they are on display in the shops and readily available for customers to buy. In consequence, a considerable amount of merchandising activity is aimed at retail outlets and the company's sales force to ensure that the public campaign is well backed-up at point of sale. Some larger agencies have specialist staff to advise clients on this vital work or, where the advertiser does not have experts in this field, to mount complete merchandising campaigns for him.

Sales Promotion Just as larger agencies have specialist staff to advise clients on merchandising, many have special Sales Promotion sections – reflecting the great increase in direct marketing.

Marketing Like merchandising, marketing may be the province of the agency as well as the advertiser. Some agencies have special marketing staff who co-operate with clients in analysing and assessing consumer wants and needs and devising marketing programmes to satisfy them.

Some agencies have even gone to the extent of establishing their own retail outlets which operate independently on a profit-making basis. Such shops provide the agency with invaluable first-hand information about the market, and can be used for testing products, packaging, or other elements of the marketing mix.

Public relations As we have already seen, PR may be added to the responsibilities of the advertising manager or may be delegated to a specialist section of the agency. A number of agencies have a PR department, fully staffed by experts who work in co-operation with their clients: others may provide a similar service through associated or subsidiary companies. Either way, the aim is still a 'deliberate, planned and sustained effort to establish and maintain mutual understanding between the organisation and its publics'.

International With so many organisations tending to operate internationally, a number of advertising agencies now extend their services to include advising clients on business activities overseas. This is done in a variety of ways. Some agencies have branch offices in a chain of overseas centres, staffing them with both local personnel and head-office experts. Others forge financial links by taking over the ownership of an existing overseas agency. This method has the advantage of acquiring an established business organisation which is already operating successfully with an expert staff and avoids the many problems of starting from scratch. Other agencies extend their services more informally by teaming up with similar agencies in important overseas centres, which are then described as 'associate companies', each agency helping the other, and its clients, by advice on its own market. Though each associate agency benefits from the association, the other methods described afford certain advantages that cannot be achieved by such informal links. Financial control ensures that better liaison and common thinking can be achieved than through 'associateship' alone, and there is the further assurance that the agency's operation will be kept in line with what is required.

AGENCY SYSTEMS

Quite apart from departmental variations, agencies also differ in their system of operation. Some use the 'pyramid' system, under which directors are responsible for a group of accounts (rather than for staff members) and the executive, media, creative or other staff may all work on several accounts, each of which may be under the control of a different director. Others operate on the 'group' system whereby the agency is divided into two or more separate units, each of which amounts to a self-contained agency.

The group system adopted by many larger agencies has various advantages: each account group becomes a profit centre, it enables the agency to handle competing accounts (provided clients agree), and staff can be switched between groups from time to time to bring fresh input to the accounts handled.

The media department may work on either the pyramid or group system.

Specialist agencies

Some agencies, rather than expand by diversifying their departments, prefer to concentrate their abilities, as in the case of an agency specialising in technical advertising. Copywriting for industrial products demands a degree of technical knowledge that the average consumer-product copywriter does not possess. Similarly, technical illustrations such as cross-sections of machinery may prove outside the average agency creative expertise. Specialist agencies, whose staff have the necessary technical knowledge and skills, thus take their place on the agency scene. Similarly, the particular needs of recruitment advertising have led some agencies to concentrate on this specialist area. Others have specialised in below-the-line media, sales promotion, direct marketing, or business-to-business.

Other 'agencies' concentrate their abilities in a different way. Rather than provide the full service of advertisement creation, media planning and buying, and production work, they restrict their expertise to one of these three functions, and it is thus possible to call on specialist services for creative work only. On the media side, the media independents (described in the following chapter) – the companies that undertake responsibility for buying media on behalf of advertisers (independently of the agency providing the creative work) – are now an important feature of the current advertising scene.

'Merger mania'

The advertising agency world has always been a fast-changing one, but has become increasingly so in recent years. Some agencies have taken over others, or set up specialist subsidiaries, to broaden the portfolio of services offered to clients.

Some larger agency groups have become what amounts to a conglomerate of autonomous companies and, as well as operating the full service concept, also offer an 'a la carte' or 'cafeteria' service from which clients select whatever services they wish.

Agency standards

The range of services provided – and the standard of these services – must necessarily vary from agency to agency, and so we should not leave this chapter without a brief discussion of the Institute of Practitioners in Advertising – the agencies' professional body. Whilst there is nothing to prevent someone without any real knowledge of the subject from hiring an office and putting up a sign proclaiming himself an 'advertising agent', it is a very different state of affairs if a firm wishes to announce that it is an advertising agency in membership of the IPA, because, before agencies are permitted to style themselves 'Incorporated Practitioners in Advertising', they will have to conform to the rigorous standards laid down by the Institute regarding – amongst other criteria – professional competence, independence and business experience.

The applicant agency is required to demonstrate its professional competence as an organisation concerned primarily with the services of creating and/or placing advertising. Such services can include, or represent, specialisation in consumer or business-to-business advertising, media placement, direct marketing, creative consultancy or recruitment advertising.

The applicant agency must show that it maintains an independent judgement in professional matters, and is not directly or indirectly controlled by an advertiser or group of advertisers whose advertising it handles, or by concerns wholly or mainly interested in the sale of advertising media or services. There is an overriding proviso that the agency should not have entered into any engagement which would cause it to devote its main energies to the service of any particular advertiser or limited group of advertisers.

The agency should be equipped to deal with a national advertising campaign in the UK, and should have been in business long enough to have established its experience and financial stability.

There are of course other requirements. The IPA looks at the financial resources and credit standing of the agency, its recognition by the various media trade bodies, the agency's experience, and the range and variety of accounts handled.

Apart from a few exceptions, all top-level agencies are members of the IPA, and it is estimated that these agencies handle well over 90 per cent of all the advertising placed through agencies in the United Kingdom.

Chapter 10

Role of the Media Independents

BACKGROUND

As pointed out in the previous chapter some agencies, rather than expand by diversifying their departments, prefer to concentrate their abilities. Rather than provide the full service of advertisement creation, media planning and buying, and production work, they restrict their expertise to one of these areas. These independent companies now form such an important part of the current advertising scene that they merit separate attention in this chapter.

What was originally thought to be a temporary phenomenon has turned out to be a substantial and permanent feature of the advertising industry. These organisations are no longer described, as they were originally, as media-brokers or buying shops. The term 'Media Independent' is not fully adequate but does describe these companies which specialise in all aspects of the media side of advertising, yet are independent of the traditional agency structure, and of any specialist creative or production company.

In order to understand why these specialist media planning and buying companies have prospered, we must examine both the service they provide and the clients who use it.

What service is provided? Media independents are specialised and have grown because they are cost-effective streamlined organisations which employ skilled media talent. Because they have no other distractions, and no other pressures are brought to bear, they are able to devote this talent with undivided attention to the task of media.

Why should any organisation call on the services of a media independent? There is no single answer. A number of advertisers found that conventional full-service agencies did not meet their particular needs or budgets. The economic climate forced some companies to look for alternative systems and, as media costs continued to rise, many advertisers turned with new interest to ways of stretching their budgets. The media independents offered them a system that side-stepped the fixed 15 per cent commission rate and employed some of the best media-buyers in the business. Clients with expert marketing departments could formulate their own products, select a skilled team of creative people to prepare the advertisements and appoint a separate team of experts to plan and book the schedule.

As marketing departments grow more skilful, so they are better able – and are often more inclined – to commission specific tasks, and they now have a far wider range of specialist teams from which to choose, to perform these selected tasks. Some companies adopt the system of using several creative companies to develop different campaigns for different products, and one media independent to place the advertisements. As clients become more sophisticated, and the media independents (and complementary creative services) prosper, some extremists have suggested that full-service agencies will have to hive off their media departments and run them like independents (some already have) or perhaps break down their range of services into four or five specialist departments operating like a conglomerate of independents – a self-service advertising cafeteria from which clients can select the dishes they want. There are two opposing schools of thought on this topic, with very different views held by the very people you would expect to hold them!

One extreme view – held by some independents – is that a trend has started which will mean the end of many traditional agencies, particularly those of a medium size which cannot afford to match the talents available within independents. It is argued that clients get a better service because independents employ the best talent to do nothing but media, and this in turn means that they must be extremely competitive. With a full-service agency, the client might find some services extremely good but others, particularly media, weak. The media independents point out that a small team of experts in media planning is usually better than a large team which includes some middling talent, and that a client using an independent can be sure the company is surviving by being competitively successful at one particular thing. The independents are not cheap, but claim to give better value for money: they make better use of the funds allocated to them and give their clients a better financial deal. There is an appreciable cost-saving and the money saved can be used to buy more media, which is the main purpose of the exercise in the first place. This school of thought argues that there is no reason for advertisers to use a full-service agency to plan and buy their media requirements, unless the agency is prepared to waive the fixed 15 per cent commission rate in favour of a payment system better than that offered by the independents – and, even if this were granted, the independents would still do a *better* job.

The opposing school of thought – found, of course, in the agencies – is that there will always be a need for the superior resources and fertile inter-connections of the full-service agency. Companies without internal resources of experienced advertising and marketing staff need help in straightening out their advertising strategies and marketing planning. While a media independent will perform its allotted task very efficiently, all depends on what it is asked to do, and the independent may not have the agency's wide knowledge of marketing and of the client's marketing in particular. It is not only unsophisticated companies which need full-service agencies, however. Advertisers with a wide variety of communication needs, and different levels of campaign running simultaneously for a range of different products, need a full-service agency to co-ordinate for them. But, whether the client has few internal resources or is extremely sophisticated, the underlying point is the vital one: that by using a media independent advertisers lose the benefits resulting directly from the integral structure of the full-service agency, where creative, media and account people work together as one team under the same direction. The criticism made of the independents is that everything is brought down to the lowest common denominator: cost. Furthermore, as media independents are often divorced from the creative strategy, they are less efficient than their agency counterparts in making media choices which acknowledge creative demands, and the penalty of not using a full-service agency must be measured by the loss in effectiveness of the total advertising investment.

The casting vote between these extreme viewpoints must be with the clients who appoint the media independents in the first place and decide what services they need, so it is important to recognise that it is not only advertisers who employ the independents' services. The client profile for the media independents now covers the whole gamut of opportunities – advertisers, agencies, creative consultancies and design groups, and even media-owners and management consultancies.

Many small agencies now place some or all of the media planning or buying in the hands of the media specialists, but it is not only the small firms who do this: quite a few medium-sized agencies enlist outside media assistance, particularly where TV buying is concerned. Media independents are getting business from new agencies without media departments, set up by people who are building agencies they would like to be different from the large ones they have left. They have decided not to offer clients a full service in-house but to use media independents to do their buying (and often their planning) for them, and some new agencies without media departments are viable only because of the independents. These companies are providing the top creative and account-handling experience that complement the media independents' own services to clients. Added to this, the rise of separate media-buying companies has also opened up the field for the creative consultants, whose work has multiplied over the years.

The media independents are now in a period of evolution rather than revolution, and the 'either/or' syndrome no longer applies so rigidly – advertisers and agencies recognise that the independents have a lot to offer, can save time and money and cut down administration costs.

SERVICES PROVIDED

It is interesting to note the wide variety of services now offered. Some independents work in an advisory capacity but do not plan or buy campaigns – while others specialise in international business. Furthermore, the ways in which the media independents are integrating have become increasingly flexible – they co-operate not only with creative consultancies and the new-type agencies but also work freely with advertiser/agency partnerships direct – some advertisers now use media independents working alongside their existing agencies, rather than seeing them as competitors as was the case in the past. Media planning and buying have always been difficult tasks, and the growth of new media opportunities (including the proliferation of terrestrial, satellite and cable TV channels and the expansion of selective press media) has meant increased demand on the independents' talents.

There is no longer any need to argue for the respectability of what were called buying shops – it is now firmly established that most media independents are run by professionals. This professionalism was recognised more formally, however, by the formation of the Association of Media Independents. In order to establish the calibre of companies seeking membership, the Association checks that applicants meet various criteria as laid down in its memorandum and articles.

Firstly, the applicant company must be in the business of media buying, with billings and a client list which show that its capacity extends across major media and that its practice is not unduly restricted. The company must also have received recognition by the various media-trade bodies.

A second requirement is that the applicant firms are of high professional standing: they must give a written undertaken to provide any first-hand client with copies of invoices from media-owners, showing prices at which space or time was bought on their behalf. The applicant firm must also give a formal undertaking to abide by the Code of Advertising Practice.

A third requirement for Association membership is that applicants are of sound financial standing and, to this end, must provide the last set of accounts as submitted to one of the recognition bodies.

A fourth requirement is that the applicant company be independent of any advertiser, agency or media-owner and, to establish this independence, the applicant company must submit to the Association details of its company shareholdings and corporate structure. More than two-thirds of the turnover of the independent sector is handled by AMI members.

Chapter 11

Specialist Services

This chapter is brief and necessarily overlaps with earlier material: the chapter on media research and services pointed out the possibility of special computer runs based on available data, and the media-owner chapter touched on the many additional services provided in addition to delivery of your advertising message.

The purpose of this chapter is to draw attention to the fact that it is not only advertisers, agencies and media-owners who can contribute to your effective use of media: there are other specialist services which can assist in improving your advertising effectiveness.

Media independents merited a separate chapter, which also mentioned the corresponding growth in creative consultancies. On the media side, national and specialist sales houses play an increasingly important part, enabling media-owners to sub-contract or supplement their media sales operation, thereby providing a better service to advertisers and agencies.

Computer bureaux or in-house facilities also make an increasingly important contribution, in respect of data handling. This broad heading covers not only the provision of further tabulations of existing data, but also a wide spectrum of additional data-processing activities. One end of the scale covers the relatively straightforward (but nevertheless vital) 'housekeeping' functions such as orders, schedules, vouchering, invoices, payment advice, and budget versus expenditure analysis, etc. At the other end of the scale are sophisticated media-planning operations which could include cross-tabulations and market area breakdowns, cost per thousand and cover rankings, duplication tables and cumulative coverage, schedule construction and analysis, evaluation of schedule performance over time, and the many media-planning activities discussed in detail in Part 3.

There are many firms active in the 'housekeeping' and/or media-planning aspects of data processing. Needless to say, not all of these firms offer the full range of data-handling activities listed, and others specialise in particular aspects of media service.

Other 'house-keeping' aspects of advertising can also be contracted out. It may well be vital to do so because any firm which invests advertising money in stimulating the market should gear itself up to respond swiftly to the interest generated. It would be very unwise, for example, to underestimate the task of handling the deluge of simultaneous calls which might result from featuring your phone number in a TV commercial. Specialist services not only have the technology to respond with minimal delay, but can also undertake prompt despatch of literature. Even when no 'instant' response is required, 'fulfillment houses' can relieve you of the 'mechanical' chores of storing and despatch. Such sub-contracting serves a double purpose: it reduces the risk of losing prospective purchasers by speeding up response and, at the same time, frees your own staff to concentrate on their proper functions.

While many special needs have existed for years and are covered by the services of long-established companies, the swiftly-changing nature of the business world means that new needs are constantly arising. More often than not, new organisations are set up to cater for these new needs.

Part 3
THE EFFECTIVE USE OF ADVERTISING MEDIA

Having considered the range of advertising media available to communicate your advertising message, and the organisations and individuals concerned, we can now examine the *effective* use of media under the following chapter headings:

a *Research and investigation* Gathering the company, product and market data essential for effective planning.

b *Advertising strategy* Deciding your campaign objective, which directly affects both media selection and the creative approach to be featured.

c *Budgeting* Fixing the advertising appropriation so that you spend the right amount on achieving your chosen objective.

d *Preparation of advertising proposals* Planning an advertising campaign, creating advertisements and selecting media, to achieve your chosen objective.

e *Approval of proposals* Checking, prior to executing the campaign, that your proposals are likely to achieve success.

f *Execution of these proposals* Putting your plan into effect.

g *Follow through* Ensuring that your company is geared up to cope with the response generated by advertising.

h *Evaluation of results* Checking that you received value for money, and identifying what lessons can be learned for the future.

197

These are the component tasks that overall – whether undertaken by advertiser or agency, and in which the media-owner is directly involved – make for good advertising. These tasks should be a closed loop, and evaluation of the results of this year's campaign should provide additional information on which to base next year's planning.

Chapter 12

Research and Investigation

Before you start planning to use advertising media, it is essential to have a thorough knowledge of many business aspects. You must have a full background knowledge before considering any advertising, for unless your campaign reflects these facets of your business, it cannot work to full advantage.

YOUR FIRM

A full knowledge of all aspects of your firm is essential. Is it old-established so that emphasis could be placed on tradition, or is it alternatively a newly-formed pioneer? Where is it based? Are you, in fact, considering a single organisation, or perhaps a range of companies? Do they operate nationally, internationally or multinationally? Do these companies operate individually with separate advertising identities, or does some corporate theme link them together? If the latter, this should surely be reflected in your own advertising. If the former, how are these autonomous profit-centres co-ordinated? It would clearly be a waste of advertising money to pre-empt your own companies on television rather than your competitors! Does your firm have access to the management services and skills of a parent company? Is sufficient finance available to mount an extensive advertising campaign? Clearly all these considerations affect not only the size and type of your advertising campaign but also its contents, so a thorough knowledge of these different aspects is essential.

YOUR PRODUCTS

Equally important is complete knowledge of the products or services to be advertised (both individually and over the complete range), since this can affect media policy just as much as creative content. Are they marketed individually or under a 'family' brand? Prices, sizes, colours, flavours, packing – all are important. What are the limits to the amount your factory can produce: there is no point in over-selling and thus boosting sales of competitors' lines. What does your product actually do? Does it have a single use, or are you considering a multi-ple-use product? Sales might be increased, for example, by including recipes in the advertisements, thus pointing out additional uses for your product. Is there any special guarantee, or after-sales service? Is the service element more important than the product itself, as far as users are concerned? Perhaps you are considering a service as such, and your firm is a service organisation rather than a manufacturing company.

Clearly all these different aspects have direct implications for the planning of your advertising campaign. Whether the facts are supplied to you by the production staff or, as is more likely, you try the product for yourself, you must obtain all this vital information. Furthermore, you must ensure that you are notified, well in advance, of any possible changes. Having thoroughly studied the merchandise, you can now proceed to study the potential purchasers of your goods, known in advertising terminology as the 'market'.

YOUR MARKET

You must have a clear picture of the customers likely to be interested in your goods. Are they men or women? Married or single? What ages are they? What is their income? Of what 'class' are your customers – the man-in-the-street and his wife, or the 'professionals'? Who makes the actual purchase, and who influences the buying decision? The housewife may buy, but act in accordance with the wishes of her husband or children. Perhaps your potential customers are distinguished by a particular special interest, whether of race or creed, hobby or occupation. Sometimes the buyers may be other organisations rather than individuals, but it is equally important in such cases to know who makes the purchase and who influences it and what the buying process is.

Where are your customers located – are they local, in another part of the country, or spread throughout the world? Clearly this affects where you place your advertising. When do your customers buy, and how often? This information influences the timing of your campaign, and the frequency of the advertisements. Is your product bought on impulse, or only after careful consideration? How long is this consideration period? This, too, clearly affects timing, and the type of campaign to be mounted.

What use do your customers make of your product, why do they buy it and why do they select one brand in preference to others? How strong is their brand loyalty? Are some people more likely than others to adopt your new products? How many potential buyers are there? Do some buyers use the product more heavily than others? An effective approach is to segment your market into Users and Non-users, and then further segment the former group into Light, Medium and Heavy users. And are their numbers increasing or decreasing, and if so at what rate?

Part 1 outlined the socio-economic categories into which much current research groups people, and those concerned with advertising planning have long been used to looking at demographic differences (measures such as age, income and social grade) between buyers and non-buyers. Sometimes, however, demographic measures alone fail to show real differences and, furthermore, many attitudes and interests which you might expect to relate to social grade are not, in fact, associated with grade.

Lifestyle classifications

Because of these weaknesses in the customary classifications, new techniques have been developed which try to distinguish buyers from non-buyers of a product by classification of personality type rather than conventional demographics. Life-style or psychographic research is a relatively new alternative approach to understanding your consumers. By gathering comprehensive information about people's attitudes, interests and activities, it produces generalised consumer profiles which are claimed to delineate 'real live people' in a superior way to the more traditional methods of classification. Protagonists assert that it has already demonstrated considerable potential in identifying new market segments and opportunities (as well as providing an extra creative input for advertising).

Anyone who has read the James Bond novels will recall how Ian Fleming's descriptions of 007's clothes, cars and drinking habits give a far more realistic impression of his life-style than simply describing him as an A-grade consumer. (Bond enthusiasts who quibble that he is only intermediate rather than senior managerial, administrative or professional will not argue over his distinctive life-style!). This is an extreme example, but a more down-to-earth and practical approach has been developed which classifies people according to brief 'pen-portraits' which describe their background, attitudes and habits - rather than grouping them in social grades according to the head of household's occupation.

Another approach to considering your market is in terms of *Sagacity*

Groups, a lifestyle classification developed by Research Services Ltd. This alternative way of classifying consumers takes into account the individual's lifestyle, income and expenditure, and breaks the population down into groups according to whether they are 'blue or white collar', in the dependent, pre-family, family or late stage of life; in the last two stages respondents are also classified as better-off or worse-off, thus making 12 groups in all. Each group is designed to be as homogenous as possible, and contain respondents at a similar stage of their life cycle, with similar disposable income and cultural characteristics. These Sagacity groups are found to exhibit different behaviour patterns over a wide range of markets, in terms of media behaviour and product usage. The classifications are based on National Readership Survey data and give an interesting addition to the standard demographic classifications.

Geodemographic classification

Another way of considering your market is in geodemographic terms. The ACORN (A Classification of Residential Neighbourhood) groupings classification into nearly 40 neighbourhood types can indicate different life-styles, different patterns of expenditure and different levels of exposure to advertising media. An extension of this approach is the CLS (Consumer Location System) analysis which relates people's purchasing, reading and viewing habits to the type of neighbourhood in which they live, by linking information generated by the Target Group Index, described in Chapter 4, to the various ACORN categories.

There are various other ways of classifying your market geodemographically, including:

MOSAIC, developed by CCN Systems, provides a classification system comprising 58 postcode types (e.g. *High status retirement areas with many single pensioners, High status retirement areas with married owner occupiers*, or *High status retirement areas with rented flats for elderly* through to *Hamlets and scattered farms*).

PiN, developed by Pinpoint, splits the country into 3 levels of area types ranging from 12 major *PiN* area types (e.g. *Upwardly mobile young families, Affluent households, Older people in small houses* etc) through to 60 more specific *PiN* types.

Superprofiles, developed by Demographic Profiles Ltd, consists of 37 *Super profile* consumer types which can be summarised into 11 lifestyles (e.g. *Stockbroker belt, Young metro singles*, or *Young married suburbia*)

Workforce, another variation on the 'Where' question has turned attention to where people work, by means of a classification system developed by CACI. This operates in the same way as ACORN, in that it can function as a management/media information tool, for market identification and business location, and as an aid to market segmentation.

Media Usage

Another approach to classifying your buyers and potential buyers is to think of their *media* habits and attitudes. It is always salutory to remember that the easiest way to define a fashion-conscious woman is to point her out as 'one who reads fashion magazines'. Many firms already categorise their markets in terms of heavy, medium, light and non-users, and the same thinking can be applied to their 'use' of media – are they heavy, medium, light or non-users of television, radio, newspapers, magazines or other media? Some advertisers now link their target markets with media audiences by relating them to the so-called Media Imperative groupings, which break the population down into four quartiles according to their media preference. Some women, for example, watch a great deal of television and are also heavy readers of women's magazines, others are more exposed to one of these two media than the other, while some women are difficult to reach through either medium. In this way, the population can be divided into four Media Preference Groups: Dual High (heavy exposure to both media), TV Preference (more exposure to TV than to print), Magazine Preference (those who read more than they view) and Dual Low (those with low exposure to both media). These preference groups, when related to heavy, medium, light or non-usage of your product, can be a most useful aid to media selection and planning. The classifications are based on Target Group Index data, and can provide a further interesting addition to the ways in which you can relate markets and media. Later, when selecting media to reach your chosen market, you should always bear in mind that advertising communication is a two-way process – how do your consumers use the media you are using to reach them?

In practice, you may well find that you have more than one homogenous target group, so it would be more accurate to refer to *market segments* than to *market*. For effective media planning, each segment must be clearly defined and sizes, trends and priorities established – without this knowledge, how can you start constructing a media schedule which delivers your advertising message to your selected target groups?

Knowledge of all these market factors is vital if your advertising campaign is to be effective. Considerable time and money can usefully be spent on research before planning begins, for unless you know your potential market segments you cannot select media to reach these people, nor create advertisements that will appeal to them. In addition you must bear in mind that your market is not static, but constantly changing as old customers leave and new ones come along. The replacement customers may perhaps be different and motivated by other desires, so that mere repetition of previously successful advertising may not show the same results. Market knowledge must be kept up-to-date, and your advertising policy adjusted accordingly. Study of market trends is, in fact, a never-ending task.

With knowledge of your firm and its products and market, you must now make a study – of how your company plans to sell these products to that market: in short, its marketing policy.

YOUR MARKETING POLICY

Advertising policy is affected by, and should reflect your company's marketing policy. The concept of marketing was outlined earlier, and your advertising campaign should bear direct relation to a number of marketing factors. Is the purpose of your advertising to launch a new product, a reminder campaign for an existing one, or an attempt to halt a decline in the market? If, on the other hand, your marketing decision is to increase sales, how is this to be achieved? Is the drive to be in a particular area? Is distribution of your product completely even across the entire country or is it regionally biased, or perhaps even limited to certain areas? Many companies divide their selling territory into areas, and the total marketing operation thus comprises a number of individual sales drives. A phased or 'rolling' product launch may be spread over a given time period, successively covering one area after another until national (or sometimes international) distribution is achieved. This will clearly affect media planning, since it calls for heavy initial advertising in appropriate areas during the launch periods, followed by a reminder campaign during the months that follow. Even where distribution is nationwide, your marketing decision may be to increase sales by pin-pointing a particular segment of the market (as distinct from a geographical area) for special attention, rather than attack on all fronts. Clearly, such marketing decisions directly affect media selection, and for effective use of advertising media you must appreciate the policy behind the choice made.

What is the structure of your sales force? How many sales staff does your company employ and how long does it take them to complete their round of calls? Do they call on all retailers, or rely on wholesalers to reach the smaller outlets? How dominant a role do the multiple shops and chains play? Is your product available freely or only in selected outlets? The need to feature names and addresses of local agents may have a marked influence on media selection. Are trade discounts competitive, or has your firm an advantage or disadvantage over rival producers? Promotional policies differ and manufacturers may adopt either a 'push' or a 'pull' approach – with the latter you give minimal discounts and use massive public advertising and sales promotion to pull your merchandise through the retail outlets. The retailer gets only a small amount per unit, but prospects of large sales stimulated by public advertising make him realise it will be to his advantage to stock your merchandise, so that he is ready to meet the public demand stimulated by your advertising. With a 'push' campaign, on the other hand, little is spent on public advertising, but heavy merchandising and attractive trade discounts are used to persuade the retailer to promote your goods, in view of the large sum he gets for every unit sold. In practice, naturally, it is rarely a question of operating at either extreme end of this push-pull scale but at some intermediate point, but clearly such factors determine whether or not to use the trade press and the timing of the support campaign.

With a thorough knowledge of firm and products, market and marketing policy, you must next study previous advertising.

PREVIOUS ADVERTISING

You must check carefully what advertising has appeared in the past and with what results, and see what lessons can be learned to increase the effectiveness of future campaigns. All too often money is wasted through failure to keep adequate records. Careful checking of results can lead to increased efficiency, bringing better results for the same expenditure, or achieving the same results for less outlay. Either way, the benefit to your company is obvious and previous advertising must, therefore, never be overlooked. Which advertising media proved effective in the past? What creative approaches appealed to prospective customers? What did these call for in terms of advertisement size, position, use of colour, and timing and duration of the campaign? Before planning future advertising you should check what you can learn from the past and, as has already been made clear, evaluation of the results of this year's campaign should provide the basis of next year's planning. This preliminary stage of research and investigations is thus directly linked with the final planning stage of evaluation of results, to which a later chapter is devoted.

CONSTRAINTS

In considering you, future advertising plans, you may be faced with two different types of constraint – internal and external. Both should

205

directly influence your advertising planning.

Internal The points considered here should have first arisen when reviewing your company and its activities under earlier headings. Is there a limit to the number of products your company can produce? – there is no point in stimulating demand you cannot satisfy. Will financial constraints restrict your advertising budget? Is your distribution restricted to certain areas? – this will influence your media selection. Do you have a list of dealers whose names and addresses must be featured in your advertising? – this will affect choice of media, size of space booked and your creative content.

External Advertising practice is not a free-for-all with no holds barred. There are a number of legal constraints and voluntary codes that limit your actions. In some cases the constraint is fundamental and dictates media policy, e.g. you cannot advertise cigarettes on television or radio. Clearly your researches must make you fully aware of what you are (and are not) allowed to do and say – how else can you prepare an advertising campaign that satisfies these requirements? What constraints does the Data Protection Act impose on your direct mail database? What, if any, are the implications of the Financial Services Act? How will your advertisements be affected by the Advertising Standards Authority's Code of Advertising Practice, the ITC's television code, or the Radio Authority's rulings? Detailed discussion of these legal and voluntary controls is beyond the scope of this book and, for the most part, they have creative rather than media implications.

COMPETITION

In investigating competition, you make not one study but at least six, since you must consider the competition faced from each of your rivals under the same six headings – firm, products, market, marketing policy, previous advertising and constraints.

What are the strengths and organisational weaknesses of rival companies? What products do your competitors make and how do they compare with your own? What are the strong and weak points of each? Who are your competitors' customers and how do they differ from those of your own company? And, most important, why do they purchase rival brands in preference to your own? Are your sales ahead or behind those of your competitors in the 'brand-share' table? Are you, or is one of your competitors, the brand leader and, if so, why? This may be due to differences in products or perhaps because of marketing policy, the next aspect of competitors' activity which you must study.

The marketing policy of competitive firms must be studied, item for item, against the points previously considered when investigating your own company's policy. Equal attention must be paid to the advertising campaigns of rival firms – which media do they use and what sizes and positions? How frequently do they advertise? What sales points are stressed in their advertisements and how are they illustrated? What are the constraints your competitors face? – these may give you a competitive advantage you can feature in your advertising.

During World War II, Field Marshall Montgomery had a photograph of Rommel in his caravan HQ in the North African desert. He knew that only by getting inside the mind of his opponent could he expect to out-think and beat him. In planning your advertising, it is vital that you have a similarly thorough knowledge of the competition you face from others. A clear understanding of the indirect competition which your own and rival brands face from other product groups can be equally important.

MEDIA

As you would expect, your investigations should include gaining a first-rate knowledge of advertising media, the need for which was made clear in Part 1. This investigation is best approached from the concept of 'candidate' media, which should indicate those media that merit *in-depth* study. You may consider, for example, that to reach your AB target markets you should use 'quality national newspapers', but your plan must be far more detailed than that. To select between these newspapers, and to use them in such a way that they make the maximum contribution to achieving your campaign objective, you must first study them in detail.

This in-depth investigation should go far beyond simple statistics (such as costs, circulations, and comparison of costs-per-thousand) because Average Issue Readership (AIR) is only an estimate of the number of people who have read or looked at a copy of the publication for at least two minutes during its issue period. While this information is important, you should ask if there really is such a thing as an 'average' issue? As different readers look at some pages more than others, this calls for in-depth analysis of both editorial content and advertising format. What features does each publication carry on a regular basis, on which days of the week, and is adjacent advertising possible? The same advertisement could be made more effective, for example, by booking particular positions on specified feature pages which appear on certain days of the week in any given publication. Such positioning not only pin-points those readers with interests relevant to your product, but also ensures that your advertisement reaches them when they are in a receptive frame of mind.

Gaining such in-depth knowledge of media is no small task: it calls for daily study of every copy of each relevant medium – and its competitors – over numerous issues. Hence the importance of the candidate media concept, and having neither too long nor too short a list before beginning your detailed planning. Too long a list, and you will never complete your task. Too short a list, and you could perhaps overlook a medium which, through *effective* use, could make a positive contribution.

BACKGROUND

When undertaking your research and investigations it is important to recognise that you – and your competitors – do not operate in isolation, but against the background of a national economy increasingly influenced by international factors. To assist you in reviewing this background and placing your organisation in it, there are two useful acronyms: P–E–S–T and S–W–O–T.

P–E–S–T

These initial letters represent four background areas with direct implications for the success (or failure) of your organisation: *P*olitical, *E*conomic, *S*ociological and *T*echnological.

Political This analysis is not a question of whether you vote Conservative, Labour or Liberal Democrat, but simply recognising that political decisions directly affect the day-to-day running of your business. Changes in tax structure, in capital allowances, or in development grants all illustrate how political decisions have immediate business implications. Changes in the law can be equally important.

Economic This area of course overlaps with the first, since different political parties have different policies for dealing with economic ills such as inflation, recession or unemployment. We must recognise, however, that our own economy is influenced by others – action on oil prices, changes in exchange rates, or other governments' decisions about interest rates all have far-reaching effects on the British standard of living.

Sociological Under this heading, you have only to consider the changing role of women and young people in our economy, the increasing number of single parents, general concern about health and environmental 'green' issues, or the development of Britain's multi-racial society, to realise their direct implications on any advertising or marketing campaign. In some cases, of course, sociological and political changes interact, for example, lowering the voting age from 21 to 18, or legislation regarding racial, religious or sexual discrimination.

Technological We live in an increasingly technological society – think of the constant flow of new and technologically improved products. Even if your own product is not undergoing a technological revolution, your organisation is certainly affected by technological changes, particularly as these affect advertising media. Printing quality has improved for most press media, colour is increasingly available and copy dates are shortening. Television is being revolutionised by satellite and cable technology. Direct mail has also undergone a technological revolution. To varying degrees, all advertising media have been affected.

S–W–O–T

These initial letters come from a well-known marketing analysis which has equal application to deciding advertising policy. Bearing in mind the many factors just reviewed and likely future trends, what are your *S*trengths and *W*eaknesses, and what are the *O*pportunities and *T*hreats facing your organisation?

THE IMPORTANCE OF RESEARCH

Without research into all eight points discussed above, it is impossible for you to plan effectively. Before thinking about future advertising, therefore, your first task is to make a full investigation of all these matters. Then, and only then, can you give thought to planning future advertising.

Research is vital for accurate media selection. Media planning can be likened to aiming a gun: you cannot hit a target unless you know what and where the target is, and it is research that frequently provides this information. Research also helps in timing your campaign, by indicating when your product is purchased and how frequently, and whether it is an impulse purchase or one that needs serious reflection, the latter calling for your advertising message to be delivered well in advance with subsequent reminders.

Research can equally be helpful to creative staff. Your product may have dozens of sales points, any one of which could be featured in your

209

advertising, and it is of major importance to select the particular benefit that will attract attention and lead readers to study your
advertisement more closely. Featuring the correct sales point attracts
attention and, equally, featuring the wrong 'copy platform' loses attention – and sales. Should the creative work be based on something of
lesser importance, the potential customers may not bother to read the
advertisement and will thus miss the sales point which *is* of major interest – and would have clinched the sale had they known of it.

Research can thus make a significant contribution to media planning and creative work by ensuring that it is soundly based. Its
purpose, however, is only to set the framework for media and creative
work: it will not prepare a media schedule nor the creative content of
your advertisements. Research does not dispense with the need for
good media planners or creative staff, but does provide an efficient tool
to make their work more effective.

Market research has been defined as 'the systematic study of products (and services) – existing or potential – in relation to their
markets'. You could obtain information by going out to interview
potential customers personally, but field research is both costly and
time-consuming, and the necessary information may already have
been collected by some other organisation. Research does not necessarily imply spending large sums of money calling in a professional
market research company to undertake scientifically planned investigations – although naturally the information that results from such
action can be invaluable. Research also includes your own reading, and
the number of information sources you can consult is extremely large:
there are numerous government surveys and reports, the many data
sources detailed in the chapters on media research and on specialist
sources, and there are the innumerable research documents published
by media-owners, advertisers and agencies. If to this list is added information available from analysis of your own internal records, the
research undertaken by trade, professional and technical associations
and institutions, and the reports and publications available from other
sources, then the wealth of information that is available, provided you
know where to look, will be apparent – as will the invaluable contribution of desk research. Good desk research could make field research
unnecessary by locating the information required, perhaps a bit here
and a bit there, in the many different published sources, and so not
only save the expenditure of several thousand pounds on a field survey,
but save vital time as well. Any book on media must necessarily cover
desk research and – as when field research was discussed in an earlier
chapter – there is thus an in-built tendency for it to become a book on
research as such. But a line must be drawn somewhere and so, having
drawn attention to its role in providing information on which to base
your planning, discussion of desk research will end here, other than

mentioning that a good librarian could provide you with invaluable help in locating relevant information sources, either direct or through various directories in which such sources are listed.

PLANNING YOUR PROGRAMME

It is important to recognise that, although listed as the Advertising Manager's first task, these initial investigations must be approached as an on-going programme. Situation analysis is in fact a never-ending exercise – today's newspapers may contain news that directly affects both you and your target groups, and markets must be monitored throughout the campaign.

Pareto Analysis

Many newly-appointed executives recognise that research never ends; their problem is 'where to begin?' For example, how should you set about situation analysis on joining a company with an extensive range of products, selling to numerous types of purchaser, spread across a large number of different markets? One solution is so-called 'Pareto analysis', applying the 80/20 rule based on previous profits.

Such analysis frequently shows some products, purchasers or markets to be more profitable than others, usually in an 80/20 ratio. If 80 per cent of your profits come from only 20 per cent of your product range, it is logical to concentrate initially on finding out all you can about those particular products. For those selected products, the same analysis can reveal which target groups are the most profitable, and within which particular markets. In this way, you identify the relatively small number of big buyers who merit most attention.

The converse is that 80 per cent of your products, purchasers and markets account for only 20 per cent of profits, and Pareto analysis can identify the many small buyers making only a limited contribution to profits, who merit less attention.

As we shall see later when discussing media planning, advertising expenditure can then be allocated between the more and less profitable target groups in the same proportions, according to their 'market weights' or values.

Always remember, however, that all market situations are necessarily in a constant state of flux. While the 80/20 rule is a sound starting point, do not overlook that its very opposite – 20/80 analysis – can often make an equally positive contribution. Hence the importance of a never-ending study of trends, to identify those products, purchasers or minority markets which, although making only a small profit contribution at present, are the 'big earners' of the future. Fighting competitors for today's markets should not prevent you from cultivating tomorrow's profitable target groups, which your rivals may not yet have identified.

The alternative approach

Pareto analysis, which implies that past profit figures are available for analysis, may be inapplicable for entirely new products. How could you set about planning to launch – with no previous data – a revolutionary new service, highly relevant to a wide range of possible purchasers within a large number of different market segments? Conventional research is both costly and time-consuming and, in any case, in which of these many markets should you begin your investigations? An alternative approach is to formally recognise this absence of data, spend your money on advertising rather than conventional research, use advertising as a research tool, and plan your campaign on the 'shotgun' principle. If both purchasers and markets are unknown quantities, it is clearly impossible to mount a focused campaign, and your objective must therefore be to get possible prospects to identify themselves. Accordingly, your campaign can then feature a large number of small direct-response advertisements spread over a wide range of candidate media. Your initial advertising serves a research function: those market segments requesting further information clearly merit attention, and future campaigns can be focused accordingly.

THE NEXT STEP

With your initial investigations complete, you now have a firm base on which to undertake your next task. This is determining your advertising strategy, described in the next chapter.

Chapter 13

Determining Your Advertising Strategy

With a thorough knowledge of your firm and its products, its market and marketing policy, your previous advertising, the various constraints imposed, the competition you face, candidate media, and business background, you can now commence more positive action – problem analysis and determination of your specific advertising objective.

Advertising is a means of achieving an objective. Your firm may have more than one reason for advertising, and thus need to run two or more concurrent advertising campaigns. The underlying purpose of these campaigns may also change from time to time, with circumstances.

There is a remarkably wide range of reasons for advertising - one well-known analysis[*] contains a checklist of 52 advertising tasks! Even the more fundamental reasons are, surprisingly enough, a blind spot to many advertising people, who are so engrossed in the detail of their work that they overlook the need to define clearly the basic purpose of their advertising. Many times, when you enquire about the the objective of a proposed advertising campaign, you receive a surprised look and the answer 'Why, it's to increase sales, of course' – as though you had asked a foolish question. But how are these increased sales to be achieved? 'Increased sales' is not a business objective but only an optimistic hope for the future. If these increased sales are, in fact, to be realised, then there must be a definite objective for, as you will see later, this will affect the type of advertising campaign, the media used and its creative content.

A useful exercise is to take a random selection of advertisements and

[*] *Defining Advertising Goods for Measured Advertising Results* by R. Colley (see Chapter 19).

213

try to 'read back' from the creative content just what was the *specific* objective. Very few participants in this exercise will achieve a 100 per cent strike rate, which surely proves two points:

1 Many advertising people have a blind spot when it comes to analysing advertising effectiveness.
2 Many advertisements are not effective, simply because those responsible for the campaign failed to establish a clear objective.

This may be a 'Heads I win, tails you lose' argument, but why else should we not be able to achieve a 100 per cent success rate in analysis?

In no way should you underestimate the importance of creativity in advertising, but creativity is functional only when it contributes to achieving your campaign objective. Specification of a clear objective assists creative people by setting the parameters within which they should work: it gives a strong indication of the creative approach necessary, quite apart from being essential for good media planning. This book concentrates on direct media aspects, but these cannot be treated separately from creative considerations.

ANALYSIS OF SPECIFIC OBJECTIVES

Analysis of advertising campaigns in a wide range of media revealed a large number of different specific objectives: these are discussed below, but not necessarily in any order of importance. The list is not exclusive, nor should the objectives be considered as separate 'water-tight' compartments. You may wish to achieve two or more purposes simultaneously – or perhaps your company has an objective not included in the list (I readily admit my own blind spot). The main point is the essential need to set out clearly, before starting to plan your campaign, *precisely* what you hope to achieve. Planning and creativity will then follow that much more easily. Some critics have argued that any systematic analysis must restrict the creative process. On the contrary, it should liberate creative staff, by ensuring that their efforts are concentrated on providing the ideal creative solution to the *real* problem facing the advertiser. Possible campaign objectives might include the following.

Reminding existing users

You must constantly remind users of your wares. Why 'must'? Well, human memory is short, and frequent reminders are necessary. Moreover, there are innumerable distracting factors which soon make memory fade. In some cases, it may be the advertising of rival firms.

There is also the competition for attention faced from makers of totally different products: television sets face indirect competition from washing machines, holidays abroad, or new furniture. Taking a still wider view of the many factors competing for public attention, there are thousands of non-selling influences at work to make people forget your products – the latest news at home and abroad, the activities of family and friends, new events at work and the latest films and television programmes. The manufacturer who expects to be permanently remembered amid this host of competing calls on public attention is more than optimistic. An apocryphal story tells how Wrigley, the chewing gum magnate, was once asked during a train journey why he spent so much money on advertising. Surely, his questioner asked, everybody knew Wrigley's chewing gum and everybody chewed Wrigley's chewing gum? Why the need for such heavy advertising? Wrigley supposedly replied that he would answer if the questioner told him how fast the train was going – and promptly denied he was changing the subject. When told that the train's speed was about 70 miles an hour, Wrigley immediately asked 'Why keep the engine on the front?' Reminder advertising maintains momentum in the same way and, if this is your objective, there are clear implications as to choice of media and creative content. Furthermore, constant reminders through advertising can enhance your firm's reputation and standing, and play their part in cementing customer loyalty. Reminder advertising is, however, quite distinct from the need to reassure previous purchasers – another specific purpose discussed below.

Reassuring previous purchasers

The need to reassure previous purchasers is a task quite different from that of simply reminding existing users. For many products, particularly where major expenditure is involved, current owners are key figures in the decision process of potential purchasers. If you reflect on any major purchase you have made, you will realise that in almost every case you sought the advice of somebody who had already bought the product. *Their* view was far more influential than any salesman, and much current advertising therefore takes account of the theory of 'cognitive dissonance'. This theory is based on the idea that if a person knows various things that are not psychologically consistent with each other he will, in a variety of ways, try to make them more consistent in order to reduce this dissonance. To illustrate how advertising planning should allow for this, take the case of someone who so dislikes waking up in ice-cold rooms that he installs central heating. After some months, the unpleasantness of cold mornings will fade from his memory, and all he remembers is the previously non-existent heating bills. Ask such a person for his views on central heating and you will hear how expensive it is to run and not a word about the benefits. As such negative reactions would put off prospective purchasers, much advertising recognises this and aims at reassuring previous purchasers just as much as attracting new ones. If your product comes into this category, the need to 'keep customers sold' has clear implications for both media choice and creative content.

Countering the natural decline in the market

Reminder advertising can be most effective in maintaining sales, but you must face up to the fact that your existing customers, through no fault of yours, are steadily decreasing in number. The manufacturer who claims there is no need to advertise because he has all the business he needs ignores the fact that people leave the area or the country, change their circumstances or just stop using his product. The quality of your product may remain as high as ever, but sales will steadily decline through the natural diminution of the existing market. As Lord Keynes once pointed out, in the long term we're all dead! New customers must be attracted to counter this decline, and advertising is one of the means available to achieve this end.

Informing the constant flow of potential customers

The population is ceaselessly changing, not ony in size but also in composition. As they grow older, people change from schoolchild to teenager, to young married to parent, and perhaps to grandparent. As they move from one consumer group to another, so their needs change; they become potential customers for goods which previously were of no interest to them. Similarly, in the technical field, firms change in size and in the scope of their operations, and need to purchase new plant, equipment or facilities. They become new prospects, and advertising can convert them into customers. Many firms mistakenly assume that, just because they have been advertising for years, people must know about the merchandise they have to offer. This ignores the fact that many prospective customers entered the market for the first time *today*, and earlier advertising therefore had only a limited effect. Research has proved that people look at advertisements for products which interest them, and ignore others. Yesterday these potential purchasers were not in the market, so were unlikely to respond to advertisements for the merchandise in question.

The constantly changing market

The fact that the market is ceaselessly changing is a blind spot for many advertisers. Markets steadily decline through natural causes, there are always potential new customers in need of information and, in the meantime, you need to remind and perhaps reassure existing customers. If you consider your own journey through life, the practical implications of this obvious statement become apparent. In your infancy you were, through your parents, in the market for nappies and talcum powder. As you left this market, the manufacturers of these products needed new customers to replace the sales lost when you no longer needed their merchandise. Your life can, in fact, be described in terms of products which you use for the first time, others about which you need reminding, and those which you eventually no longer need. Such a list would include school clothing, bicycles, razor blades and cosmetics, engagement and wedding rings, homes and furniture, baby clothes and prams, and so on through to false teeth and hair pieces. Such analysis has been extended to describe markets in terms of the dependent, singles, mating, breeding, full nest and empty nest stages. Population trends are important here, in recognising the increasing numbers of 'golden wrinklies', for example. We all finish up in what has been given the macabre title of the coffin and cremation market! At every stage of our lives we represent, simultaneously, lost customers for one producer and prospective buyers for another. Advertising planning, if it is to be effective, must take account of these never-ending changes in the market.

Information about new developments

Present customers may know of your goods, but do they know of any improvements made, or of new lines added to your range? Firms devote a great deal of time, money and effort to improving their products, but this is of little purpose if customers are left in the dark about them. They must be informed about new or improved products, new packs, or the delivery of eagerly awaited goods. Prices and products are constantly changing, and it is a great mistake for any manufacturer to believe that, just because *he* knows about these things, his customers are equally well-informed. Potential customers will not become purchasers unless they know of the new developments, and advertising helps to keep them informed. Furthermore, changes in your product line may open up new market segments, for whom your earlier products were not of interest. Again, there are clear media and creative implications.

Stabilised production

For a number of advertisers, their objective is not to increase sales but to stabilise demand. If demand for your product is unsteady, your factory has to work at full capacity – perhaps even overtime – while sales are high, but when demand falls off machinery lies idle. A sales graph with great peaks and troughs makes for uneconomic production. Advertising can help to even out the graph in two different ways.

One solution to problems arising from uneven production is to plan your advertising to fill the troughs. There is a net increase in sales but you stimulate the market only at specified times of the year. The other way of levelling out your sales graph is by shifting sales from peaks to troughs: in this latter case there is no increase in sales but, by using advertising to persuade consumers to make their purchases in slack rather than peak periods, expenses are reduced with an obvious increase in profit. Stabilised production as an advertising objective can be applied not only seasonally but also between days of the week or even hours of the day.

Advertising can facilitate making the most efficient use of your resources and such considerations directly affect the timing of your campaign and its creative content.

Fighting declining sales

The purpose of your campaign may be not to increase or stabilise sales, but to hold off a decline. This overall category, in fact, masks various types of decline, for which different advertising approaches are necessary. One advertising campaign may have as its purpose countering the natural decline in the market, mentioned above. Another purpose might be to sustain an existing brand against competition. Other purposes might be to slow down a permanent trend, or to reverse a temporary decline.

Where the market for your product is steadily diminishing, it is unwise to expect advertising to work miracles and reverse the permanent trend: it may, however, be able to make some contribution by slowing the rate of decline, thus giving you time to seek new opportunities in other directions. Where advertising can make a far more positive contribution is in countering temporary falls in sales. The Chancellor's budget, for example, may introduce tax changes in relation to specific groups of products, or impose hire-purchase and credit restrictions which inhibit sales. Positive advertising, emphasising value for money, can help people adjust more swiftly to the new conditions.

Increased advertising is one method you can adopt to avert a slump, but the underlying causes call for different types of advertising campaign.

Overcoming resistance

Many companies seem to assume that the public is merely waiting for a suitable advertising message to stimulate them into buying the product. But people are wary of buying unfamiliar products, and retailers equally shy of stocking lines unknown to their customers. More than this, people may even be hostile: consider, for example, the reluctance of many drivers and passengers to use seat belts and how the 'clunk click' campaign set about trying to solve this problem, and also the subsequent contribution advertising made to publicising the law which made use of seat belts obligatory. A further campaign followed when the law was later extended to rear seat belts. If your product encounters such resistance, advertising can do much to overcome this sales barrier by building up a favourable image in the public mind.

'Prestige' advertising

The popular 'title' for this type of advertising covers allied uses – you will come across references to mood-selling, image-building, corporate or institutional advertising. Certainly some organisations may need to concentrate on their image rather than their products but, alas, in many cases this approach is misused, or even taken as an easy way out! Many cynical creative directors have remarked that, when all else fails, you can always rely on the old stand-by of an aerial view of the factory and a picture of the Chairman to keep everybody happy! But for this type of advertising to be effective, you must ask very fundamental questions. Whose opinion are we concerned about? What opinion do these people hold now? If your image is bad, is this, in fact, well deserved? If it *is*, then no amount of so-called prestige advertising can rectify matters: the true solution is to put things right and only then set about advertising. For this type of advertising to be effective, you must know who constitutes your market, what these people think now, and precisely what you want them to think in the future. Unless you have the answers to these questions you can neither choose media nor decide upon creative content.

Whilst in the general area of consumer opinions, you should also consider those cases where manufacturers attempt – perhaps at the same time as achieving the main aim of 'selling' their products – to change consumer attitudes. In such circumstances, it is vital to distinguish between basic beliefs and short-term behaviour. Many consumers have deeply entrenched views based on their total experience of a product – or product group – perhaps going back to their childhood days. As you would expect, it is no easy task for advertising to shift such views, which may be paralleled by market trends. Whilst advertising can be very effective in influencing short-term buying behaviour, changing long-term beliefs or market trends is a very different matter. Advertising can rarely reverse a negative trend (see 'fighting declining sales' above) but it can help encourage a positive one.

'Umbrella' campaigns

The underlying purpose of many corporate campaigns is not prestige as such, but to link various separate activities. Examples are often found where organisations are active in various fields, with separate divisions marketing separate products to separate markets via separate advertising and selling campaigns. Many such organisations realise that linking their self-contained business operations would benefit all the component companies. To illustrate how this applies in practice, divisions A, B, C and D might each have sales campaigns for their separate industrial markets, with appropriate advertising in the relevant professional or technical press. National press would normally be ruled out as too few readers come within the specified categories of buyer. But as many industrial purchasers buy not only product A but also perhaps B, C and D as well, the separate advertising campaigns in specialised press can be made more effective by an 'umbrella' campaign in more general media, on the creative theme of 'If you need advice on A, B, C or D, we are the experts'. Sales representatives from the individual companies then cross-refer enquiries, as necessary. Such an advertising objective clearly has a much more functional aim than a so-called 'prestige' campaign, and there are clear implications for both media choice and advertisement content. The same effect can apply, however, even within a single company, as is explained in the following section.

Benefit to other lines

A similar effect to an umbrella campaign may apply within a single organisation. One obvious effect of advertising is to increase sales of the item featured, but a secondary result may be increased sales of *other* lines. A retailer, for example, is likely to find that people make more than one purchase when they call at his shop to buy an advertised product. Multi-product manufacturers also benefit correspondingly when the publicity afforded to their brand name by advertising one item helps other lines in their range: hence the importance of establishing, at the earlier investigation stage, whether there is any family branding or corporate communication theme which links the autonomous profit centres which produce your various products.

If advertising is likely to have a beneficial 'spin-off' for your other products, this added advantage must be borne in mind when planning your campaign. The chapter on the advertiser mentioned the existence of 'brand managers' and the question then arises of whether a company with this marketing structure is likely to adopt such a co-ordinated approach.

Launch a new product or service

For new products or services, reminder advertising is clearly inapplicable: here the task is one of basic education – informing potential customers of the benefits they will reap by purchasing your new product. A side effect of this may well be, in due course, a counter campaign to fight declining sales by the manufacturer whose product is no longer in favour.

Market Research

The previous chapter pointed out that, on occasion, the Advertising Manager must accept that the information necessary for an effective product launch is not available. In such circumstances, two possibilities present themselves. One is to commission the necessary market research. The alternative is to proceed despite this lack of data, spend money on advertising rather than field surveys, use advertising as a research tool, and prepare a campaign (often on a 'shotgun' basis) to make prospective purchasers identify themselves. Consumer response is then carefully evaluated, to identify target groups ripe for subsequent development through focused campaigns in targeted media. As the database marketing section pointed out, this alternative approach – planning campaigns in such a way as to obtain all necessary information – could replace conventional market research in some product areas.

Even for those firms not able to develop their database so directly, this advertising objective clearly links with the later planning stage of *Evaluation of Results*. As Chapter 19 makes clear, evaluation is a vital stage, whatever your campaign objective.

Extending distribution

In some cases, your advertising may be aimed not at the public but at stockists. A manufacturer who finds his product in insufficient outlets will seek to widen his distribution and would use advertising as a tool for this purpose. Trade press advertising is obvious in this respect but consumer advertising is equally effective, when sales representatives take round specimen advertisements which they employ as a most persuasive argument in getting retailers to stock and display your merchandise. If extended distribution is the purpose of your campaign, it is often to your advantage to book advertisements of a larger size than is strictly necessary to convey the creative message, simply because of the impact this larger size has on retailers in getting them to anticipate a heavy demand.

Stimulate existing distribution

As with the previous case, advertising is used for its effect on retailers rather than the general public. The difference is that your product is widely distributed but you consider the stockists insufficiently active in promoting sales. To rectify this, you can use heavy local advertising to persuade hitherto passive retailers to give your products more window and in-store display. As before, larger sizes than are strictly necessary can be most helpful when using advertising in this way as a sales tool for representatives. In both this and the previous case you may find it advantageous to feature the names and addresses of stockists, perhaps on a co-operative basis. Such considerations clearly influence the choice of media, and the way in which you use it.

An extreme example which shows clearly how the need to influence distributors can affect media planning concerns a less than active builders' merchant. Booking poster sites immediately facing and adjacent to his stop contributed markedly to overcoming his former apathy!

Back-up for sales representatives

As in the previous two cases, the underlying target for your advertising is not the general public – here, its aim is to stimulate your representatives. Salesmen, in the field all day and thus out of contact with your sales office, soon feel cut off and may become dispirited. Advertising can give them a much needed psychological boost. Where representatives sell to industrial buyers rather than to retailers who then sell to the public, this back-up role can be vital. Advertising aimed at extending or stimulating distribution can also be considered under this heading, for its indirect effect in boosting your salesmen's confidence and thus encouraging them in their efforts. A classic McGraw-Hill advertisement, designed to promote advertising in its specialist publications, showed a steely-eyed industrial buyer looking at the reader and saying:

'I don't know who you are.

I don't know your company.

I don't know your company's product.

I don't know what your company stands for.

I don't know your company's customers.

I don't know your company's record.

I don't know your company's reputation.

Now–what was it you wanted to sell me?'

MORAL: Sales start before your salesman calls –
with business publication advertising.

McGRAW-HILL MAGAZINES
BUSINESS●PROFESSIONAL●TECHNICAL

Leads for sales representatives

This use of advertising differs from the previous instances in that it is
aimed at the consumer, but the salesman is still a key figure because
the purpose of the campaign is to provide him with sales leads on
which to call. Salesmen's time is valuable and at a premium, and following up contacts who have indicated positive interest by, for
example, returning a coupon is far more productive than cold canvass-
ing. This was the main advertising function for one client whose
account I handled: the aim was a steady stream of leads to keep sales
staff busy. Although planned on a long-term basis, scheduling was extremely flexible with advertising activity being stepped up when
necessary or cut back when the representatives had more business
then they could handle. For this client, effective advertising clearly
demanded flexible media planning.

Direct selling and mail order

Much the same type of strategic planning may be necessary for those
who sell direct to the consumer, using advertising to spread informa-

tion about their products and to solicit orders. As was the case when keeping representatives supplied with sales leads, a flexible media plan is necessary to keep demand and supply in balance. This objective links clearly with the concept of database marketing discussed earlier – as does the next objective.

Building up a mailing list

Some advertisers have found it profitable to vary this pattern when selling direct. The initial mailing list is built up by public advertising, and direct mail then used to obtain orders from those who have expressed interest. Direct marketing is the primary aim of the campaign, and general advertising is used to 'top up' the mailing list from time to time since this must necessarily suffer the natural decline inherent in every market.

Clearance of surplus supplies

Advertising is often used on an occasional rather than regular basis, and the 'sales' which feature so prominently on the retail scene reflect this. Sales advertising often serves two quite distinct purposes – one is to boost sales at an otherwise slack period (as described above) while the other purpose is to clear shelves of last year's stock to make way for new merchandise. The retailer makes the old stock more attractive by cutting prices, and makes this reduction known through his Sale advertising. Additional benefits come from the fact that valuable storage space is cleared to make way for new merchandise, and cash provided to pay for it.

Dispose of by-products

In other cases, the purpose may be to market by-products rather than to clear dead stocks. In manufacturing its main product, your company may produce a by-product which it wishes to sell at a profit.

This exercise differs from the main selling operation in that sales volume is dictated by the main product, demand for which determines production levels, which in turn control the amount of by-product produced. The aim of the by-product advertising campaign is thus to sell just so much and no more, since there is little purpose in stimulating a massive demand for this secondary product when supplies could not be increased without creating an unsaleable surplus of the main product. Any promotional plan thus has a 'cut-off' point dictated by the main sales programme, which your media scheduling must clearly take into account.

Utilising other marketing strengths

There are other circumstances in which advertising planning is determined by your company's overall marketing programme, rather than by demand for the single product for which you are preparing a campaign. This can occur when manufacturers review their product range and make a work study of sales force effectiveness. A producer may find, for example, that his representatives are not working to full capacity: this is no reflection on his sales staff and their efforts, but simply recognises that the present product range does not keep them fully occupied. There is thus spare sales force capacity, and the question then is: 'What additional product, which would be of interest to current buyers, could your salesforce carry and sell effectively?' If a further item is added to round out your company's product line, this is another case where promotional planning will be determined by factors outside the usual considerations, depending on the main marketing programme.

Advertising as an aid to buying

Advertising has been defined as 'making known in order to sell' but on many occasions your aim may be the very opposite – not to sell, but to buy. Many business needs are put out to tender, the contract being advertised and the order going to the firm submitting the best bid. Similarly, 'Situations Vacant' advertisements are the recognised way of locating suitable applicants to fill staff vacancies. At the start of this chapter mention was made that the various reasons for advertising should not be considered as water-tight compartments, and that two or more purposes may be applicable at any one time: 'Situations Vacant' is an example of where this applies. Many firms realise that, whilst a small classified advertisement might be sufficient to convey the bare facts of a post, they face competition for the best applicants who are more likely to respond to a prestige advertisement which conveys that they would be working for the leading company in the field. Employers realise also that not only potential applicants see these advertisements but also many others, including the public at large, suppliers, shareholders and customers. Such positive recruitment advertisements can also help weaken competitors' morale!

Arbitrary reasons for advertising

This section should not be here but, alas, it would be unrealistic not to recognise the sad fact that, whilst there are many sound reasons why advertising can be the most effective way of helping you achieve your purpose, there are also a number of other 'reasons' for advertising which are less rational. To give one example, it is not unknown for a producer to advertise out of personal pride: it gives him satisfaction to see his name (together with his picture and an aerial view of his factory!) in print or some other advertising medium, and to feel that his friends and acquaintances think of him as an important man.

Media selection can also be influenced by arbitrary factors - the advertiser's motivating force may perhaps be tradition: his firm has always used the medium in question. Alternatively, he may feel 'forced in' because he does not wish to be the odd man out. Or again, he may feel he has a 'duty' to support the relevant trade magazine or exhibition. Sometimes this latter aim is not as irrational as it appears: some firms realise they *need* the publication or exhibition, and equally appreciate that the media-owner's sales revenue from copies or admissions is insufficient to make the venture commercially viable. Since the manufacturers have a clear need for this particular means of communication they support it, and advertising thus has in it an element of subsidy. In other cases, by booking space in special programmes, firms use advertising as an indirect means of making donations to charity.

Increased sales

This reason for advertising has deliberately been left until last: not because it is unimportant – far from it – but because it demands greater attention and more detailed analysis than the other reasons so far discussed.

The so-called aim of 'increased sales' is perhaps the most frequent blind spot in the whole advertising and marketing process. It is a great weakness that many firms, both large and small, regard 'increased sales' as a sufficiently clear objective on which to base an advertising campaign. But 'increased sales' is *not* a specific objective – it is only a wish for the future. What percentage increase are you aiming for? By which date? Where are these increased sales to come from? How are they to be achieved? The lucidity of the answers to these questions will influence the effectiveness of your advertising campaign, and directly affect not only media choice but also the way in which the selected media are used in terms of size, position and frequency. Equally fundamental is the influence of these answers on the advertising content, in terms of creative approach.

Too many people overlook the fundamental fact that different routes to increased sales call for different types of advertising campaign, in terms of both creative content and media strategy. One well-known marketing matrix suggests four basic ways of increasing sales:

- existing products to existing markets
- existing products to new markets
- new products to existing markets
- new products to new markets.

These possibilities can be evaluated against a 'risk' scale, with the fourth clearly being the most risky.

While this matrix can assist marketing planning, it is unsatisfactory for advertising purposes since it fails to take account of competition, nor does it consider campaigns which persuade customers to switch brands. An alternative approach is therefore necessary, and the matrix below facilitates both media and creative planning.

A first essential is to stop thinking in terms of increased sales, and to think instead of increased *purchases* – or, more specifically, possible purchasers and their buying patterns. Viewed in purchasing terms, there are three ways in which you can increase sales of existing products.

1 Increased purchases by existing users Such a campaign will convert light into medium users or medium into heavy, and your aim is to extend the range of uses they make of your product, or increase their frequency of use. This will increase the value of the market, but not its size in terms of people.

2 Purchases by new users With such a campaign, your aim is to educate non-users (who have not used your own product nor that of any rivals) about the benefits of your product, thus converting them to its use. Advertising of this type will increase the size of the market in terms of people, as well as its value. But see the warning note below.

3 Purchases by competitors' customers Your campaign aim here is to persuade buyers (existing or potential) of rival products to switch brands. This will not increase the 'size of the cake' – only the way it is divided.

These three routes to increased sales of existing products facilitate advertising planning more effectively than the earlier matrix which suggested only two markets – existing and new – and ignored opportunities for brand-switch sales.

The new matrix does not yet allow for *new* products. This term could encompass replacements for existing products, or extensions to an existing range, as well as entirely new product lines, so clearly advertising analysis must now extend beyond the three possibilities so far considered. A full planning matrix should also allow for:

4 Purchases of new products by existing customers There are many advantages when planning such a campaign – you know who your present customers are and can perhaps reach them through, for example, direct mail. Furthermore, your advertising messages can build on existing knowledge: there is (hopefully) a wealth of goodwill to assist in launching your new product.

5 Purchases of new products by new users This is similar to the second possibility (purchases of existing products by new users) in that the target group has not used the new product and needs educating about its benefits. One significant difference is that as the product is *new*, there is no track record on which to build: the testimonial approach of 'thousands of satisfied users' is not applicable. Secondly, there is no goodwill from which to benefit. And there is, again, a warning note, discussed below.

6 Purchases of new products by competitors' customers Although similar to route No 3 (purchases of existing products by competitors' customers) the differences are again significant – there is again no track record on which to build, and furthermore you must fight established goodwill to rival companies.

If the new product is a multi-use one, this six-route matrix can be extended by subsequent campaigns which suggest new product uses (or, for a single-use product, reasons for more frequent use). This completes the circle by returning to the first route to increased sales – existing users to use more.

A warning note

In considering sales to 'new users' – and indeed *all* purchasers – you must be careful to distinguish between long-term basic beliefs and short-term current needs. Advertising can be most effective in influencing short-term buying behaviour but, as earlier paragraphs made clear, changing beliefs is a very different matter. A simple example is wedding dresses, which at first sight would appear to be 'purchases by new users'. In the strict sense this is of course true, but you would be very unwise to plan your advertising appeal on this basis – there is no need to 'educate non-users about the benefits of your product, thus converting them to its use': women *know* the use of a wedding dress! Equally, no woman is going to rush out and buy one because of new styles, low prices or easy credit terms: the purchase of a wedding dress depends directly on her long-term views on marriage, on accepting a proposal, and on her deeply entrenched views about white weddings. In this sense, the sale of a wedding dress is a brand-switch operation: the woman's decision is made, and your objective is to persuade her to buy a wedding dress from your company. The same reasoning applies to another example, this time for the (mostly) male market – a new exhaust system for your car. This time there are few (if any) 'basic beliefs' but in no way will you spend money on a new one until it is essential to do so: the decision to replace your exhaust system is made for you by circumstances, and your task – aided by suitable advertisements – is to decide where to go to get it. In this case you will actually seek out information, so this is another example of how people *use* advertisements that are being used to reach them. Both examples illustrate the need to consider the long-term and short-term effects of your advertising, as well as consumers' entrenched beliefs and short-term needs – your immediate campaign aim might be to attract possible customers who are in the market for a product *now* but, at the same time, your advertising will also be seen by others who – although they have no need of your product at present – may want it in future and, when the time comes, may recall your company name in this respect.

Wedding dresses and exhaust systems are extreme examples and, in most cases, 'sales to new users' means just what it says, and your task is to explain to non-users the benefits they will get from your product. If your analysis is correct, they should be grateful for the information and buy the product, to your mutual benefit.

If the increased sales/increased purchases analysis is reduced to the most fundamental level, it will be apparent that media policy and basic creative content can then be entered on a chart as shown overleaf.

A campaign designed to meet one of these objectives is unlikely to be as successful in achieving the other five since they call for different advertising in terms of both media and creative content.

From the creative standpoint, a campaign aimed at existing users, suggesting further uses for your product, may not be understood by new users who are unaware of your product's basic function, let alone additional uses. A campaign designed to explain your product's basic benefits to potential purchasers may bore existing users, who are already well aware of its function. Neither will it be effective in influencing the brand loyalty of buyers of rival products. Equally, a campaign prepared to persuade buyers of rival products to switch brands, by stressing the advantages of your product over others, is likely to be less successful in educating new users to the product group's basic benefits. Campaigns for new products call for similar basic differences in creative content.

Much the same can be said of media policy: to increase sales to your

Type of sales increase	Media policy	Creative content
EXISTING PRODUCTS		
1 Existing product to existing users	Maintain insertions in current media	Suggest new uses for your product, or reasons for more frequent use, building on existing contacts and goodwill
2 Existing product to new users	Consider new media	Explain the basic benefits of your product, and your company record, to people unaware of them
3 Existing product to users of rival products – brand-switching	Consider competitors' media patterns	Comparison campaigns pointing out the advantages of your product over rival brands, and of changing established buying habits
NEW PRODUCTS		
4 New products to existing customers	Maintain insertions in current media	Explain basic benefits, building on existing contacts and goodwill
5 New products to new users	Consider new media	Explain basic benefits, and company record in other fields
6 New products to competitors' customers	Consider competitors' media patterns	Explain basic benefits, and overcome established goodwill

existing customers you would clearly wish to continue (but strive to improve) your present media pattern, whilst to reach new prospective buyers you may have to use new media. Playing 'follow my leader' rarely results in effective advertising but, if you seek brand-switch sales, clearly you will wish to influence your competitors' customers and would *deliberately* aim at the same market – and are thus likely to use the same media. This is a very different matter to blindly following your rival's lead, for lack of anything better to do.

Advertising should thus be seen in context as part of your total marketing operation. It is not a separate activity but must be based directly on marketing objectives, which should be clear and detailed. Sales force activity must equally be aimed at achieving the identical marketing objective: advertising and selling should be complementary.

Thus different types of sales increase the call for different types of media schedule as well as different creative content. Like most fundamental truths this is all very obvious – once it has been pointed out. But for too many organisations it appears to be a blind spot. Of course, the matrix over-simplifies for ease of analysis, and the six types of increase are not self-exclusive. Furthermore, there certainly *are* advertisements which achieve sales in two or more of the possible ways simultaneously. Much successful advertising recognises the distinct ways of increasing sales and accordingly the campaign is not a single entity but comprises several interrelated components, each aimed at one distinct target group. These components are not only successful in their own right but, because they are clearly linked, each component reinforces the effectiveness of the others. Synergistic advertising such as this can be achieved only by design, never by accident.

Summary

The essential message of this chapter is the need to define clearly, before starting to plan your advertising, precisely what the underlying objective of the campaign is to be. It is more than obvious to state that you cannot hit a target unless you know what that target is – why should it be less obvious that it is impossible to prepare advertising proposals to achieve an objective unless you know precisely what this objective is? A great deal of current advertising is, alas, ineffective simply because this fundamental truth has been ignored. Analyse your marketing objectives properly and your advertising effectiveness must increase.

A later step will be to convert these advertising objectives into communication objectives – what information must you convey and what should be you say, to achieve your desired campaign objectives?

THE NEXT STEP

Having decided what you hope to achieve, you can now proceed to the next step – deciding how much you should spend on achieving this objective.

Chapter 14

Budgeting

The first essential for effective use of advertising media was gathering information on which to base your planning. Next came problem analysis and determining your specific advertising strategy. With these two tasks completed, you can now tackle your third problem – deciding how much to spend on achieving your chosen objective. It is appreciated that not all readers will be directly involved – they may be on the receiving end, and have to work to a budget set by someone else. Nevertheless, it is helpful for them to appreciate the ways by which the advertising appropriation can be decided. Furthermore, if their advice is sought on whether a proposed sum is suitable, or if any agency or media-owner hopes to persuade an advertiser to spend more, then this knowledge is even more important.

ADVERTISING AS AN INVESTMENT

Advertising is a cost, but it is usually incurred in increasing sales, from which come profits. If sales are increased by the advertising campaign, then profits are increased, and the extra profits can more than pay for the advertising. Increased sales can also lower costs, and thus enhance the margin of profit. Production in large quantities spreads overhead costs over more units of output and brings other economies of scale (such as better terms for purchasing raw materials in bulk) which lower the cost per unit produced, and thus make possible lower prices.

Increased sales, as we have seen, is by no means the only possible reason for advertising – stabilised sales make for more economic production and thus lower costs, higher profits and/or lower prices. Advertising can make a positive contribution to profitability in many ways, depending on your particular business objectives. The number of firms which imagine that advertising adds to the cost of goods, and that therefore they risk being undersold by competitors who do not advertise, are few: most firms realise that advertising is a cost, but a cost which brings savings in its wake. The problem lies not in deciding whether or not to spend money on advertising, but in deciding *how much* to spend. This, strangely enough, is another blind spot for too many organisations.

It is important to consider the advertising budget in context, as part of your total complex business operation. There are in fact several stages to the financial planning involved. First and foremost is the marketing plan – that you manufacture a product (or provide a service) with your product policy, advertising, distribution and selling effort all geared to achieving sales in a chosen market.

An overall allocation of funds is then made: so much for plant and equipment; so much for raw materials and labour; so much for selling effort; so much for advertising support, and so on. In this way a total budget is drawn up, showing the various financial commitments involved. It soon becomes apparent that fixing the advertising budget is a *management* decision, and part of a process of balancing expenditures when different activities compete for funds.

It is, therefore, desirable to approach this exercise from the viewpoint of ROI (Return On Investment) or ROC (Return On Capital) rather than spending money. For management to approve an advertising budget, you will need to convince your directors that advertising, rather than any other use of funds, will be the most productive form of expenditure, and make a positive contribution to profitability. Should your Board view advertising as spending without results, you are unlikely to have any budget approved.

BUDGET DEFINITION

The amount to be spent on advertising is known as the 'appropriation' and appropriation policy is usually initiated by the advertising manager and then confirmed by the Board, some three months or so before the start of the marketing year.

The term appropriation can be defined as 'the total amount to be spent on advertising during a given period'. Like all definitions it sounds simple, but two points merit special comment – for very practical reasons.

One point relates to 'a given period'. If you have an advertising budget of £X,000, you can have no idea whether this is a sufficient sum, or too much or too little money, unless you know the period of time for which this amount must provide advertising support. Most appropriations are for twelve-month periods, either the calendar year starting on 1 January or the financial year commencing on 5 April. Some appropriations are longer term whilst others are for shorter periods, say three months, with four appropriations per year, but the annual appropriation is more usual. Often, accounting practice makes this inflexible, so that towards the end of the period you are not permitted to 'borrow' from your next year's budget: equally, accounting practice forbids your carrying over any unspent funds. You must, therefore, be clear as to the time period to be covered by the money available, otherwise you cannot budget to cover it effectively. This, surprisingly enough, is less of a problem than the second point regarding the definition, namely the meaning of the word 'advertising'.

In its broadest sense, advertising could be taken to include anything featuring your company name or symbol, but more usually it is restricted to the conventional forms of advertising: press, posters, cinema and television and radio commercials and so on. Firms take differing views of what they include under the heading of advertising and may depart from the ASA's definition of 'paid-for media space or time'. Some exclude production costs for leaflets or display material, the money for these coming out of a separate budget. Others include them, together with such items as postage on direct mail, all of which come out of the advertising appropriation. In some firms the salaries of advertising personnel are set against the advertising appropriation, whilst in others they are considered as general staff costs. Public relations activity may have a separate budget or come out of an overall promotion budget, and the same applies to merchandising and sales promotion. In short, there is no hard and fast rule as to what comes out of the budget and what does not, and practice varies from firm to firm. However, the point is a basic one – if you are responsible for the appropriation you must have a clear idea of what it does and does not cover. It would not do for you to plan carefully how to spend your appropriation and then, towards the end of the period, get an unexpected invoice for something you did not consider as advertising, but which the accountants do.

There are many sad stories to illustrate the practical need for this clear understanding. A newly appointed advertising manager was told, three-quarters of the way through the year, that he had overspent by several thousand pounds. Even after repeated checks he still considered himself well within budget, and the difference of opinion arose because he considered sales literature as coming under the sales manager's budget, whereas the accounting staff considered it an advertising charge. As a result, the advertising manager was obliged to cancel some insertions, in order to make up the amount of money in dispute, so upsetting his carefully planned schedule. This deprived his company of valuable advertising support at a time when it was greatly needed, which resulted in lost sales which, in turn, meant loss of profits. A clear understanding of what his appropriation covered would have prevented this.

This is an extreme case, but even minor items can pose a major problem since many activities do not fit neatly into one category or another and soon add up to a considerable total expense. Is the new shop front or the new sign outside your factory an advertising expense, or should it come out of general building costs? What about the charges involved in special painting of delivery vans? Is the cost of 'Situations Vacant' advertisements to be charged against your advertising budget? There is a tendency for other departments to pass unwanted invoices (and who wants invoices anyway?) to the advertising manager, and if these are paid for out of the so-called advertising appropriation there is less money available for genuine media expenditure. The possibility of invoices being 'passed sideways' is, of course, increased by the fact that different departmental heads compete for funds. It is therefore directly in your own interest that you are absolutely clear about what your budget does and does not cover.

THE NEED FOR A PROPER BUDGET

With the period of the appropriation and what it is to cover clearly defined, you can then make plans, and so fixing the budget is clearly a vital step. On what basis can you avoid spending too much or too little on advertising? Before reviewing the various methods, consider three alternatives.

1 No budget It is vital that your advertising is carefully planned. Sometimes you may encounter a manufacturer who suddenly feels 'It's time we had an advertisement' or, occasionally, you may come up against one who advertised simply because a media representative asked for an order! Such an off-hand attitude is unlikely to bring results. If the manufacturer does not plan his advertising, the chances are that a bit of money will be spent in one medium and a bit more in another, some this month and some the next. Before long, someone will get round to adding up how much has been spent on advertising: he will usually be horrified at how expenditure has mounted up, and decide that advertising is a waste of money. And, face facts, advertising in this way *is* a waste of money. To be effective, your advertising must be planned, and planned well in advance. Your plan should be flexible rather than rigid to allow for the opportunities – and setbacks – of business, but a plan there must be. Advertising is not a separate activity unconnected with your company's other activities: advertising, sales and display effort must all be co-ordinated. When this is the case, retailers' windows, in-store displays and shelves feature the merchandise you are advertising, and selling activity ties in with your advertising and display effort. With effective planning, sales staff have advance information about the merchandise advertised, and have been coached to draw attention to these goods. In this way your prospective customer's interest is awakened by advertisements, displays give effective reminders, and the sale is completed by counter staff. When sales staff are ignorant of the advertising, sales are lost and bad impressions created. Think of the occasions on which you asked a shop for an item currently advertised, only to find that sales staff knew nothing about it: your impression – correctly – is that the shop is slack and inefficient which, of course, it is. This is more than likely the result of unplanned and uncontrolled advertising expenditure.

2 The arbitrary 'guesstimate' Picking a figure out of the air, by hunch or whim, rarely leads to successful advertising. This method is adopted by fewer and fewer advertisers, and most give careful thought to the amount they spend. But beware of those who disguise this approach to budgeting by claiming that 'My twenty years' experience tells me that we should spend £X,000'. Has this individual really had 20 years' experience – or only one year's experience twenty times? Certainly, as will be seen later, true experience can make a most valuable contribution, but all too often the term is used to defend what is, in truth, only a guess. The 'method' still exists, however, and so it must be mentioned – if only to point out that it has little in its favour.

3 'Chairman's Rules' This 'method' is encountered in companies where the advertising manager has no say in deciding the appropriation, but a figure is dictated to him by his Board. In many cases, the company *does* know what it is doing, but in some instances there is no real basis for the Board decision. A figure is decided, but those concerned have little idea of whether they are budgeting too much or too little. The 'method' nevertheless exists and so must be mentioned if only to stress that – like the 'arbitrary guesstimate' – it has no sound basis.

The last two methods, however, are not entirely without merit. Both methods set a sum for advertising, and this in itself means that someone is *forced* to undertake at least basic planning. Somebody will have to ask fundamental questions such as 'There are twelve months of trading, so how shall I spread my spending over the year?' and 'There are x products needing advertising support: how much shall I allocate to each?' From the planning point of view, he will be forced to apportion his money between media, and decide which to use and so, in that these two methods are likely to result in some fundamental planning, they are not without merit – but, either could result in too much or too little being spent on advertising.

Most readers will know the saying attributed to Lord Leverhume – 'Half the money I spend on advertising is wasted – the trouble is, I don't know which half'. Whenever I hear this story, I always recall my visit to the merchandising vice-president of a gigantic one-stop shopping centre in Midwest America. In reply to my question as to how many people worked in the centre, his laconic reply was 'About half of them'.

Your aim must be to ensure that *all* your advertising money is working for you and, if the 'no budget/arbitrary guesstimate/chairman's rules' methods have so little in their favour, what alternatives are open to you?

There is no single best way to decide on how much to spend. A great deal depends on circumstances: for established products, fixing the appropriation may be an annual ritual, while with the launch of a new product it may be regarded as a capital investment. Many methods are in use, each with its advantages and drawbacks, and all are used with varying degrees of success according to the circumstances in which the company operates.

BUDGETING METHODS

Though there are many different methods, they can be considered under seven main groupings. Each of these categories has numerous variations – in some cases the necessary arithmetic can be done on the back of an envelope whereas in other instances the same method is applied in a more complex manner using a computer to undertake intricate mathematical calculations: it is, nevertheless, the same basic method. The fundamental choices open to you are outlined below, together with their advantages and drawbacks.

1 Percentage of last year's sales

Many advertisers take a set percentage – say half per cent or five per cent – of the previous year's turnover as the basis for their appropriation. If you use this method it has the advantage of safety, as you are spending money in accordance with established sales. There are, however, two drawbacks to this method. First, there is the problem of deciding what percentage it should be – half, one, two or five or more per cent? When you consider that some industrial advertisers spend less than a quarter of one per cent of sales on advertising, while consumer product advertising could account for up to a quarter of the selling price, this gives you a more than wide range from which to choose! Some categories of firm have an advantage in that trade statistics are published showing the average for their particular industry. But this advantage is not as helpful as it seems, since an average is only an *average*. Remember that half the people in the UK are below average height (the other half are above average height: that's why there is an average!). If there is an average percentage, that it because many firms are, quite rightly, spending more than the average and others, equally correctly, are spending less than average. The first drawback to this method is determining what percentage *you* should spend.

The second basic weakness of the method is that it looks to the past rather than the future. A bad year means lower turnover and so even less on advertising – in a never-ending downward spiral. The answer to lower turnover might be for you to spend *more* on advertising rather than less, to counteract the decline, in the belief that advertising causes sales. Even if sales do not drop the method still has weaknesses: if your market is, in fact, growing by 25 per cent a year, then a sales increase of only five per cent means that you are losing out by some 20 per cent each year. Furthermore, it is a chicken and egg situation – did sales rise because you spent more on advertising, or did you spend more on advertising because sales had risen? In spite of its weaknesses, this method is, nevertheless, used by a large number of organisations. Others prefer to look to the future and use expected sales as their criterion.

2 Percentage of anticipated sales

This method can lead to a realistic appropriation if, for example, your aim is for a marked increase in sales. It suffers, however, from one of the same drawbacks as the previous method, that of deciding just what the percentage should be. A second drawback is that future sales cannot be precisely estimated: the sales have yet to be made and over-estimation could lead to over-spending on advertising. Examination of the 'expected sales' decision-process will reveal three broad categories:

(a) Solo decisions In many small firms all management decisions are taken by a single individual. Since he is responsible for all aspects of his firm's activities, he usually has his finger on the pulse of the market, and takes a realistic approach.

(b) The sales versus advertising split With some larger firms, responsibility for the two functions is divided, the sales manager being responsible for the buying/selling operation, and the advertising manager for the advertising: this can lead to considerable problems in practice. Most sales managers have a strong optimistic streak – the nature of their job calls for it! Consequently, they frequently over-estimate unintentionally. Problems begin when expected sales are not achieved, since the advertising manager will blame the sales manager and *vice versa*. The advertising manager will point out that the advertising cannot work miracles, and he is not to blame if the sales manager chose poor merchandise. The sales manager, in his turn, will ask how on earth can he be expected to sell merchandise with such piti-ful advertising support? When the unsold stocks come to management attention the old game of 'pass the buck' commences and, in 'pecking order', sales usually ranks above advertising. The managing director will reprimand the sales manager, who vents his wrath on the adver-tising manager, who promptly takes it out on the agency, the account executive finds fault with the media department, and blame eventu-ally passes to the media representative, whose medium has 'proved' itself ineffective! This is a game in which nobody wins but unfortu-nately is played all too often, as most media representatives will confirm.

(c) **The marketing approach** Here the decision is again taken by a single individual, but this is a very different matter to the one-person approach described above, since the marketing director has reporting to him executives responsible for sales, for advertising, and for market research. The sales *versus* advertising problem just described has led manufacturers to devote considerable time and effort to sales forecast-ing, in order to better decide the appropriation, as well as the more obvious benefit of fixing production levels with greater accuracy.

3 The unit percentage method

This approach uses detailed cost analysis as the basis for deciding the amount to spend, thus overcoming the problem common to the last two methods, of arriving at a suitable percentage figure. A costing study is made of the product: so much for raw materials, so much for direct pro-duction costs, so much for overheads, so much for packaging and so on. These figures may total, say, 35p, and if you wish to sell to the retailer for 40p this leaves a 5p margin. Of this, you can decide to keep 4p as profit and spend 1p per unit on advertising, keep 3p and spend 2p, keep 2p profit and spend 3p per unit and so on. This costing exercise can be extended to include distribution charges through to your final selling price to the public rather than stop at the factory gate but, in essence, the advertising appropriation is fixed as a residuum with profit: the difference between the selling price and all charges is a fixed amount which you spend on advertising or retain as profit. If you use this method, you are unlikely to overspend, since with a 5p margin you would never dream of spending 6p per unit on advertising. By the two previous methods, however, you could unintentionally overspend, as we have seen.

Even this method, scientific as it may appear, is not without its drawbacks. It is strictly inward-looking, since it is based on the factory floor and takes little account of the outside market. Even within the factory there is the danger that the amount per unit may not be revised as conditions alter, raw materials change in price or wage rates increase. Furthermore, overheads vary with output: the more units there are produced, the more widely costs are spread and the smaller the charges that must be borne by each unit.

Finally there is the fundamental point that all these figures are costed with a certain level of sales in mind, whereas it is possible that you may not achieve these sales. However, providing you estimate sales accurately and revise costings whenever necessary (so that the unit percentage is not passed down over the years without alteration) this method can provide a useful guide to what you can afford.

The three methods so far discussed are alternative answers to the question 'How much shall we spend?' The next method asks a very different question: 'How much are *they* spending?'

4 Competitive parity

Another way to fix your appropriation is to look at what competitors are spending and to decide your own expenditure accordingly. This method can be useful when entering a new market, for in such circumstances competitors' spending provides a useful indication of the amount of money you need to inform the market.

The weakness of the method is that although your competitors are similar they are not *identical* but vary in product, market and marketing policy and their problems are therefore different. Moreover, there is the difficulty of finding out just what competitors *are* spending. Press advertising expenditure can be calculated to a reasonable degree of accuracy and without too much trouble, simply by checking competitors' advertisements against publishers' rate cards. For the more important advertisers the task is even simpler in that you can look up their expenditure in the standard reference publications listed in Part 1; these also contain television billings. These figures are, however, usually at rate card cost, while efficient media-buying may well have achieved considerable discounts. For other media, such as posters, direct mail or display material, it is even more difficult to estimate the

scale of competitors' financial expenditure. And, even if this information is available, who is to say that the rival companies were correct in
the first place? One advertising manager remarked, with some justification, that basing expenditure on your competitors is like cheating in
an examination by copying the candidates next to you – you can't see
all that clearly, and you don't know that they're right anyway! A
further drawback to this method is that a new entrant to the market
must have some effect on competitors' sales, with the result that they
may spend more on advertising, so forcing the newcomer to increase
his appropriation. This method, then, gives a useful opening indication, but should not be allowed to lead to an advertising 'war' wasteful
to all parties.

5 Advertising share

A variation which overlaps several methods already discussed is the
'Share of Voice' approach which looks not only at your advertising expenditure in relation to your competitors, but also at your relative
sales. Earlier chapters indicated sources you can consult for this information, and in both cases the figures are examined in terms of
'share'. The question then is 'Are the sales for your product the same
share of the market as your advertising share?'

Analysis of this kind may result in interesting information such as
an average advertising-sales ratio for the product group and whether
you are 'working harder' (in terms of advertising expenditure) than
your competitors and – much more important – what result is this
having on sales? Observation of what happens in the market place may
reveal, for example, that firms which increase their share of advertising also increase their share of the market. (Or, of course, *vice versa*.)

This study of advertising and market share may be extended over
time by what has been called the 'dynamic difference' approach which
looks at

Sales share in one year less sales share in the previous year

as against

Advertising share in one year less advertising share in the previous
year

The overall weaknesses of this method are those already outlined
under the 'competitive parity' method and, furthermore, it does not
prove that increased expenditure results in increased sales. Even if a
sales rise is associated with increased advertising, the question then
arises of *how big an increase?* One firm, for example, might increase its

share of advertising, but at a *lower rate* than its main competitor who might have stepped up his advertising expenditure for some very good marketing reason which has no immediate connection with advertising.

6 The marginal method

The methods so far discussed all have one thing in common: they ask the same question, namely 'How much shall we (or do they) spend?' The marginal (sometines called *zero-based*) method poses a very different question, and asks 'How much *extra* shall we spend?' Attention is shifted from deciding a total amount to deciding 'layer by layer', and each additional expenditure must justify itself. The claim that 'Advertising will increase sales' is frequently made: the manufacturer using the marginal method asks *how much* will it increase sales? The method is an extension of the unit percentage method, and is based on a careful assessment of the results of each *additional* amount spent on advertising. If, for example, a manufacturer makes a profit of £10 per unit sold, then an advertisement costing £1000 must sell at least 100 additional units if it is to pay for itself. 'Increased sales' of only 50 units would be of little appeal to this advertiser, since this would involve a *loss* of £500. If you can relate sales to advertising in this way, the marginal method can prove extremely helpful. But do bear in mind just *what* you are evaluating, since the advertisement's content clearly influences its effectiveness. Your money has, in fact, bought you the most useless thing in the world – a blank space! There is no point in blaming a medium for proving ineffective in bringing increased sales, when the fault lies really in the use you have made of the space purchased. Some advertisers, in the fortunate position of having a direct response they can measure, extend the marginal method to measure creative aspects as well as media, checking creative idea A against creative idea B, headline C against headline D, illustration E *versus* illustration F and so on. Returning to the media aspects, however, the marginal method can be applied more specifically. Colour costs more than black and white and special positions are more expensive than run of paper insertions – are they worth it in terms of increased returns? Economists talk about the 'Law of Diminishing Returns' and supporters of the marginal method check this out in practice – large advertisements cost more than small ones and weekly insertions are some four times as expensive as a monthly appearance, so is it worth it? The fundamental question asked by those applying this method – who are in the fortunate position of being able to evaluate the answer – is 'If it costs x per cent extra, do returns increase by more than x per cent?' A later chapter covers evaluation of results in more detail but it should already be apparent that this method is ideal for those who can make their advertising 'sit up and beg' when it comes to measuring response. Many advertisers, however, are unable to establish so direct a connection and must therefore look to other methods of fixing their appropriation.

7 The target sum method

This means of determining your appropriation is on an entirely different basis from all the methods so far considered. Instead of asking 'How much (or how much extra) shall we spend?' the target sum (often called *Objective and Task*) method asks 'What will it cost?'.

In short, the method jumps ahead to the next planning stage - Preparation of Proposals – and then works back from media-owners' rate cards. If you decide that to achieve a given level of sales you need, say, half-pages every week in a selected list of publications, your appropriation can thus be calculated by multiplying the cost of these advertisements by the number of insertions. Thus a schedule of weekly advertisements costing in total £10,000 for each appearance in a selected list of publications gives you an appropriation of $52 \times £10,000$ or £520,000, plus production costs. In practice, of course, the schedule would be more complex and the arithmetic more involved.

The method is realistic in taking into account the cost of advertising – ignored by all the previous methods. A weakness common to the other methods so far considered is that if media rates increase by, say ten per cent, the outcome is that you are forced to book ten per cent less space or time, since no allowance is made for actual media costs.

The problem with the target sum method lies in deciding the variables – who is to say that half-pages are the correct size, that weekly appearances are necessary and which media should be included? The danger obviously lies in being greedy: what most advertisers would really like is saturation campaigns comprising full colour pages every day in every publication, posters on every hoarding, heavy television and radio campaigns, leaflets distributed door to door, and so on! In such circumstances, *all* your company's money would go on advertising. However, if you take a realistic view of what weight of advertising is really needed to inform your potential customers, this is a sound method of fixing your appropriation.

8 The composite method

This chapter began by stating that there were seven main groups of methods for fixing your advertising budget, so you may well be surprised at arriving at number eight! The eighth 'method' is, however, simply to use two or more of the previous methods together and strike a figure somewhere between those produced by the several calculations – which in any event are unlikely to be vastly different. When reviewing the various methods of fixing the budget against your own particular situation, some will immediately appear more relevant, and others less practical. By making the necessary calculations for the selected methods, you arrive at a range of figures giving your minimum and maximum expenditure levels. To 'pick a figure' somewhere in this range may sound haphazard, but consider what you have in fact achieved. Rather than any arbitrary guesstimate you have determined that, under no circumstances, should you spend less than a certain sum. Equally, you have scientifically and logically calculated a maximum figure. Your range of uncertainty has thus been narrowed down in a most practical manner, and it is at this point that experience becomes truly valuable.

This chapter warned earlier against those who made claims that 'My experience tells me we should spend £X,000' but there is a vast difference between vague guesses and the practical application of true experience. And it is experience in assessing the overall marketing situation which will tell you where, within the prescribed range, you should fix your own particular appropriation. For example, an advertising manager might consider that, with a depressed economy and consumers having little disposable cash, the signs indicate that a high budget is necessary. On the other hand might be the facts that his company's merchandise has a distinct product and price advantage, and that his main competitor's sales force and distribution are currently weak. Taking into account the strengths and weaknesses of the situation, he might decide to fix his appropriation at the lower end of the scale rather than the higher level which at first appeared necessary. Your own experience can be invaluable in reaching a decision relevant to your own particular situation, and certainly the results of your previous year's advertising should be considered also. Advertising policy thus becomes a 'circular' procedure, the results of one year's appropriation serving as a basis for establishing the subsequent year's expenditure which, in its turn, will also have to be revised to meet the needs of the following year.

In search of the perfect method

Any reader mistakenly seeking the impossible – a single universally applicable method of fixing the advertising budget – will be disappointed. I often recall, however, a colleague taking issue with my earlier writings on this subject – why was I so general, when his brand-leader organisation calculated its budget precisely? When I enquired how, he proudly presented a complex mathematical model calling for estimates of some dozen variables, and a lengthy computer run to resolve them into a recommended budget figure. When I pointed out that most advertisers did not have estimates of so many variables, nor a formula to inter-relate them even if such data was available, and that the research budget to acquire this information (let alone the cost of devising the mathematical model and then processing the data) far exceeded most companies' total advertising expenditure, he did admit that his 'perfect' method was specific to his firm, and that having a brand-leader's budget did make quite a difference!

Completing the loop

Even if there were a single perfect method, there is considerable difference between fixing a budget and then a) using it and b) spending it. The circular procedure of last year's results helping determine this year's expenditure should also be influenced by two later stages in the planning process: preparing and executing your advertising proposals.

When using your advertising budget, how strong will your creative proposals be? A powerful selling proposition, made to 'come alive' in a compelling way, will produce results with less expenditure than a weak creative campaign.

Equally important is the efficiency with which you buy your advertising. A good media buyer, by hard bargaining, will get you more for your money or, putting the same thing another way, will buy you the same amount of advertising for a smaller budget.

Various budgetary methods, all with many variations, are thus currently in use, each with its advantages and drawbacks. The outlines given perhaps over-simplify some variations, which are based on econometric approaches and complex mathematical models. In the absence of a single perfect mathematical model, however, these are the main methods from which you can choose. Indeed, any method is preferable to the 'bit-here-and-a-bit-there' approach, in that it must lead to planning and thus to more effective advertising.

Budget divisions

Before leaving the matter of your appropriation, various additional points must be made. One is that your company, rather than have a single figure, may require several appropriations, one for each of its products or divisions. It may even need an additional appropriation to promote an 'umbrella' campaign for the group as a whole, rather than for any individual line.

Furthermore, the appropriation may be divided into two – for 'above the line' expenditure by the agency and a 'below the line' budget retained by the advertiser. Also, part of the budget – described as a 'Contingency Reserve' – may be set aside to cater for unexpected opportunities or setbacks. These sub-divisions within the overall appropriation are discussed elsewhere.

You may also encounter division of the budget for yet another reason: to set aside funds for manufacturer/stockist co-operative advertising. Many firms find it productive to share with retailers the cost of advertisements in local media, announcing that they stock the merchandise featured in the campaign. When retailers consider their advertising budgets, they should clearly take into account this possible source of additional funds. Some advertisers also set aside funds as a contribution to a co-operative advertising campaign mounted on an industry-wide basis, to increase demand for their product group as a whole.

The question 'Who pays for a pan-European advertising campaign?' often proves a vexed one. Similar questions are also asked about funding corporate or umbrella campaigns within a single country. Many multi-national companies have for years adopted a philosophy of decentralisation, with individual operating companies generating their own advertising budgets. In many cases, a central advertising budget did not exist. The availability of satellite-delivered pan-European television has lead many multi-national companies to institute new procedures for funding advertising campaigns which appear simultaneously in different countries. There are two alternatives: 'top down' funding (a central advertising budget above and beyond those of the operating companies) or 'bottom up' (whereby the operating companies contribute to the central fund). Similar 'top down' or 'bottom up' considerations apply to the funding of corporate or 'umbrella' advertising campaigns.

Long-term planning

Finally, mention must be made of long-term budgeting. The various methods described all imply an *annual* appropriation, but the custom of yearly decisions is largely an artificial one arising from accounting practice, and many companies now take a longer-term view. When launching a new product, they accept that it will be impossible to realise a profit within a calendar year. It is unrealistic to expect a new venture to show a profit situation within a day, a week or a month – why should you expect to move into a profit situation within a year? It is long-term prospects which are important, since your company plans to be in business long term. Accordingly, the marketing plan covers four or more years, for example, depending on the estimated time needed to capture the market. The first year of operation may involve a considerable loss, in the second year the company breaks even, the third year shows a sufficient profit to offset the first year's loss and a true profit is not made until the fourth year. The first-year loss is a calculated situation, and that year's appropriation is regarded as an investment to be recouped by subsequent sales. Some conventional accountants resist the concept of advertising as investment, since they see no tangible assets they could sell off in the same way that they can dispose of production plant. But since machinery is purchased not to sell but to produce, surely advertising should be treated in the same way? Accountants are more than accustomed to the concept of 'depreciation', spreading capital expenditure over a number of years, so it is surprising that many find it difficult to adopt this approach with advertising.

Long-term budgeting calls for a 'pay-out' schedule. In simplest possible terms, the company calculates two cash flows – the rate at which money is being spent, and the rate at which it is coming in. As we all know from personal experience, we soon run into difficulties if cash goes out faster than it comes in, and the same applies to companies. They must therefore work out how much capital is needed to keep things going until a profit situation is reached: it would be more than unfortunate to run out of capital on the very eve of showing the first true profit. So this is where the accountants should come into their own – a marketing-orientated accountant can make a most valuable contribution.

Equally, any advertising and marketing executive will find a knowledge of financial skills and terminology a most useful asset - even if only in arguments with the more conventional accountants whose instinctive reaction in times of recession is to cut the advertising budget. Most advertising and marketing people have this argument more than once during their careers!

At the start of the chapter, mention was made that fixing the appropriation is a management decision, and it is to this point we must return before concluding. The appropriation is decided at director level, and advertising and marketing staff must learn to live with this figure. There is always a temptation to ask for more money to take advantage of some special offer. This temptation should be avoided, for the appropriation was decided after very careful thought. Even if you do decide to ask for more money, there may be no Board meeting for some weeks and, in any event, is the Board likely to view this special offer – a very minor event in the total company operation – with the same enthusiasm as you do? Covering such events is the function of the contingency reserve described later: this is a very different matter from a *major* overall review of company policy. Should the economic situation, for example, change to such an extent that your company's marketing plans are no longer valid, the Board would swiftly meet to deal with the new situation as a matter of urgency, and would review all aspects of business activity – production levels, prices and, of course, advertising. Such a major review is a very different matter from coping with the temporary and minor setbacks which are an unfortunate but unavoidable feature of business life.

THE NEXT STEP

Now that your budget is known, your next task is preparation of campaign proposals to achieve your advertising objective.

Chapter 15

Preparation of Advertising Proposals

Advertising planning is only part of overall marketing, and for effective use of media you must think in terms of your marketing objective – that you manufacture a product (or provide a service), with product policy and advertising and distribution and selling effort all geared to achieving sales in a chosen segment of the market. To talk of campaign planning is misleading, however, since this implies a *single* campaign, whereas effective planning is more complex. Quite apart from the need to 'aim' your product correctly, including its branding and packaging, your promotional activities must also seek to achieve the same marketing objective and here it is usually more correct to talk of *campaigns* in the plural.

Before the purchaser can buy your product it must be available; before your product can be in the shops your sales staff must put it there; and before they can do so they must be fully briefed. Any successful campaign, therefore, has at least three components – a campaign to potential purchasers, a second to distributors, and a third aimed at your own sales force. Each of these groups could be the target of several types of promotional activity: advertising, created media, merchandising and sales promotion, and public relations. This book is concerned with the advertising aspect alone, but you must consider this in context, if you are to plan effectively. Media planning, although vital, is only one part of your overall promotional campaign, and must interlock with the others.

THE MEDIA BRIEF

If you ask any media planner to tell you, in confidence, what causes the most problems, the majority will say it is a request for media proposals unaccompanied by adequate information. Many will complain of clients – or even agency executives – who rush in to demand 'a £750,000 schedule for new product X'. Such individuals fail to appreciate that a full briefing is essential for the effective use of advertising media. The adequacy of this briefing directly affects the effectiveness of the media planning. If an inadequate briefing is given, there is no firm basis on which to evaluate the advantages of the different media, or on which to construct an effective schedule. For this reason, it can be vital for the media executive to contribute to the formulation of the media brief, rather than play a passive role 'on the receiving end'.

The earlier chapters on research and investigations and on problem analysis detailed much of the information you need if you are to prepare the most effective media plan. Part of your media brief has yet to come, however – the creative aspects.

CREATIVE/MEDIA INTERACTION

The two aspects of preparation of proposals – choosing the media and creating the advertisements – are complementary activities and, whilst this book is concerned primarily with media, you are directly affected by creative considerations. If your schedule provides for half-page advertisements in certain publications, this implies a creative decision that the insertions are to be of half-page size in press media and, at the same time, it is equally a media decision – to book half-page advertisements in selected publications on certain dates at a cost of £X. Creative and media decisions are therefore usually taken simultaneously, but the dominant aspect may be either media or creative. For example, media selection may be determined by the creative need to show your product in colour or to employ a medium which demonstrates its use. Alternatively, creative needs may take second place to the market requirement of informing a clearly defined target group, which one medium covers more effectively than others.

The attention factor

Media decisions overlap with creative considerations in another way, when attracting potential purchasers' attention to your advertising message. It is insufficient simply to place it before them by choosing a suitable advertising medium: you must also decide how to attract their attention. The first essential for effective advertising is attention, for without this your advertisement cannot communicate. There are various devices for attracting attention: some of them concern creative work alone, but others have media implications.

All these devices have one thing in common, however: their full utilisation implies a media knowledge which goes far beyond circulation or readership statistics alone. Hence the importance of the concept of 'candidate media' discussed earlier, and the need to study each of those in depth. What is the format of the medium, and what regular (or occasional) features does it have? What advertisement positions are available, and on which pages? These factors in fact suggest an alternative title for this book: The *Creative* Use of Advertising Media. Creativity and media planning/buying should be considered as interactive, rather than treated as separate activities.

Size

A large advertisement in itself attracts attention (and is more impressive to those who see it, as well as giving greater scope for creativity and the inclusion of more information). The creative/media decision to use advertisement size as the attention device has clear scheduling implications. You should always bear in mind, however, that sheer size is no substitute for creativity and may be extremely wasteful – full pages in broadsheet newspapers may be *too* big to be read comfortably, except at arm's length. For this reason, many media-planners prefer to book 'page killer' sizes: solus positions large enough to dominate the page.

Position

A press advertisement on the front page, or facing or next to editorial matter, or in a solus position without competition from other advertisers, is likely to be seen by more people than one appearing alongside others within the body of the publication. Positioning on particular pages also serves as an attention filter, by placing your advertisement before those readers who, by the very act of reading the selected editorial, indicate that they are likely to have an interest in your product. Additionally, such positioning is more likely to attract attention, simply because these self-selecting readers are in a receptive state of mind. Again, the decision to use position as an attention device directly affects your media plan.

Colour

Colour is often used as an attraction device. Printing in a second colour can attract (and highlight parts of the advertisement) while full-colour advertisements also permit you to show your product in its natural colours which, with some merchandise, is a vital factor in influencing consumers' buying decisions. The creative need for colour to attract attention clearly influences media planning, particularly if creative staff stress high quality colour reproduction.

Illustration

A product well-illustrated is often more than half sold, and advertisements featuring illustrations usually have greater impact than those without. 'Action' pictures, showing your product in use with people enjoying its benefits, have strong attention value. Whilst these are mainly creative considerations, it is obvious that the quality of reproduction required directly affects media selection.

Movement

Movement, as in a moving exhibition display or a unit which lights up from time to time, attracts attention through contrast with the static background.

Demonstrating your product in use can also attract attention through movement, and not all media permit this. Once again, creative requirements have strong media implications.

Sound

The human voice can quickly attract attention and also convey a message. Music and other sound effects can similarly attract attention as well as influence the mood of the listeners, who become more receptive to your advertising message. The need for sound to fulfil these functions again influences media selection.

Headlines (and body copy)

Writing headlines which serve as an attention device is the copywriter's speciality, as is producing interesting and compelling text for the body of the advertisement. There is a simple formula which provides a helpful checklist in preparing (and evaluating) advertisements. It is expressed mainly in terms of press advertising, but the points made apply to most advertisements, subject only to adaptation for the medium in question. There is an easy way of remembering the formula

– the initial letters of the four checkpoints form the title of an opera: AIDA. These creative checkpoints – all of which have media implications – are:

Attention
Interest
Desire
Action

AIDA is not the only model of how advertising works – another suggests an Awareness/Comprehension/Conviction/Action process, while the ATR model is an analysis based on Awareness, Trial and Reinforcement. Detailed examination of these models is outside the immediate scope of this book, but the purpose of mentioning them is to point out their relevance to media planning. Taking the AIDA model as an example, the first and last checkpoints have immediate media implications. The use of media planning (rather than creative devices) to attract attention has clear scheduling implications, and the same is true of many 'Action devices'. If your advertising objective is consumer *action* (rather than, for example, reminder advertising or image-building) this has direct media implications, since this may demand selection of a medium which facilitates action by your potential consumers. Examples such as coupons in press advertisements, reply cards in magazines or direct mail shots, or reply services on television and radio, all clearly illustrate how the final action checkpoint has media implications which are just as direct as the opening attention factor. Even the other two checkpoints – interest and desire – cannot be considered as having creative implications only, and thus not influencing media selection: never forget that the mood of your potential purchasers, when your advertising message is received, is an important criterion for media comparison.

Advertising strategy determined your campaign objective. This must now be translated to communication objectives: what must you say to whom, and how, for your advertising to be successful? Effective media planning and creation of persuasive and attention-getting advertisements are thus complementary activities and both are essential for effective advertising. Clearly there is little point in placing your advertising message before those who are not potential buyers, nor in buying media if your advertisements fail to capture attention or feature the wrong sale propositions or are not sufficiently persuasive. It is, therefore, vital that both media and creative staff agree that the market could best be reached by advertisements of a certain size, in an agreed broad group of media. The media staff must feel that this broad plan gives them sufficient scope for effective scheduling, and the creative staff must similarly consider that the plan permits them to express the selling message persuasively. Creative and media departments then work independently, the creative staff preparing their copy and design proposals, and the media planners calculating the scheduling possibilities within the broad media groups agreed. The next step for the media staff is to plan in detail how to spend the appropriation so as to get maximum effect for every penny spent.

MARKET WEIGHTING

Your media problem is not simply to decide whether or not Medium A is to appear on your schedule. The problem underlying all media planning is how your appropriation should be allocated over time, how it should be divided between the different sales areas and what weight of advertising should be directed to different segments of the market. This is sometimes decided on what is described as the 'case rate' method, by which expenditure is in direct proportion to sales. Thus, if Sales Area A accounts for 30 per cent of total purchases, it would seem logical to devote 30 per cent of your budget to media that will stimulate that area. The spread of expenditure across the year may be decided in the same way, according to each month's sales figures: months when the market is ripe in terms of actual purchases will thus receive heavier advertising than the months in which sales figures indicate that the market is not in a buying mood. Case-rate spending thus provides a sound basis for media scheduling: as we shall see later, however, there are often good reasons for departing from this planning base.

MEDIA ALLOCATIONS

A first step in constructing the schedule most suitable for achieving your marketing objective is often to divide the overall appropriation into separate allocations for each of the different media groups on which your campaign is to be based. Amounts are allocated to individual media groups – so much for television, so much for national and local press, so much for posters, and so on. This is sometimes called the 'Media Split' stage, or the 'inter-media' decision.

Newcomers to advertising are often surprised that media planning is both precise and empirical, and that the perfect media schedule is rarely produced at the first attempt. There is in fact no one right answer, and so media planners consider innumerable ways of spending the appropriation, assessing one schedule against others, before making final recommendations. The schedule that is finally booked may well be the end result of first calculating and then contrasting perhaps dozens of possible alternatives.

The same practice applies when allocating between different media. Should the appropriation be divided, for example, between press and television, then possible schedules will be constructed for these two media groups and the overall costings compared: if good press coverage can be achieved without spending the provisional allocation in full but additional money is needed to obtain an adequate television schedule (or *vice versa*) then the media split will be changed and the inter-media allocations adjusted accordingly.

DETAILED PLANNING

Within any group of media, the same constructing of different schedules, and consequent adjustment, is also the rule. Taking into account the duration of your campaign, the advertisement size selected, the required frequency of appearance, and the list of candidate media that initially appear most suitable (probably on a cost ranking basis, as described below), the first step is to cost a preliminary schedule. The chance of this basic arithmetic resulting in a sum that exactly balances the allocation is small, so several possible schedules are costed out. Should the preliminary costing exceed the allocation, then expenditure must be cut back and you must evaluate the best way to do this. In the simplest possible terms, there are just four ways in which your preliminary schedule can be adjusted. These are:

1 Advertisement unit One solution might be to reduce the size of your advertisement, or to abandon the use of colour, of special positions or of peak time. If essential creative or other considerations make this impossible, then you must consider other alternatives.

2 Frequency Another approach would be to reduce frequency and have, for example, alternate week instead of weekly insertions. Marketing requirements, however, may make this solution unacceptable and you must, therefore, consider other possibilities.

3 Duration Another alternative would be to curtail your campaign and maintain it for only (for example) 11 months instead of a full year, omitting periods when the market is dead. There is, however, a fourth possibility you must consider.

4 Media list Another solution is to reduce the number of candidate media included in your schedule, in order to maintain the weight of advertising in those retained.

The variables you can use for media planning permutations are thus basically four: dominance (in terms of size, position or colour), frequency of appearance, duration/continuity of campaign, and the media list. In every case, except the last, you must take into account *non-media* considerations, since the advertisement unit can be changed only after consultation with creative staff, and the frequency of appearance and length of campaign are determined by marketing factors such as how often your buyers must be reminded, and the duration of your selling campaign. These problems are magnified by the fact that rate cards tend to be only indicative of cost, and are really often only a starting point for negotiations at the later buying stage.

Often, these considerations lead inevitably to a reconsideration of the case-rate spending method. Case-rate spending, with expenditure proportionate to sales, can be likened to a chicken and egg situation. Should you spend 30 per cent of budget to maintain the 30 per cent of sales – or have you achieved 30 per cent of sales in that month or this area simply because you have always devoted to it 30 per cent of your advertising expenditure? This leads to a marketing-cum-media re-examination of the cause-and-effect of the case-rate situation: from this re-examination two other strategies may arise. The two alternatives – increased or decreased expenditure – are both based on consideration of *potential* as distinct from actual sales.

1 Increase You may decide to boost a particular month or area by devoting *more* than the case-rate amount on the assumption that, although according to past sales figures it merits only, for example, ten per cent of expenditure, there is in fact a far greater potential which would respond to added stimulation. Hence the media/marketing decision to step up the advertising in the selected area, market segment or time of year. But with limited funds, where is the additional expenditure to come from, if not from the standard four variables already mentioned? The other alternative to case-rate spending, in fact, releases funds rather than calling for additional expenditure.

2 Decrease Here, your assumption is that demand is relatively stable: in economic terms, it is 'inelastic'. People have perhaps got to buy a certain minimum amount of your product. After heavy Christmas spending, for example, many people have no funds to spare and keep their spending to a minimum. No amount of heavy advertising can persuade them to buy more, since they just do not have the cash to do so. Conversely, however, there is a minimum amount they must buy – and would do so even without any advertising stimulus. Alternatively, on a more positive note, you may consider that one particularly brand-loyal market segment would maintain its level of purchases, despite a reduction in advertising frequency. Hence you may take the media/marketing decision to reduce advertising activity in a particular month or market in the belief that demand is inelastic and sales will remain at that level even when advertising is cut.

OTHER VARIABLES

The balancing of advertisement unit, frequency, duration and media list, and re-examination of these four variables against the case-rate method, by no means exhausts the media scheduling possibilities open to you. Other variations should also be considered.

Multiple-size campaigns Many campaigns call for more than one size of advertisement so that, rather than use one uniform size throughout, you plan your media schedule using two or more sizes – and a new possibility in the media 'balancing act' is thus open to you. For example, you may open your campaign with a half-page advertisement, followed by quarter-page advertisements in each of the following three weeks, reverting to a half-page advertisement and more quarter-pages in a repeating pattern. Use of two sizes enables you to get the best of the two worlds of impact and repetition, and many campaigns are based on this principle. Sometimes a third and very dominant size, perhaps a full-page advertisement, may be used to launch your campaign, simply to impress retailers and assist your salesmen in persuading them to both stock and display your merchandise.

Multiple sizes can also be used with other media such as television, where you will often see a combination of longer commercials and shorter 'edited' versions. This is yet another example of where media and creative staff must work together. Research has proved that such creative/media co-operation can be most effective. When shown a shortened version, many of those interviewed often respond with total recall of the full commercial screened earlier!

Drip versus burst A variation on the increase versus decrease and multiple-size approaches is to base your planning on 'Burst' rather than 'Drip' advertising. A campaign based on the drip approach calls for steady advertising over a period, on the premise that 'constant dripping wears away a stone'. The burst approach on the other hand concentrates resources into a limited number of weeks to achieve greater impact (larger sizes, greater frequency or more extensive media list) within the period. A typical burst campaign might consist of four weeks on/twelve weeks off/four weeks on, in a repeating pattern. This variation of the multiple-size campaign incorporates the boost versus abandon approach to planning, the difference being that one of the multiple 'sizes' is zero, i.e. advertising is abandoned in certain weeks in order to boost the others. Although the burst approach offers advertising advantages by concentrating campaign impact, it can present marketing problems by complicating the retail stock control of advertised products. There is also the problem of 'decay' – will your market forget you in the intervals between bursts?

Media in combination Few campaigns are based on a single advertising vehicle but rely on various media used at the same time. Economists refer to the 'Law of Diminishing Returns' and this applies just as much to media planning as to other types of expenditure. You may feel that one medium has received a sufficient weight of advertising, and that it would not be worthwhile spending any more money in it. You therefore consider other media for this reason, and also because it permits you to reach the same market but by other means, for fresh impact. The chapter on budgeting outlined the marginal method of deciding your appropriation, and this approach can be applied to the use of media in combination – will the last £X,000 spent on your first medium bring as good a result as the same £X,000 spent on the alternatives?

The term 'media in combination' masks two separate considerations: *inter*-media and *intra*-media comparison. The former concerns the 'media split' stage, and thus refers to multi-media campaigns which cover, for example, newspapers *and* television *and* magazines. The intra-media consideration concerns media *within* a group e.g. within press using publications A *and* B (*or* C?). With both aspects of the term, you encounter the problem of distinguishing between 'duplication' and 'net extra coverage'.

Duplication Duplication means reaching the same market by different media. To some extent all media duplicate since people read newspapers and magazines, watch television and see posters, and advertisers contact them through all these media. Duplication, viewed from another standpoint, represents an increase in one of the four basic variables: frequency. If monthly contact with prospective buyers is your aim, monthly insertions in two media whose coverage overlaps means that those who see both media see two advertisements each month instead of one, and therefore receive double the frequency you think necessary. Two alternatives are open to you: to maintain monthly insertions in one publication and delete the other from your schedule, or to use the two publications in alternate months, thus maintaining regularity but giving this part of your market a monthly stimulus through alternative means, for variety of impact.

Net extra coverage If duplication and thus unwanted repetition is to be avoided, you will seek media giving you the greatest net extra coverage. Two additional candidate publications may be under consideration, one of which has a much larger readership than the other and therefore, on the surface, seems a better proposition. However, if most of this larger readership is already covered by media already on your schedule, this means you would contact these people with higher frequency than is necessary. If, on the other hand, the publication with the smaller readership gives little duplication, then by using this medium you will reach entirely new prospects to whom no advertising message has yet been delivered. By seeking net extra coverage, you thus increase the overall *penetration* of your campaign.

The two factors of duplication and net extra coverage reflect contrasting marketing objectives. If your marketing aim is to reach as many prospective buyers as possible (even if with only a single advertising message) then you should aim for net extra coverage and thus maximum penetration. If, however, your marketing objective is to achieve maximum repetition, duplication of coverage is preferable. In practice, however, you are unlikely to want to operate at either *extreme* end of this scale.

Cumulative coverage (or reach) Coverage is the proportion of the target group who have at least one opportunity of seeing your advertisement. Although the number of people reading the average issue of a publication remains constant, the same people do not always read every issue. Thus additional advertisements in a series can add new readers, thereby increasing your cumulative audience (as well as giving those already covered an additional opportunity to see your advertisement). Cumulative cover in this sense reflects the penetration of your campaign.

Opportunities-to-see How many advertisements will your target groups see? The average frequency is often called the average 'OTS' or opportunities-to-see (or hear), and is defined as the number of potential exposures received by the average reader/viewer/listener. Any average OTS or OTH figure must be treated with care when considering a possible schedule, for it can mask wide variations in the number of opportunities received by different members of your target group.

Frequency distribution This will give you a more detailed breakdown of opportunities-to-see across your target groups in terms of coverage. Coverage is very often linked with the levels of opportunities-to-see, *viz* 2+, 3+, 4+ and so on, showing the number (or percentage) of the audience likely to have that stated number of opportunities to see your campaign. Frequency distribution should reflect the marketing priorities of your market segments, and the market weighting discussed earlier. The vital need for a full media briefing is again apparent.

SOME UNCHARTED TERRITORIES

The fact that you can pump statistics about net extra coverage *versus* duplication through a computer to see the effect of adding publication A rather than publication B to your schedule has led many people to think the 'science' of advertising is at a very advanced state. And, taking data-processing aids into account and setting aside any research weaknesses (what *is* a reader/viewer/listener?) then our industry has made enormous strides in recent years – and is light years ahead of those countries which do not have authentic circulation figures, let alone reliable viewing, reading or listening figures.

It would be a false kindness, however, to omit mention of any weaknesses. When it comes to the basic matter of how advertising *works* and how the whole marketing communications/purchasing-decision process operates, it must be bluntly stated that there is a great deal more to know before we can claim complete mastery of advertising as a business tool. It would need another book to discuss these uncharted areas in full, so they can be touched on only briefly here. The fields in which we need more knowledge include the following:

Campaign period

This is not a matter of whether your campaign runs for 6, 8 or 12 months, but of the campaign's effects on consumers. What is the 'life' of an advertisement or of a campaign, and what would happen if you stopped advertising? Chapter 13 described the natural decline built in to any market and the need to remind those remaining but, should you stop advertising, how fast would its effects 'decay' and how swiftly would your sales start to fall? How strong is brand loyalty to your products, and what part does advertising play in maintaining this loyalty? As campaign duration is a basic variable in your media-balancing act, more information is needed. Under this heading – but beyond the scope of this book – you should also consider the creative use made of the space booked. How quickly will your current campaign 'wear out', and how swiftly should you replace it with a new one? This may in turn be affected by the next factor – the frequency with which people see your advertisements.

Frequency

This is another basic variable, but little is known *in detail* about its effects. It is all very well to have rules-of-thumb about weekly reminders for weekly products and so on, and these do perhaps give a guide to the minimum frequency required. But what about *maximum* frequency? Is increased frequency necessarily beneficial? Can you always equate heavy usage of your product with heavy exposure to your advertising? And can you, in fact, dissociate this from your campaign's *creative content*? Will over-exposure perhaps be counter-productive? People have argued, for example, that some heavily repeated television commercials have an irritation factor which harms rather than helps sales. All of us have seen humorous commercials which were extremely amusing at first viewing but for which we dreaded subsequent screenings and, with some people, hard-sell commercials have the same effect. Cultural differences may be important, since different things irritate (or motivate) different groups. There is very little published data on this area.

Multi-media campaigns

You can compare with relative accuracy the results – in numerical terms – of adding Newspaper A rather than B to your schedule, or Magazine C instead of D. When it comes to comparing different media groups – comparing *Newspaper* A or B with *Magazine* C or D – you are on less certain ground. And when it comes to assessing these in comparison with a totally different medium – whether this be television, cinema, radio, outdoor or any other media – you are in largely uncharted territory. While *intra*-media research (comparing publication A with B) is relatively advanced, *inter*-media research is still at the experimental stage. When looked at in terms of the way advertising works and the purchasing-decision process, there is certainly no 'map' to help you find your way. There are, however, a few 'pointers'. If, as the Law of Diminishing Returns suggests, you should use more than one medium or one media group, it is best to examine the possible ways which you could use them, and then evaluate these alternatives against your advertising objective. In making such an assessment there are marketing and creative as well as media considerations. Multi-media schedules can achieve various objectives.

1 Additional coverage By adding new media you can increase your cumulative cover and thus the total penetration of your campaign. A variation on the same theme is to rectify any weaknesses in the coverage of those media already on your schedule. Clearly this is a matter of marketing/media rather than creative considerations.

2 **Added frequency** Through a multi-media campaign, your target market may have more opportunities to see your advertisements. This again has mainly marketing/media considerations, but you should consider how your customers will react to this increased frequency.

3 Different media The aim here is the very opposite of (1): rather than increase penetration, you wish to reach the same people. It overlaps with (2) but, even though you may deliver the same message more often, your target audience receives it through a *new* medium, often with a different environment (at home or work or while travelling) for fresh impact. This is not a simple matter of added frequency and there are important creative considerations, as some media groups are more complementary than others when used in combination. The term 'synergism' (or visual transfer) is used to describe, for example, the degree to which people exposed to a given TV campaign can re-create the visual component with only the TV soundtrack to trigger their memories. TV *plus* radio is the obvious example, but the same principle of beneficial 'transfer', with one medium reinforcing the other, applies to other combinations. Some combinations, eg TV and Radio, have considerable 'built-in' synergism, while others have it to a lesser degree. Where there is minimal media synergism, this should be achieved by creative means.

4 Strategy variations All three variations so far described assume your advertisements have the same creative content: the variables are *who* you reach, *how* you reach them and *how often* – not *what you say*.

Should this be so, or should you consider variations in creative strategy? The concept of 'mood' is nothing new in media evaluation, and the same is true of creating advertisements to suit the media that are to carry them. Even if reaching the same people in demographic terms, many advertising practitioners put these two concepts into practice, and develop different creative approaches to suit the different media. Others ask if you will, in fact, reach the same *kind* of people, even if the standard demographic characteristics are similar? Are the people you reach through one medium more (or less) likely to buy – or try – your product than the people you reach through alternative media? The Media Preference Groups' analysis described earlier has shown marked differences in the purchasing patterns of people reached by different media, even though the demographic descriptions are the same. Should your media selection and creative content change accordingly?

Added cost

In addition to considering these possible ways of mounting a multi-media campaign, you must also bear in mind you have changed yet another variable: cost. Quite apart from the fundamental cost of buying an additional medium there is the added expense – in terms of time and effort as well as money – of preparing advertisements for the new medium.

Multi-media campaigns thus have implications far beyond media choice alone, and these fundamental questions give a new importance to problem analysis and the vital need to establish a *true* campaign objective. Before leaving these relatively uncharted areas, you should bear in mind that a great deal of exploratory work is being done – with some very interesting results, so you should keep up-to-date with new developments. However, much of this pioneer work is undertaken to gain a competitive advantage and, understandably, the results are not always published. But Part 1 listed sources of media news, and you should therefore consult these regularly to keep up-to-date with new developments.

RESPONSE FUNCTIONS

Balancing cover against repetition has always been a difficult planning problem, and most decisions have been taken after analysing schedules rather than applying a 'Response Factor' in advance when preparing the media proposals. Given a fixed budget, the variable of cover as against repetition is the amount of advertising each individual receives and, when a mathematical response model is used, you must state the objectives of your campaign in numerical terms. These numbers describe the response you expect from the individuals exposed to your advertising.

A response function is a weighting system for overall schedule construction, based on your subjective judgment of how your advertising works and specifically how many exposures are necessary for your advertising to be effective. A *cumulative* response function is a set of numbers defining the relative value to the advertiser of an individual in his target group receiving one, two or more advertising impressions, and must be distinguished from the corresponding *additional* response function – the added value given by each separate additional exposure.

Response functions are often employed when using a computer optimisation program (see below) to construct a schedule. Although expressed numerically to give the computer a weighting factor for each successive advertising exposure received by the individual, graphs are often used in formulating response functions and as a basis for discussing the type of advertising campaign best suited to achieve your chosen objective. Such discussion must necessarily be general, involving creative and marketing considerations as well as media. In that these graphs reflect the 'shape' of your campaign, five possible response functions are illustrated here, rather than in the later discussion on computers.

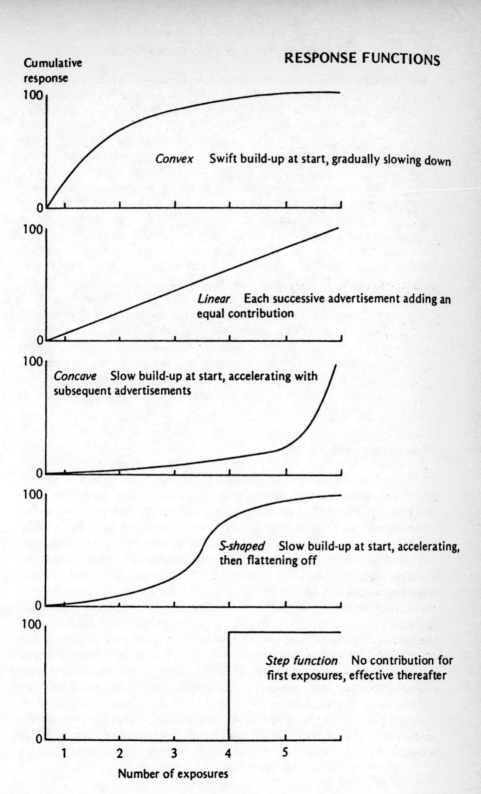

Cumulative response

100

0

Convex   Swift build-up at start, gradually slowing down

100

0

Linear   Each successive advertisement adding an equal contribution

100

0

Concave   Slow build-up at start, accelerating with subsequent advertisements

100

0

S-shaped   Slow build-up at start, accelerating, then flattening off

100

0

Step function   No contribution for first exposures, effective thereafter

1   2   3   4   5

Number of exposures

RESOLVING THE INEVITABLE CONFLICT

In balancing all these variable factors, there is necessarily some element of conflict, and you must be aware of the danger of trying to meet *all* requirements, since it is unlikely that you can meet them all. Somebody once said that a camel looks like a horse designed by a committee. Similarly, if you try to balance the variables by merely reaching a compromise, the result is likely to be an ineffective schedule. In another sense, however, all media planning is necessarily a compromise – if you satisfy the requirement for one of the variables in the media balancing act, you are likely to fall short on the others. It is important, therefore, for you to establish whether coverage is more important than repetition, and the relative priority of other factors. Trying to please everybody may lead to the appropriation being so widely dispersed that your advertising ceases to have any solid impact.

A generally accepted rule is to give each medium a sufficient weight of advertising before adding others to the schedule. One way to avoid a weak compromise is the well-established 'concentration-domination-repetition' principle advocated by many practitioners. For this reason, the suggestion that you cut back 'just one' insertion in one medium to permit inclusion of another in your schedule, is unlikely to result in effective advertising.

The shotgun principle

The very opposite approach to media planning is the 'shotgun' principle often followed by advertisers launching new products into unknown markets. The same approach can be applied by those whose fragmented markets cannot be defined in terms of age, sex, social grade, occupation, geographical location or any other conventional demographic criteria. How can you communicate advertising messages to clear but widely diffused markets (such as people who need glasses, have bad breath or back trouble, or suffer from haemorrhoids) when there may be no medium, or group of media, which gives particular coverage of these target groups? If it is impossible to achieve concentration, domination and repetition, one alternative is to pepper the market on the shotgun principle, often with a wide spread of small advertisements which, through their headlines, select potential purchasers from the total audience reached by the media in which they appear.

As we have seen, 'shotgun' schedules can also be used as a market research tool. In such cases, the actual campaign would be executed on a flexible basis, according to results. Three 'separate' planning stages – preparation of proposals, execution, and evaluation – are thus all directly inter-related.

Scheduling stages

There are thus two distinct stages in scheduling. First, there is the arithmetical work of costing and balancing alternative schedules taking into account cost ranking and other variables discussed below. Second, and more important, is the work of evaluating these schedules to select the best. The second task involves just as much arithmetic as the first, in assessing facts about coverage and cost per thousand, quite apart from value judgments about qualitative factors such as the means of transmitting your message, and the mood of prospective purchasers when they receive it. The process of schedule construction, calculating possible alternatives and contrasting each to see which gives the best results, means a tremendous amount of work in evaluating media research data and in sheer arithmetical calculations. Many advertisers, agencies and media-owners therefore now use computers to make these calculations.

THE COMPUTER IN MEDIA-SCHEDULING

Most data processing experts stress that a computer is nothing more than an incredibly fast and accurate idiot, which does exactly what you tell it and nothing more. The way in which a computer is instructed is known as a 'program': note that this is spelt differently from the conventional theatre 'programme'. The names of these programs are often acronyms based on initials: thus AASAM stands for Area Allocation System for Advertising Money, SORBA stands for Systems for Optimising Regional Budget Allocations, BAR stands for Budget Allocation by Region and BAT for Budget Allocation over Time – all four programs are variations on the case-rate spending method, which take into account a wide range of different variables. One leading agency even developed ABACUS (Advertising Budget Allocation and Co-ordination Utility Systems), IMPART (Intrinsic Model for Predicting Audience Reach in Television), PREFACE (Predictive Formula for Audience Coverage Estimation), RASCAL (RAdio Schedule Coverage ALgorithm) and SESAME (System for Evaluating, Setting and Allocating Media Expenditure). The computer experts even have a name for the program which reveals the computer's idiocy – GIGO, standing for 'Garbage In, Garbage Out' or, in more British terms – 'Ask a silly question and you get a silly answer'.

The term computer is a catch-all expression and covers the huge mainframe machines down to the miniest microcomputers, and includes both users' own installations and use of external service bureaux. Computers have influenced the effective use of advertising media in various ways, one of which is simply accounting and control. A great deal of straightforward office work has been transferred to computers. In essence this amounts only to shifting the burden of work rather than venturing into new fields, but there are further repercussions. The computer can lead to far greater efficiency in normal office routine with faster, more up-to-date and accurate paperwork. Speeded-up paperwork can lead to invoices being paid more promptly. The computer cannot extract money, but it can 'invite' people to pay earlier, simply by sending out invoices more quickly. Similarly, payments can be made by the computer which can also write out cheques. Many of these points apply to all those concerned with the effective use of media – advertisers, agencies, media-owners and specialist services.

Computers can, however, make a more positive contribution to effective use of media, but it is important to bear in mind that the underlying principles of media planning remain the same whether or not a computer is used: data processing merely helps you to work more efficiently. The contribution the computer can make to media planning depends on the information it is given and the calculations it is asked to make.

Input

The information supplied to a computer, as the basis for its calculations, falls into two broad categories.

1 Factual data Research statistics, such as the size and composition of the media audience and the wealth of data described in Part 1, can easily be put into the computer's memory, as can information about costs.

2 Quantified value judgments This involves you in assigning 'weights' to various qualitative factors, such as whether you think mood and the time spent reading a publication make magazine readers more 'valuable' than newspaper readers. Similarly, you might wish to assign relative media values to high quality reproduction, or to colour as against black and white, or to availability of sound and movement and so on.

If you value a magazine reader as 1½ units and a newspaper reader as only 1, because you believe that magazines are better able to communicate your advertising message, this will clearly bias the results in favour of magazines. Value judgments are not infallible simply because they are processed by a computer. Effective use of media is still based on media research data backed up by media judgment, a situation no different from that encountered in the past. The task is basically unchanged, once the veil of mystery that surrounds computers is removed.

Calculations

You can instruct the computer to perform various types of operation:

1 Cross-tabulation The computer can cross-tabulate the data contained in any readership or market research survey, to provide additional analyses not included in the standard tables.

2 Cost ranking Candidate media can be ranked in cost-efficiency terms against your target market, taking the price to be paid for the space available and relating this to the readership. In this way the computer establishes an order of priority for candidate media to appear on your schedule, expressed in terms of cost efficiency. If desired, you can include your own weights for the demographic constituents of the market and for the media themselves.

3 Schedule optimisation Because of the speed of operation, it is possible for the computer to contrast literally thousands of possible schedules within a very brief space of time, and select the best according to specified criteria. If maximum coverage of a selected market group at the most economic cost is your aim, you can instruct the computer to calculate the combination of media which, for a given expenditure, produces the highest total coverage at the lowest cost per thousand. Value judgements, as well as research data and costs, can also be taken into account if required.

4 Schedule evaluation The purpose of this approach is not to say whether a schedule is the best possible, but to estimate what a schedule will achieve. You can use it, for example, to estimate what total coverage would be achieved for each market group for each month of your schedule. An evaluation program can compute the coverage, the gross opportunities-to-see, the average frequency, the schedule cost, the cost per thousand opportunities-to-see and the frequency distribution of these opportunities. Evaluation techniques tell you what you get for your money, leaving you to make your own decision.

5 Performance evaluation The computer can be instructed to evaluate schedule performance over time (comparing the results of one advertising period with another) to improve advertising scheduling to suit marketing objectives.

Whichever task the computer performs, you are free from the chore of innumerable mathematical calculations, and can concentrate on your main task of planning. Consideration of alternative schedules need no longer be limited by the work involved in producing them.

An indirect advantage of using a computer is that media are no longer vaguely assessed. To use the computer, you must draw up precise criteria by which to judge media, and you no longer evaluate them by loose 'experience and judgment'. Media planning moves from vague personal preferences into the area of facts, clearly stated value judgments and specific performance criteria.

THE NEXT STEP

With your campaign proposals prepared, your next step is to evaluate them as carefully as possible, to ensure to the best of your ability that they will achieve your chosen objective.

Chapter 16

Approval of Advertising Proposals

Approval of proposals is a far more complex a matter than it appears, and you will need time to review the proposals overall, to check the reasoning behind the media schedule, to study the creative proposals, and to ensure that all the component parts of the plan interlock. When your campaign is a large and complex one, this task may take some weeks. Sometimes, campaign approval is an on-going procedure rather than a single task but, even with relatively simple proposals, it is rarely possible to give an instant OK, since approval has repercussions far beyond advertising alone.

Before you can approve campaign proposals, you must check them from several different standpoints. The approval process has both interesting and routine aspects: where many executives slip up is that in their eagerness to consider the more glamorous creative aspects they sometimes overlook checking the duller internal and external background on which their campaign is based. In consequence, basic errors often pass unnoticed.

While it is important to scrutinise proposals meticulously before giving your approval, it is equally important to do so as swiftly as possible. Early approval gives more time for execution, thus preventing the mistakes which so often occur with rush jobs. Delay in approving proposals, quite apart from increasing the likelihood of expensive errors, can result in missed deadlines. What a waste of money if you have no advertisement to appear in the spaces for which you are legally liable to pay! Swift approval can also lead to cost savings: undue delay could result in your finding all the best positions already booked by competitors, and having to bid at high rates for the few remaining spaces!

INTERNAL ASPECTS

Before planning any advertising proposals, your first step was investigations into firm and product, market and marketing policy, previous advertising and competition. You must bear in mind that preparation of proposals took time and that things may have changed since the investigations, on which your proposals were based, took place. For example, the original plan might have been to market your product in a choice of colours, but subsequent production problems necessitate a reduction in the range. Clearly your creative proposals must be amended, for there is no point in stimulating prospective customers into demanding a colour which will not be available. Such action is likely to result in disappointed buyers and perhaps an increase in sales of competitors' products. This is only one example of changes that may have occurred since your original investigations.

In addition to checking your proposals from the product/creative changes standpoint, you must also ensure that the media aspects still dovetail in with your company's marketing activities. If your advertisements are to list branch addresses and phone numbers, has the list changed since the initial briefing? Many an advertising executive has been castigated for giving out-of-date details, for lack of attention to this very point! Campaign timing is vital, for consumer advertising must not appear before your goods are in the shops, ready for people to buy. Your campaign plan must therefore allow for the delivery time needed to get goods to the shops once the order has been received, and further allowance must be made for the time needed by salesmen to get orders. To assist salesmen in their work, your consumer campaign may be supported by trade advertisements, and further help provided by heralding your salesman's call with a letter. The timing of each campaign stage must match the other marketing and promotional activities.

The timing of these many aspects of your overall marketing campaign does not depend on the advertising manager alone and, accordingly, you must check to ensure that your proposals interlock with salesforce movements and with other parts of the overall plan. Delivery dates might have changed since your first investigations – will the product in fact be in stock and on display when your advertising breaks, or has there been some unexpected hold-up? If for some good reason or other things are not proceeding according to the original plan, then clearly you must take action to remedy the breakdown in the plan or alternatively amend your proposals to take account of the changes.

Advertising proposals are designed to solve a particular problem, and the facts of this problem may have changed: you must therefore check these marketing aspects before executing your campaign proposals. Clearly, approval cannot be given overnight, for you may need to consult the sales manager, production manager, transport manager, and many others.

EXTERNAL ASPECTS

Before considering your campaign's more creative and media aspects, it is necessary to check proposals from another less interesting but nevertheless crucial aspect: that of background constraints.

This is a creative/marketing matter for the most part, but it is nevertheless necessary to discuss it in some detail, and for you to remember the numerous legal and voluntary controls which affect advertising, and thus your own campaign proposals.

You should certainly obtain a copy of the *British Code of Advertising Practice*, which is under the general supervision of the Advertising Standards Authority and has the support of the major organisations representing advertisers, agencies and media-owners, whose representatives constitute the Committee of Advertising Practice (CAP). The Code is published by CAP, whose address is Brook House, Torrington Place, London WC1E 7HN. CAP is responsible for advising the industry, and you can get free and confidential advice from the CAP Secretariat, based at the ASA office.

As the Code itself points out, its rules are not the only ones to affect advertising. There are many provisions, both in the common law and in statutes, which can determine the form or the content of your advertisements. The Code is not in competition with the law: its rules, and the machinery through which they are enforced, are designed to complement the legal controls.

TV commercials

The *British Code of Advertising Practice* does not apply to broadcast commercials. Television advertisements are subject to a separate, closely related code administered by the Independent Television Commission (ITC) at 70 Brompton Road, London SW3 1EY. The ITC works closely with the ITV Association, which is responsible for much pre-clearance work. The ITV Association is a member organisation of CAP, as is the Association of Independent Radio Companies (AIRC).

The ITC *Code of Advertising Standards and Practice* is a comprehensive document of general rules, and five main appendices deal in more detail with advertising in relation to children, finance, medicines & treatments, charities and religion. There is also a supplementary *Code for Teletext Transmissions*.

A specialist advertising copy clearance group set up by the programme companies under the aegis of the ITV Association work in close co-operation on the examination of more than 16,000 new television advertisement scripts per year.

The scripts are considered in relation to the Code, with the help of independent consultants in special fields; and discussion of any seemingly doubtful points ensures that the television commercials in their final form are likely to comply with the Code.

At the end of these discussions and investigations, eight out of ten television advertisement scripts are found to meet the requirements of the Code as originally submitted. The other 20 per cent are returned for amendment to bring them into line with the accepted interpretation of the Code. In due course the specialist staff of the ITC and the programme companies both view the finished commercials on closed circuit television before they are accepted for broadcasting, to ensure that they conform with the agreed script and that there is nothing unacceptable about the tone and style of presentation, or other aspects of the film treatment of the subject. Between two and three per cent of finished commercials need revision before final acceptance.

Radio commercials

Control of radio advertisements is equally thorough, and all commercials must comply with the Radio Authority's *Code of Advertising Standards and Practice*. Special arrangements for copy clearance are necessary, however, in view of differences between the two media. Some 90 per cent of television advertising is for nationally-marketed products, and most is planned many weeks prior to transmission dates. This enables the central copy-clearing machinery to ensure that all TV commercials comply with the ITC code.

Much radio advertising, however, is local – in some cases the proportion is higher than 70 per cent, and even national advertisers often give a 'local' flavour to their commercials. Equally, much radio advertising is mounted at short notice, taking advantage of the medium's operational flexibility. Because of this, there is a different control procedure.

Copy clearance is a voluntary system operated by the radio companies and designed to protect both advertisers and radio stations, just as much as listeners, as no fewer than 58 Acts of Parliament (together with detailed regulations made under them) affect radio advertising! The commerical broadcasters – both television and radio – therefore operate a Joint Copy Clearance Secretariat (based at the ITV Association) which examines and approves scripts for both radio and TV commercials.

Central clearance Secretariat clearance of radio scripts is obligatory for all 'national' advertisements, defined as commercials intended to run on more than five stations. Central clearance is also required for commercials in certain specified categories (medical products, contraceptives, financial, consumer credit, alcoholic drinks, environmental claims, charities, religious and pilot or test campaigns).

Regional clearance A commercial intended to run in only one region (up to a maximum of five stations) can be submitted for clearance to a nominated senior executive at one of the stations in that region.

Local clearance Commercials booked by local advertisers to appear on one station only (and not falling within the special categories listed above) can be cleared by the station in question.

These procedures help ensure that scripts are swiftly processed and commercials transmitted with minimum delay, allowing advertisers to take full advantage of the radio medium's speed and flexibility.

Other media

Cinema commercials are checked by the Cinema Advertising Association which is the trade association of cinema advertising contractors in the UK. Its role is partly one of a watchdog, acting to ensure that professional standards are met and maintained by the cinema advertising industry. It is responsible for vetting all commercials prior to screening in cinemas, in order to ensure that they conform to the Code of Advertising Practice. Commercials of 30 seconds or longer must also be submitted to the British Board of Film Classification for certification. Direct mail is monitored by the Direct Mail Standards Board for possible investigation by the ASA. Other media may have their own special standards.

The need for careful pre-clearance

Pre-clearance of advertisements for media implies a thorough knowledge of the Codes *prior to preparing your proposals*, quite apart from the need to check your proposals against them afterwards. The earlier chapter on research and investigations stressed, under 'Constraints', the need for you to be aware of the legal and voluntary controls which affect advertising, but these controls are not static: like your product or the marketing situation they too may have changed since your first investigations, so a rechecking, under the general heading of approval of proposals, is a necessary safety measure. Quite apart from being desirable in its own right, such double-checking can avoid the unfortunate consequences of failure to comply – two to three per cent of finished television commercials being unacceptable may seem a small proportion, but consider the position of those advertisers who find themselves deprived of advertising support through lack of any commercials to screen, quite apart from the considerable funds wasted in producing a useless commercial. Careful attention to this matter will ensure that you are not numbered among this unfortunate few.

ADVERTISING ASPECTS

Checking campaign proposals is something that *everybody* thinks they can do – show an advertisement to a layman and he can always suggest improvements! Too many people look only at the pieces of paper in front of them and fail to 'think back' to see how these integrate with the marketing objective which underlies the whole campaign. Before approving any media schedule or at creative proposals, you should ask four fundamental questions:

1 What is your specific advertising strategy? As was made clear earlier, it is no use hoping that an advertisement will 'increase sales'. Where are these increased sales to come from – increased purchases by existing users, conversion of new users, or brand-switch by the buyers of rival products? These and many other possible objectives were discussed in Chapter 13: your specific campaign objective affects media selection as well as creative content. A good advertisement clearly indicates the advertiser's marketing policy and whether increased sales are to be achieved by a brand-switch from competition, by bringing new users into the market for the first time, or by persuading existing purchasers to use more of the product.

2 What fundamental proposition has been selected to appeal to your target group? Of the many appeals you could make to potential buyers, which is the correct copy platform, key attribute or unique selling proposition that will trigger them into action? Cheapness? Effectiveness? Value for money? Better performance? If you select the wrong proposition, out of the many benefits which your product offers, clearly you will fail to achieve your objective. This question is a creative one and thus outside the scope of this book, but the answer has media implications: there is little point in constructing an effective media schedule, only to have it deliver the wrong message to your potential purchasers.

Good creative work is vital for effective advertising, but you must avoid the mistake of seeking creativity for its own sake. Your campaign must relate to your specific strategy and, when approving any proposals, you should beware of advertisements which sell creative gimmicks rather than your products.

A good advertisement gives a clear portrait of the target purchasers and their motivation in buying the product.

3 How effectively will this proposition be conveyed to the selected target group? This in turn breaks down into two separate checking operations – creative and media. Could the creative proposals be improved – does the illustration convey the selected appeal effectively, and is this backed up by equally persuasive copy? Has the single-minded selling proposition been made to 'come alive' in a compelling and memorable way? Will the advertisement convey your message to maximum advantage as regards printing or transmission? Equally important, and more the subject of this book, is checking your advertising proposals from the media standpoint – is the schedule as effective as possible in media selection and in the way the selected media are used – sizes, positions, frequency and dates, and duration of campaign? The chapter on preparation of proposals outlined the two-stage process – construction of various possible schedules, followed by evaluation to select the best, so there is no need to describe this process again. What *is* necessary is to set this checking operation in the context of the two preliminary questions – what is your specific objective, and what appeal did you select for your target group? Only after the answers to these two questions are clearly established is it worth checking the efficiency of the media schedule – a missile aimed with great accuracy at the wrong target does not win any battles, except by accident!

4 Are your proposals comprehensive and cohesive?

Comprehensive This book concentrates on the effective use of *advertising* but, if your campaign is to make its maximum contribution, it should be supplemented by optimum use of all forms of marketing communications. Chapter 3 stressed the importance of the editorial route, of possibly creating other media, and of considering the full range of your target market's message sources.

Cohesive Approval must also ensure that the various components of your campaign all fully interlock. This may mean checking each campaign component separately, but an overview is essential. Your marketing communications efforts will be wasted if the advertising campaign delivers one promotional message while public relations adopts a different theme, and merchandising and sales promotion follow separate paths. Under such circumstances, your target market would be very confused.

Rather than such fragmented efforts, you should strive for a synergistic approach whereby the separate campaign components reinforce each other, thereby multiplying the media effect.

Similarly, your proposals should be cohesive over time, so that all new marketing communications build on and benefit from earlier campaigns.

THE NEXT STEP

Once you have approved your campaign proposals from these three standpoints – internal, external, and advertising aspects – and are sure that your advertising proposals in their final form will make the maximum contribution to achieving your campaign objective, the next step is to put them into effect.

Chapter 17

Execution of Advertising Proposals

Once you have approved your campaign proposals, the next step is to put them into effect: this is a more difficult task than it would appear at first sight. Some campaigns may include hundreds or even thousands of individual advertisements in a whole range of media, and the execution of such a plan calls for meticulous attention to detail.

The task of converting a media schedule – which is nothing more than a plan on paper – into formal orders placed with media-owners is discussed below, but mention must also be made of the creative side, which also calls for considerable detailed work – commissioning artwork and marking-up the copywriter's words for typesetting. Appropriate material must be sent to the selected publishers, and advertisement proofs checked. Other media call for similar creative and production work.

Accuracy is vital in its own right, but the need for accuracy is emphasised by the time limits imposed by the media-owners' 'copy dates' which allow little or no opportunity to correct errors. If a media-owner's copy date is 1 September, this means that material for the advertisement is needed by that date if it is to appear on time. Media-owners' copy dates are difficult if not impossible to postpone.

The task of executing creative proposals may, like the work of preparing them, be undertaken in a variety of ways. The advertising department may do the work itself, it may be handled by an agency, or it may be divided between the two. Some smaller advertisers may rely on the media-owner's service facilities for help in implementing the proposals as well as advice on preparing them.

IMPLEMENTING YOUR MEDIA SCHEDULE: PLANNING VERSUS BUYING

The task of converting your media plan into firm orders placed with media-owners is more than simply an administrative task, and here the difference between media planning and media buying becomes all important. For example, your approved media schedule might show a series of television commercials to be transmitted in various time segments on certain dates. When the plan was drawn up, however, it was impossible to know the programmes that would be transmitted or the viewing figures that would be achieved many months ahead. So a great deal of skill is called for in negotiating the best possible spots at times when your commercials will be seen by the largest number of people in your target market group. Similar detailed negotiations will be necessary with the owners of other media.

The up-to-the-minute buying function contrasts sharply with the earlier planning stage, which produced only an outline plan to be implemented in the light of subsequent information. Media buying calls for a highly competitive cut and thrust approach which many find more exciting than the abstract planning stage which, in contrast, seems a rather boring arithmetical exercise. The buying role is complex and skilled: it involves diplomacy and negotiation skills, and a detailed knowledge of the market place. A good media buyer, with a good working relationship with media-owners, can save many tens of thousands of pounds, and perhaps get preferential treatment over competition. Some practitioners argue that the personal qualities called for in planners and buyers are so very different that few individuals can do both jobs properly.

The vital importance of the buying side is illustrated by the growth of the media independents, by the separation within many agency media departments of the planning and buying functions, and by the fact that advertisers have been known to move their accounts from one agency to another simply because of its better buying performance. In such cases, media considerations clearly have just as high a priority as the creative side of advertising.

SCHEDULE IMPROVEMENT

Few advertising campaigns ever appear exactly as originally planned, and you should keep your schedule under constant scrutiny and make whatever improvements are possible. A marginal improvement of, say, ten per cent in coverage is equivalent to a ten per cent increase in your appropriation, so you should keep your schedule under review and adjust it in the light of subsequent information.

The next chapter deals with evaluation of results as such, but it would be very wrong to consider this an exercise to be undertaken only *after* your campaign: you should monitor performance throughout and, with television advertising, schedule improvement is just as important as the original plan. Changes are less frequent with press or other media but the case for schedule improvement is just as valid. The publication of new circulation or readership data, the issue of a new rate card or the launch of a new publication, for example, should lead you to re-examine your current media plans. The media world is a fast-changing one with new information becoming available almost day by day. Under these circumstances, it would be true to say that anyone who executes a media plan exactly as written, without effecting any changes or improvements, must be asleep on the job!

OTHER CHANGES

In addition to the normal on-going work of schedule improvement, it may be necessary for you to make other changes, to cater for the inevitable set-backs – and unexpected opportunities – which occur from time to time in normal business practice. These can be considered under three main headings – minor, on-going and major changes.

Minor changes Although media planners always complain that the appropriation is never sufficient, you will find they rarely budget to spend *all* the money at their disposal. In preparing your own advertising campaign, you would be well advised to keep back part of your appropriation, in recognition of the fact that no amount of forward planning can predict every possible future event, and that some unforeseen eventuality is bound to occur. Rates may increase or attractive offers be made by media-owners, and a 'Contingency Reserve' allows for such events, and also for unexpected set-backs.

In a highly volatile market, it may be desirable to keep back a considerable contingency reserve, while in a stable marketing situation a nominal reserve may be quite sufficient. In fixing your contingency reserve, you are in fact attempting to predict the unpredictable: this is a most difficult decision, for if contingencies are under-estimated and call for more than the amount set aside then you must cancel some advertising to provide the necessary money, and your carefully planned schedule will be ruined. If on the other hand you over-estimate the amount, there is a temptation to fritter away this too large reserve at the end of the year, rather than leave it unspent and face criticism from your firm's financial staff when seeking budget increases in the future. There is also the danger of this contingency fund being seen as surplus to requirements, and 'taken back' when things get tight, thereby removing your ability to make tactical moves. The correct amount can perhaps be determined only through trial and error over the years.

Other advertisers take a different approach and, rather than establish a contingency reserve in advance, build one up over the campaign period. Aggressive media buying, while executing the media plan, provides another way of coping with the unexpected, the money saved being used to fund a contingency reserve. In some cases, however, the unexpected may occur on such a scale that no contingency reserve, however large, can possibly cope. Such an eventuality is discussed below, under the heading of 'major changes'.

On-going changes When launching new products or services into diverse and unknown markets, with no previous data on which to build, and when the research to provide market information would be unduly expensive, some campaign plans are often deliberately left open-ended. Rather than book a series of 12 advertisements (which would secure a series discount, but commit expenditure to media or market segments of yet unknown value) the initial space order is for only a few insertions in candidate media, with the bulk of expenditure deliberately held in reserve.

Response to these advertisements is then evaluated: those media giving value for money remain on the schedule, while those with poor response are removed. The 'Shotgun' approach, referred to earlier, involves peppering the market and then targeting specific campaigns at those market groups which, through their response, revealed themselves as likely purchasers. In such circumstances the four stages of investigation, planning, execution and evaluation are inseparably linked, with advertising serving a market-research function.

Major changes You may bestow great care, time and effort on preparing your advertising campaign only to have your work wasted, through no fault of your own. One advertiser's national campaign was at proof stage when a new competitor unexpectedly changed the marketing situation to such an extent that the whole advertising campaign had to be scrapped. The thinking behind the proposals had been correct at the time they were put forward, but the unexpected changes meant that the campaign no longer applied to the new marketing problem. Similar situations have arisen following major economic changes or governmental action such as alterations to tax structure or credit and hire-purchase restrictions. The task then is to produce another campaign to deal effectively with the new situation, in the shortest possible time. In such circumstances, resilience and the ability to 'bounce back' when all your work is scrapped are just as important as being able to handle the new situation with a clear head and without getting flustered. Hopefully, however, there will be no major upheavals and contingency reserves will enable you to cope with such unexpected changes as do occur.

In other circumstances, however, major changes may take place that make no call on contingency reserves: to the contrary, you are forced to cut back your advertising. The outbreak of fire or an explosion or strike which stops your production line all illustrate this point, for in such unfortunate circumstances you might well call a halt to advertising aimed at stimulating a demand your company is incapable of satisfying. After an initial advertisement announcing the cause of the delay, you might cancel all advertising other than interim reminder advertisements, until your production line is rolling again.

If all goes well, however, such problems will not arise and your task in implementing your media plan will then be as described earlier – part administrative and part buying/schedule improvement.

MEDIA ADMINISTRATION

The agreed schedule shows an overall picture of your proposed campaign: for press media it will include name of publication, size of advertisement, whether this is run-of-paper or a special position, black and white or colour, together with the cost per advertisement, number of insertions, total cost and dates of appearance. For other media, similar details are given. A television or radio schedule, for example, shows region and contractor, length of commercial, the time segments in which the commercials are to be screened, cost per transmission, total cost and transmission dates. For other media, this information pattern is adapted to show the relevant details. The schedule, however, is nothing more than a plan on paper and must now be converted into firm bookings.

In preparing media proposals you frequently make advance contact with media-owners to check if certain sizes or positions will be available on certain dates, for it is a waste of time to prepare suggestions if these are not realisable. The agency which obtained its client's consent to book a certain schedule, for example, only to report later that few of the spaces suggested were in fact available would look more than foolish in the client's eyes. The same would be true of an advertising manager who obtained Board approval only to report later that the plan could not be put into practice. Accordingly, you may have sought the media-owner's co-operation by asking that certain spaces be reserved for a given length of time pending formal approval. In any event, no firm bookings have yet been made and you now have the considerable task of sending out confirming orders to all media included in the schedule.

You should not under-rate this routine task of converting a single document into a number of individual orders, for accuracy is vital. A media schedule may include insertions in a large number of individual media: on more complex schedules there may be dozens of different publications – national and local newspapers, consumer and trade magazines – as well as transmissions on television and radio, and bookings for cinema, posters, exhibitions or other media. Some media groups may offer some form of central-booking or single-order service, but in most cases your media plan must now be translated into individual orders for each of the media-owners concerned, who may possibly total a hundred or more. Each individual order will contain numerous items of information, and must be accurate as to name of medium, sizes and positions and dates of advertisements, as well as costs and discounts.

A simple typing mistake can cause a great deal of trouble or even jeopardise an entire campaign. If your media schedule features an advertisement to appear on, say, the 9th of the month and the order to the media-owner is incorrectly marked for the 19th, your company would rightly be more than annoyed at lack of advertising support when expected, at what would most certainly be a vital time. This simple typing error could endanger the success of the complete campaign. If the fault lay with the agency, it would find itself in an exceptionally difficult position. In such circumstances the agency might, for example, be too late to cancel the booking for the 19th but would be legally liable to pay the media-owner for it, whereas the client need not pay the agency since he had not authorised it.

Similarly, carelessness in checking could bring trouble of a different kind. If, for example, the true cost of £950 for an advertisement is, by mistake, shown on the client's schedule as £590, then £590 is the amount the client has authorised the agency to spend on his behalf – or which the Board has given the advertising manager authority to spend. Or again, orders have sometimes been sent to the wrong media-owners and advertisements included in the wrong media: this is not as unlikely as it sounds, as many publications have similar names and can easily be confused. Needless to say, no client would be under any obligation to pay his agency for such unauthorised insertions. Accuracy in paperwork and meticulous checking for possible errors is therefore essential.

Even when the individual orders have been typed, checked and posted, however, your administrative work is not at an end. It is necessary to retain and file reference copies, and also to check carefully that every order is acknowledged by the media-owner to whom it was sent. Mere posting of an order does not ensure appearance of your advertising, for there is always the possibility that the order may go astray. Such a mishap rarely occurs but when it does the consequent absence of advertising support could have very damaging effects. To facilitate the order-checking procedure, many order forms have a tear-off acknowledgement slip for media-owners to complete and return. Some media-owners use these slips, while others prefer to use their own 'Acknowledgement of Order' forms: but either way the responsibility for checking that orders have been received and acknowledged still rests with the advertiser or his agency.

Even after a schedule has been planned, booked and acknowledged, changes may become necessary, for the reasons discussed above. For example, should demand so exceed supply that further advertising would be an embarrassment, it may be desirable for you to cancel some insertions. Alternatively, it may be necessary to transfer a booking from one date to another. Often there are special forms for these purposes and, when cancellations are called for, then special 'Stop Orders' – frequently printed in red for immediate attention – might be used. Similarly, there may be 'Amendment Orders' to affect changes within a series of insertions. As before, stop or amendment orders must be meticulously checked, and care taken to see that they are duly acknowledged.

Before leaving this administrative aspect of media, it should be pointed out that a great deal of the drudgery has been taken over by the new technologies. The chapter on specialist services drew attention to the computer services available to advertiser, agency and media-owner which, in addition to their positive contribution to media planning, can also do much of the 'housekeeping' work, thus freeing staff for more constructive activities. The chore of checking nevertheless remains – an incorrect order is still incorrect, even if it is processed by a computer!

THE LEGAL POSITION

Orders sent to confirm bookings and requests for cancellation both raise the legal aspects of contracts with media-owners. This is a complex matter which is admirably dealt with in Diana Woolley's *Advertising Law Handbook*, published by Business Books on behalf of the Institute of Practitioners in Advertising, by whose permission the following paragraph is quoted:

- *. . . media-owners specify in rate cards the conditions on which they will sell space or time to agencies, and it is an advertising trade custom that such conditions will apply to all contracts for purchase of space or time, even if no reference is made to them in the media booking form, which may be an extremely simple document. So, when an agency books space or time, if it wishes to avoid any of the media-*

*owner's conditions, it must expressly exclude them in its order and,
unless its exclusion is accepted by the media-owners, the agency will
be subject to all the conditions regardless.*

Although the book is now out of print, this quotation is still the best
summary of a very complex matter.

THE NEXT STEP

A final step before executing proposals is to double-check follow-
through arrangements, as described in the next chapter: there is little
point in stimulating the market, if your company does not respond to
the demand generated.

Chapter 18

Follow Through

This chapter is brief – and ideally should not even be here! It is self-evident that, if any organisation invests considerable sums on advertising to stimulate the market, it should gear up to respond swiftly to the interest generated.

In practice, however, advertising is alas sometimes not integrated with other activities. Hence this warning: any executive responsible for advertising would be well advised to double-check follow-through arrangements, and to ensure that colleagues are ready to take whatever action is necessary, whether this be coping with telephone enquiries, posting out literature, or following up sales leads.

There are many cases where, alas, advertising staff have taken 'follow through' for granted, to their cost – unacceptable delays have occurred before action was taken and, in one extreme case, there were even complaints that an advertisement had caused so much work in answering enquiry letters!

While you are not *directly* involved with efficient follow-through, this does not relieve you of responsibility: internal marketing communications should ensure that your colleagues are fully briefed in advance, and ready to take whatever action is necessary (whether this be handling telephone enquiries, despatching literature, or following up sales leads) thus averting wasteful dissipation of effort. Incredible though it may seem, one recent survey (across a wide range of product and service areas) revealed that, on average, some 90 per cent of enquiries are never followed up!

Quite apart from being sound practice, tactful reminders are also a useful form of self-defence – if sales targets are not achieved, there is always a temptation for colleagues to blame poor advertising!

If necessary, extra work can be contracted out to other organisations to relieve you of administrative chores: Chapter 11 mentioned the wide range available. For example, some external services not only handle telephone enquiries but also store and despatch literature. Alternatively, if your advertisements feature the offer of an informative booklet, the Royal Mail's *Admail* service (described earlier) can be most helpful. Subject to agreement, this facility allows you to cite your Head Office or other prestigious address in your advertising, but have enquiries redirected to a different office, or perhaps to a 'fulfillment house' (which stocks all necessary material, and posts it on your behalf). This can encourage response and at the same time reduce administrative costs, by eliminating internal re-routing of customer enquiries. It also saves valuable time, thus reducing delays in responding to these requests. But beware - are such costs to be charged against your advertising budget?

THE NEXT STEP

With your campaign now running, your next task is to evaluate its results, to see what lessons can be learned for the future.

Chapter 19

Evaluation of Results

Skill in evaluating results is an important talent for you to develop if you are to use advertising media effectively. This task should be approached from three standpoints – checking backwards, allowing for other influences and looking forward.

CHECKING BACKWARDS

Evaluation of results involves, first, the relatively straightforward task of ensuring that you got value for money. For every insertion booked, you should carefully check the voucher copy sent by the publisher (or obtain a voucher if the media-owner has overlooked sending one). Has your advertisement appeared as booked: in the selected position on the appropriate page on the correct date? Where no special position was booked, did the media-owner place your advertisement wisely, or does its position compare unfavourably with those of competitors? What about adjacent editorial matter? An advertiser of tinned food would rightly be annoyed if his advertisement was foolishly placed on a page featuring an article on food poisoning. If your advertisement featured a coupon, does this back upon another advertiser's coupon on the reverse side of the page? Should this occur, neither advertiser can obtain maximum results. What is the standard of printing? Has the illustration been reproduced to maximum effect? With full-colour advertisements, is your product shown with true colour values? For food or cosmetics, even a slight variation in colour can detract considerably from your advertisement's effectiveness. Has the publisher, in fact, inserted the correct advertisement? It is not unknown for a media-owner to repeat a previous advertisement instead of replacing it with a new one as instructed. There may be few occasions in the year when you need to take up any of these matters with media-owners but such mistakes do occur and you must, therefore, examine every voucher copy and carry out similar checks with other media.

ALLOWING FOR OTHER INFLUENCES

When keeping records, you should make a note of those events – other than advertising – which influence sales and, unless allowed for, would give you a mistaken idea of your campaign effectiveness. Such influences should be categorised under four inter-related headings – Favourable or Unfavourable, Once-off or Repeat.

A heatwave, for example, will push up sales of cold drinks and ice-cream and, whilst advertising can help channel demand towards your product, it would clearly be incorrect when evaluating results to conclude that advertising *caused* increased sales. By all means bask in reflected glory, but be sure to protect yourself against possible blame for decreased sales by noting those events which had an adverse effect. Both favourable and unfavourable influences may be regular or isolated incidents.

A whole host of events can affect your results, including special incentives to sales staff, entertainment and sporting events, strikes, fuel crises and so on. A record of such influences is vital in evaluating past performance and also provides a useful guide for future planning, indicating desirable or avoiding action you should take when preparing next year's campaign. Annual events such as the Cup Final will push up sales of some products at the same time as they depress others and, if your market is affected in this way, you should clearly make allowances in your media scheduling.

LOOKING FORWARD

Ensuring that you got value for money is important, but a far more significant aspect of evaluating results concerns checking effectiveness. Here your aim is different: your concern is not what happened in the past, but improvements for the future.

Did you achieve your objective? This question takes you straight back to the second basic requirement for effective use of advertising media. The first task was investigations, gathering information on which to base your advertising planning. The second task was deciding your specific strategy and the point was made that planning should be a 'closed loop' with evaluation of results of this year's campaign providing additional information on which to base next year's planning.

The direct link between the evaluation of results and the determination of specific objectives is best illustrated by reference to the DAGMAR concept. These initials stand for 'Defining Advertising Goals for Measured Advertising Results', an approach that was developed by R. Colley. To put this another way, unless you know where you are going, how can you know whether or not you have got there? At its most basic, the DAGMAR approach points out the vital need for a specific objective, and then asks if you achieved it. If not, why not? Failure to achieve your objective could arise from one of two reasons – either your objective was wrong (perhaps too ambitious) or alternatively your advertising campaign was at fault. This is an over simplification, as there are other alternatives – circumstances may have changed during the year, or perhaps your method of measuring is not as accurate as it should be. But, whatever the reason – wrong objective, wrong campaign, wrong evaluation or change of circumstances – the DAGMAR approach leads to a re-examination of the advertising plan and its inter-relationship with your total marketing operation. If you did not achieve your objective, it is not necessarily the advertising that is to blame - perhaps the marketing was at fault. But even if your objective was achieved, this is no cause for complacency – could your advertising have done better? Hence the need to analyse advertising results meticulously. As a first step, you must establish whether you are considering direct response or alternatively evaluating results indirectly by some form of survey of retailers or consumers.

Direct response

The improvements you can achieve by evaluating results are best illustrated by the example of those fortunate enough to be able to relate advertising directly to its results. Such is the case with many retailers, organisations with showrooms, or advertisers selling direct or whose advertisements feature reader request coupons. Direct response can also arise through various reply service facilities provided by media-owners.

When you invite such a direct response, you can 'key' each advertisement so that respondents indicate in which publication and on what date they saw your advertisement. Inclusion of a 'key number' such as 'SE7' would indicate that the coupon came from an advertisement in the *Sunday Express* on the 7th. The principle of keying advertisements is simple, but you must take care that your system is foolproof. Does 'DM13' indicate *Daily Mirror* or *Daily Mail*, and does '13' imply the date of insertion or the thirteenth appearance in that publication? You must ensure that your system tells you, without fail, the source of every coupon. Even if your advertisement includes no coupon, it can still be keyed by asking readers to write to a certain department or to address their reply to a certain individual, to Desk Number X or Room Y.

Increasing postal costs have resulted in people thinking more carefully before writing for leaflets, so many firms now take advantage of the Royal Mail's Business Reply or Freepost services whereby they rather than prospective purchasers pay the postage. It also provides a further incentive in that some potential purchasers might be willing to pay postage but simply do not have a stamp handy: these response services can help overcome this inertia on the part of potential buyers. Increased postal costs have also resulted in an increase in showroom enquiries rather than coupon response, and many advertisers therefore take care to include these enquiries since evaluation of postal response alone clearly gives a very incomplete picture.

Parallel services are available for telephone response through *Linkline* 0800 or 0345 numbers. The 0800 numbers are free to callers; whereas with 0345 numbers, the caller pays only the local rate, no matter from where the call is made in the UK.

The labour in checking keyed responses must not be underestimated, and you should ensure you have the necessary staff to undertake this vital chore. Much valuable information is thrown into the wastepaper basket for lack of staff to make the necessary evaluation – yet the improvement which could be achieved would more than pay for the labour costs involved, and even make a major contribution to profits! Should your advertising feature coupons regularly, there may be thousands or even millions to handle annually, and this necessitates establishing a carefully planned sorting and checking operation. Imagine yourself responsible for an advertising campaign which includes perhaps a hundred or more advertisements every month, all featuring coupons and appearing in numerous different publications – national and local newspapers, and magazines of various types. What could you learn from a careful study of coupon returns (or some other form of direct response) and what improvements could you recommend for the future?

Product offer Since all depends on the fundamental content of your advertisement, the product (or service) must appear at the head of the list. With direct response campaigns, the advertiser may vary the basic product offer featured and so judge the relative merits of different prices, packs, products, or product versions. Here, the old truth about making sure you get the offer right should be underlined in red. The head of a mail order company is quoted as saying

'the product has to be central to your offer and, depending on how you present that offer in your advertising, you can expect a fluctuation in

response of about ten or 15 per cent. A good offer badly presented will still bring the response.'

This quotation calls for comment. A fluctuation in response of ten to 15 per cent, according to how you present your product, certainly puts advertising into perspective, but we must not overlook the vital importance of this difference in effectiveness. At worst, it can mean the difference between profit and loss and, at best, a significant contribution to profitability. Some of the advertising factors which can account for this fluctuation include the following:

The medium The number of coupons brought in by one medium can be compared with the response produced by others. If comparing press media, for example, publications can be listed in response order and publications with poor returns could then be eliminated from the schedule and the money spent to better advantage elsewhere. When listing media in order of productivity it is important to consider not only media but also production charges. The longer the media list, the higher the production charges; thus there may be a double saving when uneconomic media are deleted from the schedule.

Area of coverage Where do the coupons come from? One medium may bring a good response when measured in numbers of coupons, but many may perhaps come from outside your sales area. For a local advertiser, or one with a restricted sales or service area, this factor is of major importance. Area response can be very important even for an advertiser with national distribution, and if one region responded more than others, you might decide to follow up this local interest by booking additional insertions in local papers. Alternatively, returns might be extremely poor in one area and this would lead you to investigate the cause of the low response. You might then discover your company faced severe competition from a small local company and that the competitive strategy in the area needed reconsideration. Another reason for weak response in a particular area is the fact that even so-called 'national' media vary in their intensity of coverage in different parts of the country: should this be the case, low penetration in a particular area might call for reinforcement advertising support in local media.

Type of response Careful analysis of the type of person returning your coupons can also yield valuable information. Are the coupons mostly completed by men or by women? Where coupons appear in technical publications, one industry might show more interest than others when judged by coupon response and therefore be ripe for specific targeting by a special sales drive.

Cost per reply Numbers of coupons, completed by respondents of the right type and within your sales area, can be evaluated in terms of value for money, and cost per reply calculated. High numbers are insufficient in themselves: coupons must be returned by prospective customers and at an economic rate. Publications with uneconomic returns can then be eliminated. The chapter on budgeting mentioned the 'Marginal Method' of fixing the budget, which is based on such an immediate evaluation of results.

Conversions Where customer response provides leads for sales force activity, you can calculate the number of enquiries which result in actual sales. One medium might have a low response rate, but if every enquiry leads to a sale it will clearly merit retention on your schedule. Conversely, if the conversion rate of another is low, you would no doubt want to cancel further insertions.

The advertisement unit: size, position and colour Large advertisements cost more than small ones and special positions or colour also increase costs. Comparison of response rates can indicate whether the added expense was worthwhile.

Frequency High frequency costs more than less regular appearances: evaluation of results can indicate if the additional cost was worthwhile. Does the profile of heavy and light users of your product match in with heavy or light exposure to your advertising? If not, why not?

Timing Timing can be a matter of seasons, weeks, or days. By analysing response records you can discover the most suitable day of the week for your advertisements, or when the buying season starts.

Non-media aspects Some response measures mentioned above clearly have *marketing* as well as media implications: they may indicate a new potential market or likely sales area, or touch on other marketing activities. Other response aspects also have implications for marketing, or for creativity. These include:

Creative theme The chapter on approval of proposals asked 'What fundamental proposition has been selected, to appeal to your target group?' The results of two alternative creative themes can be contrasted and keying used to show which is the more effective.

Creative expression The approval of proposals chapter also asked 'How effectively will this appeal be conveyed to the selected target group?' A given creative theme can be expressed in a variety of ways whilst the fundamental appeal remains unchanged – the theme can be conveyed by different headlines, illustrations, copy and typefaces. Analysis of which version pulled best has clear implications for creative staff.

Creative life Whilst an advertisement might prove itself effective, it may not last indefinitely – evaluation of results might reveal that a given advertisement had 'died' and the time was therefore ripe to stimulate your market in a different way. This may be linked to the earlier matter of frequency, in that the more often people see your advertisement the quicker it may die. For this reason, some advertisers base their campaigns on a series of advertisements, which they feature on a rotating basis for change of impact. Other advertisers, particularly those who concentrate on the constant flow of new entrants to their markets, have found the same advertisement continues to pull year after year.

Sales promotions Some campaigns 'top up' their appeal for prospective customers to respond by offering an incentive, e.g. a free booklet or gift, or a product on bonus terms. Evaluation of results can indicate the effectiveness of various alternatives, but it is essential to refer back to 'conversions', and also to give a warning. It is easy to get a response in this way, but it may be response of the wrong kind – from those who want something free, rather than to make a purchase. Care should be taken, therefore, to select an incentive which, by its very nature, appeals mainly to your target group.

Reply devices The aim of a direct response campaign is consumer *action*, but you may experiment with various alternative types of response, some of which prove more productive than others. Examples of different ways in which you can invite customer response include

1 *Post this coupon* – with or without Freepost, and with one or more addresses. Variations are advertisements designed to serve as reply-paid folders, or inclusion of business-paid reply cards.
2 *Payment method* – where the direct response calls for payment of money, various alternatives are possible, e.g. cash with order, whole sum or deposit, cheque or credit card, or Post Office Giro.
3 *Call at showroom* – this overlaps with the first category in that respondents, rather than post a coupon, will call in. Other advertisements suggest such a call directly, without use of a coupon.
4 *Telephone this number* – this can be the advertiser's own number, Freephone or LinkLine services, or a specialist answering service.

Needless to say, these types of response are not exclusive - some campaigns feature two or more. Under this heading, rather than under 'Creative Expression', it is relevant to mention action devices such as coupons featuring small scissors which serve as a visual trigger; corny perhaps, but they *can* work!

Cross comparisons The various comparisons listed above cannot be considered in isolation, as they frequently overlap. For example, people in a particular area may be attracted by one offer rather than another *and* respond more on a particular day of the week (perhaps affected by a major employer's pay-day). These regional and other differences will then be fed back, in a closed loop, into subsequent media and creative planning, and will lead to appropriately different advertising patterns.

Other types of response

The direct response achieved by coupon advertising is an extreme case, and if you have such a clear indicator to the success of your campaign you are indeed fortunate. Even where no such direct response exists, however, you must nevertheless attempt to evaluate results and to follow up leads which could improve your future advertising: this might be by sales audits or consumer surveys.

Sales and retail audits Many retail advertisers have direct results not in coupon form, but in sales. Manufacturers with showrooms take into account over-the-counter enquiries as well as coupon response when assessing overall results.

Other manufacturers without their own outlets attempt to evaluate results by analysing their salesmen's order books (another example of desk research) to check seasonal or geographical variations in relation to advertising effort. 'Sales in' to retailers are not always followed by 'sales out' however, so factory sales figures are an insufficient measure of success, since goods despatched from your factory might sit on retailers' shelves for months, with no sales resulting. Some companies therefore measure results by retail audits, subscribing to one of the research services which provide this data on a commercial basis. In essence, the idea is a simple one: if the stock held in a shop at the start of a month is known and deliveries made during the month are taken into account, the difference between this figure and the total remaining at the end of the month is an accurate indication of the quantity sold over the counter. If your advertising objective was to extend your present distribution or to stimulate your current outlets, a retail audit will give you the answer. A good retail audit will in fact give you a wealth of additional information – where are you placed in the shop and how many *facings* (numbers of your product actually on the shelves) has the retailer given you? Equally important, how are you faring in comparison with your competitors - who is winning the battle for maximum display at point of sale?

Consumer surveys Rather than evaluate results indirectly via retail audits, you may wish to measure customer action, researching purchases rather than sales. A retail audit may reveal an increase of say 20 per cent in comparison with the last period, but it does not tell you *how* this increase was achieved. If your sales increased, you need to know in which of three ways this came about – increased purchases by existing users, conversion of new users, or buyers of rival products switching brands. If the specific purpose of your advertising campaign was to persuade existing users to use more, consumer research can give you valuable information which no form of retail audit can ever reveal. Various research organisations maintain representative panels of consumers, which can make this information available to you.

In some cases, rather than measure actions such as sales or purchases, you may wish to measure changes in, for example, consumer recall of your advertisements, or in their awareness of your product in relation to its competitors. If your specific campaign purpose is to change consumers' attitudes, you may wish to commission research to ascertain their viewpoints before and after the campaign. Even here, however, a specific purpose is essential since 'attitude' is a very broad term. What precisely do you wish to change – your brand image, the degree to which people believe your product claims, their liking for your firm, or the likelihood of them buying your product?

Test marketing Evaluation of results may even extend to test campaigns. A national launch, however carefully planned, is an expensive and risky undertaking: marketing is increasingly competitive and great amounts of capital are involved. Many manufacturers therefore attempt to reproduce in advance, on a smaller scale, the conditions they will encounter on a national basis. By evaluating the results of the test campaign, the manufacturer can spot any weaknesses in his marketing plan, and adjust it prior to the national launch.

When planning a test campaign, your aim must be to reproduce the entire national campaign in miniature, in both selling and advertising. The advertising schedule must recreate in the local campaign the same proportionate weight of advertising to be mounted nationally. If, for example, the national TV campaign is to be launched with one 30-second peak time and two off-peak commercials each week, then this is the amount of advertising to be booked in the TV area selected for the test. Similarly, if half-page advertisements are to appear each week in the national press, then this weight of advertising must be booked in the local press. This general principle of using the equivalent weight of advertising applies to all media, for there is no point in forcing the campaign to be a success by mounting a level of advertising which your company cannot afford on a national basis.

In planning the schedule for your test campaign, account must be taken of the comparative coverage of the national press that would be used for the main campaign and of the local press to be used in the test campaign, and allowance made for any qualitative differences, e.g. class coverage, male/female bias, printing quality, editorial environment, etc., between them, before a realistic assessment of the 'real' national equivalent of a test campaign can be made.

One prime purpose of test marketing is to reveal any weaknesses, and to adjust your advertising plan accordingly. In other cases, two parallel test campaigns may be run, to evaluate the effect of different product formulae or prices, to select that most acceptable to the market. Different weights of advertising expenditure, different media schedules (or alternative creative themes) can be tested in the same way.

FUTURE ACTION

The purpose of evaluation is *action* and this can be of two different types.

1 Follow up leads Evaluation of results can lead to your taking action, e.g. addressing a target group not included in your original market definition but which, by its response, has proved its interest in your product. Evaluation of results thus leads to changes in marketing activity, rather than advertising alone. Alternatively, the target market may remain unchanged but, by evaluation of results, you improve the productivity of your advertising campaign by getting better results for the same money.

2 Elimination of weaknesses The reverse side of the 'better results for the same money' coin is 'same results for less money'. Elimination of weaknesses permits you to use the 'saved' money to buy what you could not afford before – and always remember that no budget is ever sufficient to do *everything* you wanted.

In defence of unproductive advertisements

An advertisement which does not bring results is not *always* a waste of money. Depending on your viewpoint, it can also be an investment.

The 'investment' comes from the fact that you found out – the hard way – that it did not work, and this prevents further waste in future. Alas, a great deal of advertising money is wasted by those who make *no* attempt to evaluate results in the mistaken belief that it is impossible to do so. In such cases, their campaigns continue repeating unproductive advertisements year after year in unproductive media: this is a very different matter from investing money to prevent future waste.

Closing the loop

Schedule improvement is as important as the original plan, and monitoring performance during your campaign is equally as important as post-campaign assessment. Advertising planning must be a closed loop: this chapter completes the circle since what you learn from evaluation of results provides the basis for your future planning. Closing the loop also raises yet again the important matter of advertising briefing and client/agency relationships, as discussed earlier. Many agencies complain of minimal feedback from clients about the results of campaigns mounted on their behalf. Without such information, how can the agency be expected to improve future advertising effectiveness.

A salutary note on which to finish is that if you tell your agency that the brief is 'the same as last year' then you should either resign or fire the agency, since 'no change' means that all the time, effort and money spent on advertising over the past year has apparently had no effect whatsoever!

THE NEXT STEP

Return to Chapter 12 (or perhaps Chapter 17) – you now have new information on which to base your future use of advertising media.

Index